33

3850
JAE

D0163260

AGING AND PUBLIC POLICY

Recent titles in Contributions in Political Science
Series Editor: Bernard K. Johnpoll

Edited by
WILLIAM P. BROWNE
and LAURA KATZ OLSON

AGING AND PUBLIC POLICY

The Politics of Growing Old in America

CONTRIBUTIONS IN POLITICAL SCIENCE, NUMBER 83

GREENWOOD PRESS
Westport, Connecticut • London, England

Library of Congress Cataloging in Publication Data
Main entry under title:

Aging and public policy.

(Contributions in political science, ISSN 0147-1066 ;
no. 83)
Bibliography: p.
Includes index.
1. Aged—Government policy—United States. Aged—
United States—Political activity. I. Browne, William
Paul, 1945-   II. Olson, Laura Katz, 1945-
III. Series.
HQ1064.U5A6334   362.6'0973   82-6138
ISBN 0-313-22855-8 (lib. bdg.)   AACR2

Library of Congress Catalog Card Number: 82-6138
ISBN: 0-313-22855-8
ISSN: 00147-1066

First published in 1983

Greenwood Press
A division of Congressional Information Service, Inc.
88 Post Road West
Westport, Connecticut 06881

Printed in the United States of America
10 9 8 7 6 5 4 3 2 1

For
ALIX LINDSEY OLSON

Contents

Tables and Figures

FIGURES

Abbreviations

AAA	Area Agencies on Aging
AARP	American Association of Retired Persons
ADEA	Age Discrimination in Employment Act
AIME	average indexed monthly earnings
AOA	Administration on Aging
BLS	Bureau of Labor Statistics
CBC	Congressional Black Caucus
CBO	Congressional Budget Office
COG	council of government
CSA	Community Services Administration
DI	Disability Insurance
ERISA	Employee Retirement Income Security Act
FCA	Federal Council on Aging
FHA	Farmers Home Administration
FICA	Federal Insurance Contribution Act
GNP	gross national product
GSA	Gerontological Society of America
HHS	Health and Human Services
HI	Hospital Insurance
HSA	Health Services Administration
HUD	Housing and Urban Development
IRA	Individual Retirement Account
LDD	local development district
N4A	National Association of Area Agencies on Aging
NARFE	National Association of Retired Federal Employees
NASUA	National Association of State Units on Aging
NCBA	National Caucus on the Black Aged
NCCBA	National Center and Caucus on Black Aged
NCOA	National Council on the Aging
NCSC	National Council of Senior Citizens
NIMH	National Institute of Mental Health
NRA	National Rifle Association

NRTA   National Retired Teachers Association
OAA   Older Americans Act
OASI   Old Age and Survivors Insurance
OMB   Office of Management and Budget
OWL   Older Womens League
PIA   primary insurance amount
PSA   planning and service area
SCSA   Standard Consolidated Statistical Area
SMSA   Standard Metropolitan Statistical Area
SSI   Supplementary Security Insurance
SUA   state unit on aging
UMTA   Urban Mass Transportation Administration
WHCOA   White House Conference on Aging

AGING AND PUBLIC POLICY

WILLIAM P. BROWNE AND LAURA KATZ OLSON

1 ───────────────────────────────

An Introduction to Public Policy and Aging

POLITICS AND AGE

Gerontologists have studied extensively the physical, emotional, and social problems of aging in the United States, usually concluding that the vast majority of the elderly population require special assistance in meeting their essential needs. Income-support systems, publicly funded medical services, homemaker and long-term nursing care, uniquely designed transportation facilities, and senior centers for organized community events are among the programs long supported by gerontologists as a means of alleviating a host of conditions plaguing older people.

Despite their emphasis on public programs and services, these analysts have sorely neglected the political dimensions of aging issues. The paucity of such political studies is rather surprising, especially given that the advocated solutions to the problems of old age all have involved—and will continue to involve—both the development of public policy and greater access to governmental resources. The combined financial and administrative resources of national, state, and local governments provide nearly all the assistance that older people receive. Nonprofit associations and the private economic sector rely on rather than supplant government. In reality, none of these other entities have the capacity or inclination to furnish the programmatic and financial support that the elderly need and have come to expect.

The politics of aging has become particularly acute in the 1980s. The number of elderly is growing absolutely and as a ratio of the total population. Twenty-three million older Americans sixty-five and over now belong to this group, which increased from approximately 10 to 12 percent of the population between 1970 and 1980. Within thirty-five years, if trends continue, 15 percent of the population will be over sixty-five years of age. Furthermore, at that time, just over two workers will be required to support each pensioner under social security, compared with a ratio of 3.2:1 in 1981. In sharp contrast, the 1950 figure was sixteen to one.

There are growing numbers of retirees—who usually have only modest savings, if any—at a time when pension systems and government budgets face the threats of spiraling inflation and persistently high unemployment, as well as low levels of overall economic growth. Both retirement programs and the public sector are experiencing severe financial pressures. In reaction, they have become increasingly less willing to continue, let alone expand, current levels of benefits or services. None of these trends seem likely to abate in the near future. The 1980s, then, begin a period when an elderly population with identifiable and generally understood needs is confronted with shrinking services while there are more eligible people to share them. This disparity makes politics important. Political leaders will continue to distribute, redistribute, and limit available dollars in the public domain without ever permanently resolving the conflict over who gets what.

In addition, despite this obvious relationship between politics and aging, there is nothing easily definable about existent political relationships. Unlike an air controllers' strike or a cotton producers' lobby, America's elderly lack a common bond with regard to how public funds should be distributed. Their needs are generalizable, not applicable to all who share only an approximate age factor. For instance, not all of the elderly are infirm or want social participation with other seniors in organized settings. Older people neither experience the same degree of income or health problems nor require equivalent levels of government support. While a small percentage of the aged live comfortably in retirement communities, others require more substantial government funding than currently is available simply to escape poverty. Not all of the elderly even identify with other aging people. Government's task thus becomes complicated by the diversity of the clientele within the group. The elderly themselves do not speak in a singular voice to demand government benefits, and they often fail to agree on what type of action is most appropriate. In short, the elderly exhibit little solidarity of political action in bringing together diverse elements of their own population.

Even without this consensus, the 1960s and 1970s were a time of social and political activism by a plethora of groups acting on behalf of older people. Indeed, such activities have been the most visible and frequently commented on evidence of a politics of aging. But a brief look at the array of groups shows their fragmented, special interests.[1] National organizations concerned with the broad social problems of aging such as the politically militant Gray Panthers and groups composed of older people exclusively such as the more conservative American Association of Retired Persons (AARP) also vigorously lobbied, with varying degrees of success, both Congress and the executive branch. In addition, affiliates of the major national age-related organizations shared center stage at state capitals with groups specific to the states themselves (for example, the

United Auto Workers Retirees in Michigan). Local groups similarly reflected diverse interests, fighting for such widely disparate issues as adult-only condominium zoning and neighborhood public health-care clinics.

At the same time, government officials were initiating services and expanding benefits for the elderly, evidencing their own interest in age-related issues. Both elected and appointed officials paid careful attention to servicing a constituency that they viewed as having strong public support. Action was taken to increase and extend Social Security benefits, the core set of aging programs. Politicians with interests other than income maintenance offered programmatic assistance in areas within the jurisdiction of their committees and agencies. When formulating and debating overall national policies related to health care, pension systems, social services, housing, and food stamps, political leaders often emphasized the particular needs of the elderly.

As more and more government attention focused on the problems and conditions of older people, aging programs that were housed in the fragmented system of congressional committees and government agencies were buttressed further by the creation of specific vehicles to consider and advocate additional government assistance, preferably of a more comprehensive kind. Congress created both Senate and House special committees on aging. The Administration on Aging (AOA) was established under the Older Americans Act of 1965. The White House, in concert with Congress, instituted a series of ongoing conferences on aging. In 1979, the President's Commission on Pension Policy was created by executive order for the purpose of developing long-range policy goals, as well as specific proposals, related to retirement income. By 1980, the broadly defined needs of the elderly were a focus of attention by politicians who had narrow and traditional issue interests of their own and by newer forces addressing the larger social problems of old age.

The elderly—both despite and because of their diversity—have become a politically significant force in American society. As a result of the momentum generated by special interest groups and by government officials, an entrenched and distinct politics of aging has emerged. It owes its distinctiveness to several factors: (1) the large and varied number of programs required to provide benefits appropriate to the diverse elderly population; (2) the overall impression of activism and political strength created by age-related interest groups; (3) the sprawling aging network—national, state, and local agencies on aging, along with service providers—which has provided an advocacy forum for aging programs within the broader context of the American federal system; and (4) the attention given to this select age group, particularly its receipt of a disproportionately large and growing share of the federal budget. By the late 1970s and early 1980s, such sufficient support had been created for programs serving older people that they were receiving approximately one-fourth of the national government's total annual expenditures.

SUPPORT STRUCTURES UNDERLYING AGING PROGRAMS

The elderly did not capture this large percentage of the budget easily. No simple explanation exists for their success. There are, in fact, several reasons for it, all of which are deeply rooted in the complexities of public policymaking. The politics of aging, which encompasses a broad range of issues, is especially intricate, with widely divergent patterns. Although these will be dealt with in greater depth in later chapters of the book, they deserve some summary comment here.

One way of looking at aging policy is in terms of its underlying support systems, which provide the initiative and continuing enthusiasm for particular policies. Analysts often view active citizen participation as the mainstay of any social program. However, unlike the "civic text" model, issues have not been brought forward by the mass of the elderly. Organized and closely managed groups have done this, usually to further their own specific interests. Active support by older citizens and threats of electoral intervention on behalf of an issue have been reserved for only a very small number of programs, such as Old Age and Survivors Insurance (OASI) within the Social Security Act.

The emerging aging network also has become an important source of policy proposals. As part of that network, specialists in aging issues within government have developed programs as well as secured the additional private-sector, congressional, and administrative support needed for their enactment. During the 1960s and 1970s, these legislative and administrative activists gained enough acquiescence on their recommendations to pass some programs without encountering serious opposition or controversy. Old-age interest groups became a functioning component of this network, or subsystem, as have gerontological professionals and their organizations and service providers.

Subsystems of this sort exist in many policy areas of government.[2] At their most powerful, as in agricultural issues for instance, legislative committees and agencies responsible for particular kinds of programs combine with interest groups concerned with the issues at hand to develop policies before they come to the widespread attention of either the public or other government officials. As long as congressional committee members view the costs of new or revised programs created through this process as falling within reasonable budgetary limits and as not likely to affect adversely programs outside the policy area, they are enacted into law. However, the aging subsystem per se exercises influence over a rather narrow range of social programs for the elderly, most of which are contained in the Older Americans Act of 1965. As such, the aging subsystem is hardly well developed and seldom in total control of a great number of issues when compared with any other subsystem.[3]

A third and historically the most important support mechanism for aging programs has a less direct relationship to the elderly. While the aging network proposes policies benefiting its own clients and professionals, there are a number of public officials who simply use the elderly to advance more sweeping programs[4] or even to enhance their own visibility and careers. Because large segments of society sympathize with the aged and tend to view them as less responsible for their plight than other needy groups, a number of policies have been sold because of their emphasis on elderly recipients, even though others will benefit as well. The ageds' popularity has encouraged public officials to focus debate on this group's needs and problems when selling and marketing a program. Often these proposals have come from other subsystems, as was the case with energy-cost assistance. But frequently such innovations were introduced by leaders who had broader interests, as in the case of Supplementary Security Income and Medicare. These external support mechanisms have been the most consequential for the elderly because, over time, they have both nurtured a great many new proposals from which the elderly now claim benefits and served to protect established programs from contraction.

In summary, the general electorate has supported, although passively rather than actively, most of the aging programs over the last several decades. Just as important, public sympathy appears to have favored the provision of at least some assistance to the elderly poor. A great many interest groups and professionals kept both the specific needs and general problems of the elderly continuously in front of the electorate and government policymakers, often to advance their own special interests. Within government, two patterns of support existed prior to the 1980s. In one corner, a number of individuals interested in promoting aging programs rose to power in many key legislative and administrative positions. Several other places were filled with policymakers who were concerned with more general economic and social issues and who paid special attention to the aged because of their popular appeal. To succeed with respect to policy, however, all of these decision makers had to gain acceptance of their ideas from the legislative majority and the White House administration. And, to complete the circle of participants, they had succeeded only by gaining acceptance as the legitimate voice of what the elderly wanted and what the public wanted for them. Over time, these political forces amassed an impressive, some would say confusing, list of policy accomplishments.

AGING POLICY

As discussed earlier in this chapter, most of the national government's maze of policies and programs that emphasize older people was enacted or expanded during the last two decades. The Social Security Act of 1935 and its amendments provide what government leaders view as a first-tier base of retirement income; Supplementary Security Income (SSI) (1972) is a national minimum income-support program for the elderly poor; Medicare (1965), a national health-care scheme for the sixty-five-and-over population, subsidizes, in part, medical services; and the Older Americans Act (OAA) of 1965 and its Comprehensive Service Amendments (1973 and 1978) represent an attempt to establish a system of coordinated social services. In addition, nearly all public-sector employees participate in a federal, state, or local pension system, and in 1974 the Employee Retirement Income Security Act (ERISA) set at least some uniform national standards for the approximately one-half million private retirement trusts. Older people also benefit from special national income-tax laws, including the double exemption and exclusion of social security benefits from taxation. Individual Retirement Accounts (IRAs), Keogh plans, and similar programs provide tax incentives to encourage workers and the self-employed to save for their old age.

Other national, state, and local programs have been instituted to serve the poverty-level population in general, and as such they provide aid to a substantial percentage of the elderly. These needs-tested programs include Medicaid; the Food Stamp Act; Title XX of the Social Security Act; various housing acts, especially the section 8 and section 202 federally subsidized housing programs; and low-income energy assistance. The elderly have become prime users of these programs. Individuals sixty-five and over, who comprise nearly 12 percent of Medicaid beneficiaries, receive over 40 percent of that program's total outlays, primarily for nursing-home care. Older people also represent 45 percent of all recipients of the low-income fuel assistance program.

Many of these national efforts are under attack as calls for fiscal restraint escalate. All have experienced spiraling annual cost inflation, many of them considerably higher than overall inflation in the economy. Outlays for Medicare alone, which totaled about $5 billion in 1968, reached over $44 billion during 1981. In that year, the Old Age and Survivors Insurance trust fund paid out $124 billion in benefits. Program costs were only approximately $16 million and $21 billion in 1940 and 1968, respectively. Steady expansion in the scope of Social Security, rising numbers of older people, and the linkage of benefit levels to increases in the Consumer Price Index (1975) contributed considerably to the program's soaring costs. Given the open-ended legislative commitments of Medicaid, Medicare, and the Social Security system and the growing number of elderly relative to the younger population, the percentage of federal resources devoted exclusively to the aged will continue to increase steadily each year.

Escalating federal expenditures on behalf of the elderly have not guaranteed their overall economic security, however. Nor have such enormous outlays of funds substantially improved their access to appropriate health-care services, adequate and affordable housing, effective social services, or good-quality nursing homes. Older minorities, older women, and older people residing in rural areas and deteriorating inner-city districts, in particular, have failed to achieve appreciable gains despite the enactment and strengthening of policies and programs for the aged.

Although Social Security was never intended to meet full retirement income needs, a substantial number of elderly who have not been able to save for their old age have been forced to rely exclusively on the program. Blacks and other minority groups and single women, all of whom are less likely than other older people to be covered by or vested in private, federal, state, or local retirement systems, often have no other sources of income. Their Social Security benefits also tend to be at the lowest levels, leaving many in abject poverty. The Supplementary Security Income program, which guarantees a national minimum income below the official poverty level, has not alleviated problems experienced by the most economically disadvantaged.

Average monthly benefits under Social Security were only $377 for retired workers and $348 for an aged widow or widower during 1981. Although Social Security benefits are deemed adequate for some retirees as a floor of retirement income, particularly for those with prior earnings at the upper end of the wage scale who continue to labor until age sixty-five, the maintenance of such benefit levels has required an increasingly burdensome, and regressive, funding structure.

Private pension plans, which reduced tax revenues by about $24 billion in 1981, have not been strengthened markedly, despite passage of the Employee Retirement Income Security Act of 1974. Over 50 percent of private-sector workers are not even covered by these pension programs. Moreover, such factors as restrictive vesting requirements, low—or no—cost-of-living increases, inadequate provisions for dependents, and extremely low benefits in general, preclude their effectiveness in meeting supplementary retirement income needs of most retirees who have participated under the systems.

Federal, state, and local employee retirement systems, which tend to provide somewhat higher pensions than private programs for similarly situated workers, are also seriously deficient. Lacking portability, immediate vesting, adequate survivor or dependency allowances, and the like, public-sector programs do not serve sufficiently workers who change jobs and geographic locations frequently or, in most cases, dependent, divorced, or surviving spouses of eligible retirees.

Tax laws enacted to encourage the establishment of Individual Retirement Accounts have aided primarily the upper classes. In 1977, although 85 percent of families with incomes under $5,000 and 70 percent with incomes ranging from $5,000 to 10,000 were eligible, only 0.2 percent and 1.3 percent, respectively, had such an account. On the other hand, 21.7 percent of eligible families with incomes ranging from $20,000 to $50,000 and 52.4 percent of families with incomes over $50,000 were participating in them.[5]

Current income-support programs, overall, produce a "pension elite," usually comprised of older people with high preretirement wages and long-term service at a particular job or firm. The vast majority of the elderly, particularly women and minorities, fail to obtain decent retirement income, and a substantial number are relegated to poverty or near-poverty conditions.

Burdensome health-care costs also continue to plague older people, as well as their publicly supported health-care programs. Medicare covers only about 40 percent of the elderly's total medical bills and does not provide for essential needs such as dental care, eyeglasses, podiatry, hearing aids, or out-of-hospital prescription drugs. A scarcity of doctors and limited medical facilities in urban ghettos and rural areas prevent both Medicare and Medicaid from adequately serving the elderly poor. Furthermore, large amounts of health dollars available for long-term care facilities have fostered unnecessary institutionalization. Medicaid funds flow into the coffers of nursing homes, many—if not most—of which are substandard, provide low-quality care, and engage in well-documented abusive practices.

Older people with low or poverty-level incomes continue to suffer from a paucity of effective social services, particularly those that would reduce institutionalization by substituting in-home support such as homemaker and chore services or day-care facilities. Similarly, federally supported low-income housing programs have not been funded sufficiently to meet the needs of the economically disadvantaged. Rising rents, energy and utility costs, and property taxes relative to most of the elderly's ability to pay, deteriorating neighborhoods and building structures where they tend to reside, and increasingly inadequate access to community and commercial services, especially in financially hard-pressed rural and inner-city areas, have all contributed substantially to housing problems experienced by growing numbers of older people.

Even the limited improvements gained from government programs are now threatened by what political leaders and the public view as an era of scarcity for the 1980s and beyond. Slow economic growth, increasing numbers of older people relative to the younger working population, and a perception that the latter is unwilling to pay higher taxes are being translated into fiscal retrenchment on social programs. Even the Social Security system recently has been subjected to political scrutiny under charges of insolvency. Earlier proposals attempting to remedy inequities, including those that discriminate against women and minorities, have been replaced by concrete efforts to reduce overall costs. Discussions over ways to improve Social Security and render it more effective in meeting older people's needs have been muted. Instead, the "new conservatives" among political leaders are advocating reduced benefit levels for early retirees and upward revision in the age of entitlement for full pension, lower or delayed cost-of-living adjustments, and other changes that would adversely affect the economic condition of a substantial number of older people. Debate over low-income energy assistance, food stamps, Medicaid, federally subsidized housing programs, social service delivery systems, and other programs benefiting the poor has also been limited to ways of reducing benefits, restricting elegibility, and other cost-saving measures. In short, program advocates seem to be gradually losing their legitimacy as spokespeople for the elderly to proponents of lean and austere budgets.

Congressional supporters serving on the Senate and House committees on aging have produced volumes of material exposing the social and economic problems of aging in the United States. Likewise, White House conferences on aging, held in 1961, 1971, and 1981, have enumerated myriad social ills, as well as proposed recommendations for meeting older people's needs. But most senior interest groups are now altering their expectations and strategies in the face of budgetary pressures. Rather than lobby for improved or expanded federal initiatives, they, as well as their allies in government, have been forced to defend existing programs from massive cuts. Moreover, diverse sectors of the low-income population, whether characterized by age, race, sex, class, geographic area, or marital status, now are pitted against each other as all needy groups, and their supporters, struggle to maintain their share of already limited national, state, and local resources.

Evidently, existing policies have not alleviated sufficiently problems experienced by the sixty-five-and-over population, particularly the more disadvantaged sectors. Given the current political and economic climate, their condition will probably worsen over the next decade, even if current programs manage to survive somewhat intact.

POLICY CONCERNS AND THE LITERATURE

Since the 1960s, along with the development of aging policy itself, there has been a proliferation of written material on old age in the United

States. Literature in the field of aging tends to utilize an interdisciplinary approach, although a sociological perspective often predominates. In recent years, economists, historians, political scientists, and others have contributed increasingly to such works as well. One of the most forceful treatments of aging issues is Robert N. Butler's seminal work, *Why Survive? Being Old in America*. Butler carefully documents the social problems of old age and argues compellingly that these are not inevitable within the context of an affluent society such as ours. In addition to refuting myriad myths about the elderly, which he argues contribute both to ageism and the current plight of the elderly, Dr. Butler offers valuable recommendations for reform. Other highly regarded texts include *Handbook of Aging and the Social Sciences*, edited by Robert H. Binstock and Ethel Shanas; *Aging in America: Readings in Social Gerontology*, edited by Cary S. Kart and Barbara B. Manard; *Social Policy, Social Ethics and the Aging Society*, by Bernice Neugarten; and three sociological volumes under the direction of Matilda White Riley, produced as part of the Russell Sage foundation's series on *Aging and Society*. Two prominent historical accounts of old age in the United States are David Hackett Fisher's *Growing Old in America* and especially Wilbert Andrew Achenbaum's *Old Age in the New World*. An important political study assessing old-age interest groups and their influence on public policy is Henry J. Pratt's *The Gray Lobby: Politics of Old Age*.

Furthermore, there is a small, but growing literature on problems faced by particular sectors of the elderly population, such as *Minorities and Aging*, by Jacquelyne Johnson Jackson, and the Social Security Administration's report on *Social Security and the Changing Roles of Men and Women*. Geronotologists and social scientists also have begun to address specific policy areas and the relevant private and public programs associated with them. In the last several years, social analysts have produced volumes on Social Security and retirement issues alone.

Two influential books on the economics of aging are *Pension Plans and Public Policy*, by W. C. Greenough and F. P. King, and *The Economics of Aging*, by James H. Schulz. Both provide a comprehensive overview of questions related to retirement income and pension systems in general. Their analyses of private pension systems are also the most thorough of any single volumes available to date. Although Greenough and King have a chapter on investments of pension funds, more provocative ideas, in our view, are put forward in *Public Employee Pension Funds: New Strategies for Investment*, edited by Lee Webb and William Schweke, and *The North Will Rise Again: Pensions, Politics, and Power in the 1980s* by Jeremy Rifkin and Randy Barber. The most exhaustive information on public-sector pension programs is contained in the *Pension Task Force Report on Public Employee Retirement Systems*. Consisting primarily of charts and tables compiled for the U.S. House Committee on Education and Labor by its staff, the document is a valuable source of data for researchers interested in federal, state, and local retirement systems. Another noteworthy publication on this subject is Robert Tilove's *Public Employee Pension Funds*.

Robert M. Ball's *Social Security: Today and Tomorrow* offers a detailed analysis of the Social Security program, including numerous options for its reform. Two other consequential works focusing on Social Security are *The Crisis in Social Security: Problems and Prospects*, edited by Michael J. Boskin, and Martha Derthick's *Policymaking for Social Security*. Derthick, who stresses formal institutions of government and its policymakers, argues that low-level conflict over specific decisions affecting the development of Social Security since 1935, most of which have enlarged the scope and cost of the program without sufficient scrutiny of their implications, has generated most of the system's current problems. Contributors to Boskin's text are concerned primarily with Social Security's economic impact on individuals and society. There are also a number of important historical narratives on the establishment of the program, including *The Struggle for Social Security* by Roy Lubove and *Social Security Perspectives*, by Edwin E. Witte.

In the area of health care and the elderly, a prominent, if somewhat sketchy study on the enactment of Medicare, is Theodore R. Marmor's *The Politics of Medicare*. Fuller discussions and sophisticated assessments of the program itself are furnished by Judith M. Feder in *Medicare: The Policy of Federal Hospital Insurance*, Richard Harris in *A Sacred Trust*, and Herman M. Somers and Anne R. Somers in *Medicare and the Hospitals: Issues and Prospects*. An excellent account of medical care and the elderly poor, focusing on the forces leading to the passage and development of Medicaid, is *Welfare Medicine in America: A Case Study of Medicaid*, by Robert Stevens and Rosemary Stevens.

The literature on the nursing-home industry tends to be the most critical of past and current public policies. Several works in particular have attempted to assess the underlying causes of inadequate facilities and their spiraling costs. Nearly all these authors point to the prevalence of low-quality care, including exploitation of patients and profiteering by bankers, realtors, doctors, pharmacists, and nursing-home operators. The most insightful books are *Old Age: The Last Segregation*, by C. Townsend; *Tender Loving Greed*, by Mary A. Mendelson; *Better Homes for the Old*, by Barbara Bolling Manard, Ralph E. Woehle, and James M. Heilman; and *Unloving Care: The Nursing Home Tragedy*, by Bruce Vladick.

Recent works on aging tend to reflect remarkably similar concerns. A common thread throughout much of the literature is an underlying empathy for the social and economic plight of older people. Consequently, the plethora of problems older people experience in areas ranging from deficient retirement income to inadequate long-term care facilities has been well documented. Students of programs such as Social

Security and Medicare generally applaud them for having improved considerably the condition of older people and for having raised a substantial proportion of the elderly population over the official poverty line. Despite a focus on program accomplishments, the literature is replete with discussions of their deficiencies, coverage gaps, inequities, and funding problems, as well as increasing concern over their burdensome and growing costs. Yet there are substantially divergent views on the causes of and potential remedies for the alleviation of problems facing both aging programs and their current and future beneficiaries. There are also sharply differing perspectives on where "power" resides for effectuating change, particularly among the few social scientists assessing the political potential of old-age interest groups.

Programs focusing on older people were enacted not only to serve their needs but to promote other policy objectives as well. They also have been superimposed on ongoing market structures and shaped by powerful and self-serving political and economic interests. In addition, programs established for older people inevitably have a direct or indirect impact on other sectors of society and as such may negatively affect younger disadvantaged groups. In fact, the aged in general are typically viewed by social gerontologists as having greater needs than the younger population and thus as more deserving of special attention. This orientation tends to divert attention from the study of certain aspects of aging programs, such as those that may transfer some resources from low-income younger people to a small percentage of high-income older adults. Moreover, a focus on the aged alone often neglects the fact that many of their specific problems, particularly among the elderly poor, stem from inadequate income, health care, housing and the like experienced during their entire life cycle. Policies also have disparate effects on subgroupings within the elderly themselves. Unfortunately, much of the literature on old age in the United States tends to avoid many of these larger social, economic, and political issues.

One of the more provocative works on aging that takes such issues into account is Carroll L. Estes's *The Aging Enterprise*, which examines the Older Americans Act and related social programs. Estes persuasively argues that the failure of these efforts, as well as the problems of the elderly poor per se, are rooted in our economic, political, and social structures themselves. She also contends that programs enacted to meet the needs of the aged not only benefit primarily service providers—that is, the gerontological professionals—but also support existing and inequitable power configurations in our society. Also, Laura Katz Olson, in *The Political Economy of Aging: The State, Private Power and Social Welfare*, uncovers some of the structural causes of the current crisis in old-age programs and explores why these programs fail to meet the needs of many of the elderly.

For additional readings on what we view as the primary issue areas in aging policy, namely political behavior, retirement income, health care, social services, housing, and nursing homes, we refer our readers to the Bibliography provided at the book's end. Although it is not an exhaustive listing, it is intended to introduce students of gerontology to a broad range of aging literature. Given the paucity of gerontological research focusing on structural causes of poverty and other social problems of old age, we have attempted to compensate for such deficiencies, where necessary, by including works ranging from studies of the medical-industrial complex to those discussing income inequality in American society overall. In order to keep the Bibliography within manageable limits, these volumes are selective. A few of the more noteworthy are *Regulating the Poor: Functions of Public Welfare*, by Francis Fox Piven and Richard Cloward; *Poverty amid Plenty: A Political and Economic Analysis*, by Harrell R. Rodgers, Jr.; *Social Stratification in the U.S.: An Analytic Guidebook*, by Stephen J. Rose; *Labor and Monopoly Capital: The Degradation of Work in the Twentieth Century*, by Harry Braverman; *Health Care Politics*, by Robert R. Alford; *Rockefeller Medicine Men: Medicine and Capitalism in America*, by Richard E. Brown; *The American Health Empire: Power, Profits and Politics*, by John Ehrenreich and Barbara Ehrenreich; *The Quality of Federal Policymaking: Programmed Failure in Public Housing*, by Eugene J. Meehan; *Main Currents in American History*, by Gabriel Kolko; and *The Fiscal Crisis of the State*, by James O'Connor. We have also included a sampling of books and articles focusing specifically on older women, minorities, and the rural poor, as well as publications assessing the politics and policies of old age from an international perspective.

We could hardly present, revise, or even cover all the important ideas of political relevance contained above, and we have no intention of attempting to do so in this book. Instead, we have a more narrow purpose: to expand the political interest and literacy of individuals concerned with gerontology. This volume is designed to be a primer on politics as it affects older people in American society. It should interest students of sociology, political science, and public administration, enabling them to learn more about their respective disciplines through an examination of aging issues. Moreover, given the infancy stage of political studies on aging, many of the ideas and conclusions contained in this volume are tentative ones. Although we don't necessarily agree with all of them, they can stimulate additional study and research. As such, this book fills an important void.

In this first chapter, we have provided an introduction to aging politics and policy, discussing such issues as the growth and diversity of the elderly population and the expansion of aging programs and their budgetary outlays over the last several decades. The various roles played by political decision makers, administrators, interest groups, and the elderly themselves have been presented briefly in order to document the complexity and fragmentation of the political process in this issue area. Although older people have become politically significant, most still face myriad unresolved social problems that are likely to worsen if the current political climate prevails. These are the primary themes of the book, and they will be expanded on by several authors in the remaining chapters.

The next four essays examine the elderly population in terms of their needs and conditions. Chapter 2, by Robert H. Binstock, Louis Stulberg Professor of Law and Politics and Director of the Policy Center on Aging at Brandeis University, surveys elderly conditions. His emphasis is necessarily on the economic condition of the elderly as a group. Professor Binstock's analysis clearly points to the dangers inherent in embarking on policies of less rather than more assistance. The great majority of older people can only be seriously harmed by such action.

Chapters 3, 4, and 5 turn to subgroups of the elderly, especially the most disadvantaged and disregarded with respect to policy. Older women who experience severe financial and related constraints are reviewed by Jennifer L. Warlick of the University of Wisconsin's Institute for Research on Poverty. Jacquelyne Johnson Jackson of Duke University Medical Center reviews the unique problems of minorities. Paul Kim, a social work professional from the University of Kentucky, looks at the rural elderly. These authors spell out the malaise of policy neglect from each subgroup, and propose policy innovations appropriate for meeting their needs more effectively.

A particular strength of these chapters is their ability to portray the diversification among the elderly. The situation of elderly women is not necessarily similar to that of older men; for instance, they tend to live longer, have lower retirement income, and find themselves alone more frequently. Minorities more often than white males contend with the compounding difficulties of ghettoization, low income, and less adequate personal services earlier in life. These, among other factors, have ramifications for those who age. Furthermore, the rural elderly are subject to neglect in the administration and delivery of services because benefits are harder to provide in rural America where people are less centralized and less visible to observers.

Chapters 6 through 9 examine the political environment which structures aging policy. The first three of these detail the relative impact of divergent political demands and governmental institutions on policy. Douglas Dobson of Northern Illinois University (Chapter 6) and Henry J. Pratt of Wayne State University (Chapter 7) are concerned with the initiation of proposals and ideas into the political arena. Dobson discusses age as it relates to political behavior and explores whether the elderly, themselves, constitute a political force. Pratt reviews the activism of older people through organized interest groups. Their collective findings indicate that the elderly are not different politically from the rest of the population in either behavior or beliefs. There is no great wave of identifiable activism on their part, nor is there any reason to believe that older people are clamoring to protect most of the services they now receive or to gain additional ones. Political action and support for most ideas and programs rely upon the interest groups that, in the case of age-based organizations, depend on a few highly active leaders for maintaining their groups' momentum. Again, fragmentation of interests among the elderly and varying perceptions of need are evident.

Dale Vinyard, also of Wayne State, and Dave Brown, of the University of Alabama's Center for the Study of Aging, shared responsibility for the material on political institutions. Vinyard examines the impact and concerns of the executive branch, presidential commissions, congressional committees and subcommittees, and key legislators. He attempts to show the restraints under which public officials operate as they work together and separately. Brown focuses on the administrative, or bureaucratic, side of government, with its responsibilities for developing, implementing, and evaluating programs. Because of the intergovernmental aspect of the Older American Act and certain other pieces of legislation, this chapter also looks at the effects of American federalism on aging issues, including the delivery of services by state and local governments. In seconding some of Professor Kim's earlier obervations, Professor Brown provides a strong criticism of program administration in the aging field.

In the last chapter, David Brodsky of the University of Tennessee attempts to predict where aging policy directions lie in the future. Three variables—the needs of older people, political support for them, and the availability of funds—are central to his analysis. In keeping with our introductory chapter, Professor Brodsky warns that a continued period of fiscal retrenchment, or even intense conflict over such austerity, will seriously affect the status of the elderly no matter where the sympathies of the American people may be. In addition, he notes that aging programs may suffer as older people lose the sympathy of others, especially young workers, who will resent increasingly the large and growing percentage of the budget allocated to the elderly.

NOTES

1. Robert H. Binstock, "Interest-Group Liberalism and the Politics of Aging," *Gerontologist* 12 (1972): 265-80; Henry J. Pratt, *The Gray Lobby: Politics of Old Age* (Chicago: University of Chicago Press, 1976).

2. J. Leiper Freeman produced the seminal analysis of subsystems. See his *The Political Process: Executive Bureau–Legislative Relations*, rev. ed. (New York: Random House, 1965).

3. Donald E. Gelfand and Jody K. Olson, *The Aging Network: Programs and Services* (New York: Springer, 1980).

4. Robert B. Hudson, "The 'Graying' of the Federal Budget and Its Consequences for Old-Age Policy," *Gerontologist* 18, part 1 (October 1978): 428–40.

5. U.S., President's Commission on Pension Policy, *Coming of Age: Toward a National Retirement Income Policy* (Washington, D.C.: President's Commission on Pension Policy, February 26, 1981), p. 35.

ROBERT H. BINSTOCK

2

The Elderly in America: Their Economic Resources, Income Status, and Costs

An axiom of public rhetoric in America, from the Townsend Movement of the 1930s until the late 1970s, was that most older persons are poor. By the end of the 1970s, however, this axiom had been rather suddenly discarded. Beginning in 1978, the American public was flooded with media stories and social policy analyses that portrayed the elderly as having been "lifted out of poverty" by government programs, private pensions, savings, and employment opportunities. Typical of such portrayals was a 1980 cover story in *U.S. News and World Report*, which proclaimed:

Stereotypes die hard, but few are as stubborn as America's outmoded images of older people: The impoverished widow, the decrepit man banished to a nursing home.

   Those situations still exist, but they have become increasingly rare. . . . retirees are not too badly off.[1]

   At the same time that the stereotype of poverty among the elderly was being transformed, journalists, scholars, and public officials began to recognize the economic implications of an aging population. Attention was directed to the "graying of the budget," that is, the demographic age changes and public program benefit structures that have led to a situation in which the federal government currently expends more on aging than on national defense.[2] Moreover, on the basis of reliable predictions of increases in the number of older Americans and assumed continuity in present program benefit structures, projections were made that the 25 percent of the federal budget that was expended on the aging in 1981[3] would reach 40 percent early in the next century[4] and 63 percent by the year 2025.[5] On the basis of such projections, some journalists began to suggest that American society could not afford to maintain collective public efforts to sustain the economic burden of an aging population.[6]

Taken together, the new stereotype of the economic status of the aging and the recognition of the budgetary implications of population aging began to suggest that older Americans are living off the fat of the land and pose a threat to the American economy. The business-oriented *Forbes* magazine expressed the notion in an exceptionally hyperbolic fashion in a 1980 feature entitled "The Old Folks": "The myth is that they're sunk in poverty. The reality is that they're living well. The trouble is there are too many of them—God bless 'em."[7]

Concern for the present and future costs of an aging population was also heightened in the late 1970s by projected short-term and long-term deficits in the Social Security trust funds. Despite substantial increases in Social Security taxes enacted in 1977,[8] the transition of the American economy to slow growth and high rates of unemployment and inflation indicated that the pay-as-you-go funding of Social Security, with taxes from today's workers paying for benefits of today's retirees, would not be viable in 1982. Long-term problems with the funding of Social Security in the twenty-first century were identified in relation to the changing demographic age structure of the American population. The ratio of Social Security beneficiaries to taxable workers is projected to rise sharply when the post–World War II baby boom begins to reach retirement age after the year 2010.[9]

Public proclamations of concerns about the solvency of the trust funds have apparently undermined another long-standing axiom of American politics; widespread public faith in the mythology of the Social Security program. Most Americans have long believed that Social Security benefits are like insurance annuities that they have paid for with premiums deducted from their paychecks through Federal Insurance Contribution Act (FICA) withholdings. They have paid their payroll taxes while trusting that something on the order of a contract exists that binds the U.S. government to pay them retirement benefits in accordance with their earlier payroll tax deductions. But in the context of growing official proclamations about the capacity of the Social Security system to meet future benefit commitments, public trust has been undermined. A 1979 nationwide survey indicated that more than four employees in five have less than full confidence that Social Security will be able to pay the benefits "owed them" when they retire.[10]

After several decades of relative immunity from political problems,[11] income-maintenance policies affecting the aging have suddenly become a major social policy issue on the agenda of American politics. Little attention was paid to aging policies in the three 1976 Carter-Ford presidential campaign debates,[12] but in the 1980 televised debate between Carter and Reagan a major issue was their respective views on the future of financing for the Social Security program. In the first year of his administration, President Reagan put forth major proposals for policy changes substantially affecting benefits available to current and future generations of older Americans through federal income-maintenance programs.

In light of this swiftly changing scenario, the purpose of this chapter is to provide a context in which contemporary discussions of income-maintenance policies toward the aging can be interpreted. To be sure, many broad and specific issues bear upon the politics and policies of the economics of aging. Not the least of them are the value assumptions concerning the division of collective and individual responsibility for income adequacy in old age. But, given the scope of a single chapter, the most essential issues would seem to be those that bear upon current assertions that the aging are relatively well off and that American society may soon not be able to afford programs that sustain the economic security of the elderly.

Accordingly, three central topics will be addressed in a brief, overview fashion. First, What are the economic resources available to the elderly in America? Second, What is the income status of older persons? And third, Can American society continue to bear the economic costs of maintaining an adequate income status for its older citizens?

ECONOMIC RESOURCES OF THE ELDERLY

In order to consider the income status of the elderly as well as the cost implications of maintaining or enhancing their status, it is useful to review briefly the different kinds of economic resources available to older persons in America.[13] These resources include earnings from participation in the labor force; a wide variety of public and private programs that pay cash and in-kind benefits; special tax exemptions for the aged; intrafamily transfers; and assets accumulated by older persons.

EARNINGS

About 8 percent of persons sixty-five years of age and older are active in the work force. Their earnings constitute about 23 percent of the aggregate money income received by older Americans.

The distribution of earnings as an income source for older persons has narrowed steadily over the past three decades. In 1951, for example, over half of the couples sixty-five and older in the United States received income from earnings; by 1976 this percentage had declined to 40 percent. For single men the decline in this period was from 34 to 21 percent.

Although the proportion of single older women receiving earnings rose from 13 percent in 1971 to 23 percent in 1962, by 1976 it had declined to 14 percent.

SOCIAL SECURITY

The largest of the economic resources available to older Americans is the national Social Security program. Old Age Survivors Insurance (OASI) benefits paid under the Social Security program constitute 38 percent of the aggregate money income of the older population.

Participation in the Social Security system is compulsory for employed Americans except for those in certain excluded groups, such as employees of the federal government. The program , established in 1935, is funded through a flat-rate payroll tax contributed in equal amounts by employees and employers (in 1982, 6.7 percent from each on wages and salaries up to $32,400 annually). The system is financed on a pay-as-you-go basis, with a limited reserve.

Workers become eligible for OASI benefits by choosing among several retirement-age options available to them. They can receive the full benefits to which they are entitled, starting at age sixty-five if their earnings are below a specified ceiling used to determine their retirement status. They can opt for earlier retirement at age sixty-two, but receive reduced benefits throughout their remaining years. Or they can delay retirement beyond sixty-five, adding to the amount of benefits to which they are entitled (and receive benefits at age seventy-two, and beginning in 1983 at age seventy, regardless of the amount of additional income they receive from earnings).

The amount of benefits paid is calculated through formulas based upon the worker's history of participation in the system. In January 1982, the monthly benefit for an individual with maximum covered earnings and retired at sixty-five was $679.30; a worker with an average earnings history received $535.40; a worker with an earnings history equivalent to the nationally established minimum wage recieved $355.30 in retirement. The total amount of OASI benefits paid out in fiscal year 1981 was estimated at $97.1 billion.

PUBLIC EMPLOYEE RETIREMENT SYSTEMS

A variety of government employee pension plans make up 6 percent of the aggregate money income of older persons. These include retirement systems for civilian and military personnel of the federal government as well as employees of states, municipalities, counties, school districts, and other special district governments.

The federal civilian employee retirement system was first established in 1920. Today, it encompasses sixty-eight retirement systems for federal personnel, covering virtually all employees of the national government. In fiscal 1981, retirement benefits to federal civilian employees totaled an estimated $16.7 billion. The military retirement system currently awards benefits of 50 percent of pay after twenty years of service. In fiscal 1981, total military retirement expenditures were $13 billion.

More than six thousand public employee pension plans are administered by the state and local governments of the United States, covering 85 percent of their workers. Although such plans began in the nineteenth century, their major growth took place in the 1940s and 1950s. By 1978, the total benefit outlays of these systems were estimated to be ten billion dollars. State and local government workers can also elect to be participants in the national Social Security system; currently, about 70 percent of state and local employees are covered by Social Security in addition to their own plans.

PRIVATE PENSION PLANS

About one-half of the private work force is covered by private pension plans, but they constitute only 7 percent of the aggregate income of the elderly. Coverage is primarily limited to large, unionized manufacturing firms. In 1981, total retirement benefits paid through private plans was estimated to exceed twenty billion dollars. About 21 percent of the retired population sixty-five and over is receiving income from private pensions. The national government regulates certain aspects of private pension plans through provisions of the Employee Retirement Income Security Act of 1974, which affects vesting (for job changers), funding, and management of pension funds.

MEANS-TESTED CASH ASSISTANCE

A national cash-assistance program, Supplemental Security Income (SSI), pays benefits to older persons whose other sources of income do not bring them up to a designated income level established by the federal government. SSI is funded from general tax revenues. Eligibility and benefit amounts are determined through income and assets tests. State governments are encouraged (and in some cases required) to add their own benefits to the federal benefits. In fiscal 1981, the national government paid out an estimated $2.6 billion in SSI benefits.

IN-KIND INCOME PROGRAMS

In-kind income consists of goods or services available to the aged without expenditure, or at least at a rate below the market value of the service. The federal government's Medicare and Medicaid health insurance programs are important examples. Another is subsidized housing. Still another is the nation's food stamp program, through which more than one million persons age sixty and over receive coupons that can be used to purchase food in retail stores. The value of coupons received depends on both the income of recipients and the number of persons in a family, and eligibility for the program is means tested.

In fiscal 1981 the federal government expended an estimated $45 billion in in-kind benefits to the aged. Medicare accounted for $35.8 billion; Medicaid expenditures were estimated at about $6.0 billion; public housing subsidies comprised about $2.3 billion.

While in-kind benefits do not contribute to the money income of the aged, they clearly are an important economic resource for older Americans. Measuring the value of these benefits, however, poses some difficult conceptual issues. For instance, the value that recipients themselves place on some in-kind services and goods (such as medical care or housing) may well be substantially less than the market price. Consequently, as will be made evident below, assessments of the income status of the aged can vary considerably in accordance with different interpretations of the impact of in-kind benefits.

SPECIAL TAX EXCLUSIONS

Substantial benefits are provided to the elderly through a variety of national, state, and local tax provisions. One important tax exemption for older persons is the nontaxation of Social Security benefits. Another is property tax reductions, which are granted in all states for elderly persons. The most common type of reduction is a "circuit breaker," through which tax relief is tied to need as defined by taxpayers' income levels in relation to their property tax liabilities. Another common method of property tax relief is the "homestead exemption." Under this mechanism, before the tax rate is applied, a state excludes a portion of the assessed value of a single-family home from total assessed value. A few states allow deferral of property taxes until an elderly owner dies or sells his or her residence, and a few freeze the tax rate in force when the aged person reaches a certain age, usually sixty-three or sixty-five.

INTRAFAMILY TRANSFERS

Another resource to be considered is intrafamily transfers of money, goods, and services to the aged. But very little is known about the magnitude and nature of transfers among family members (for example, from children to parents, or vice versa). In the most recent study, economist Marilyn Moon found that intrafamily transfers altered the well-being of about 28 percent of aged families.[14] However, relatively large transfers flow both ways—with slightly more aged families receiving assistance than assisting younger children.

ASSETS

Many of the aged own assets that provide housing, serve as a financial reserve for special or emergency needs, contribute directly to income through interest, dividends, and rents, and generally enhance the freedom with which they spend their available income. Assets provide about 19 percent of the aggregrate money income of the aged.

Most assets can be sold and thereby converted to money that can be used to buy goods and services. But one should distinguish between liquid assets and nonliquid assets. Nonliquid assets usually require more time to convert. If an aged family has significant nonliquid assets, such as housing, as long as they are determined to keep that housing and not sell the property that asset is not convertible into income to be used for day-to-day living. In effect, the asset is "locked in."

In fact, a high proportion of older people own a home or have an equity in it. About 80 percent of elderly couples and 57 percent of one-person elderly households live in an owned home. The amount of mortgage debt on those homes is usually very low; in fact, about four-fifths of elderly homeowners own their homes free of any mortgage.

Until recently in the United States, there was no available financial mechanism that would permit people to sell the equity in their home, get back money over a period of time, and still be able to live in the house. Since January 1, 1979, however, the Federal Home Loan Bank Board has allowed federally chartered savings and loan associations to offer reverse annuity mortgages. Under this type of mortgage, a homeowner may sell some equity in the house, receiving in return a fixed monthly sum based on a percentage of the current market value of the house.

INCOME STATUS

Given these various economic resources, how well off are the elderly? Two principal approaches for addressing this issue are, first, to examine the distribution of income among the aged and, second, to apply various measures of income adequacy.

INCOME DISTRIBUTION

The aged, as a group, have cash incomes significantly lower than the incomes of the younger population. In 1979, the 8.8 million householders sixty-five and older had a median income of $11,316, compared with a median income of $21,201 for families with householders younger than sixty-five; unrelated individuals sixty-five and older had a median income of $4,653, compared with a median income of $9,706 for younger unrelated individuals.

Table 2.1 shows that the majority of aged households in 1979 had cash incomes of less than $10,000 a year; only slightly over 13 percent of aged units had incomes higher than $20,000. A breakdown of income distribution by race, sex, and marital status, as depicted in figure 2.1, shows that incomes tend to be lower among older women, members of minority groups, and single persons.

Table 2.1
Distribution of Money Income among Aged Households, 1979

Income	Total Households (thousands)	Percent of All Households
Under $5,000	4,985	31.0
$5,000-$9,999	4,961	31.0
$10,000-$14,999	2,708	17.0
$15,000-$19,999	1,360	8.0
$20,000-$24,999	758	5.0
$25,000-$29,999	503	3.0
$30,000-$34,999	276	2.0
$35,000-$39,999	175	1.0
$40,000-$49,999	214	1.0
$50,000-$74,999	151	1.0
$75,000 and over	61	0.3
Total	16,152	100.0*

SOURCE: U.S., Bureau of the Census, *Current Population Reports*, Series P-60, "Money Income and Poverty Status of Families and Persons in United States, 1979. Advance Report (Washington, D.C.: Government Printing Office, 1980).

*Percentages do not add to 100 because of rounding.

Figure 2.1
Median Money Income for Population Sixty-five and Older, 1978, by Sex, Race, and Marital Status

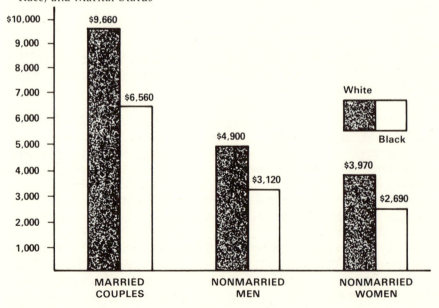

SOURCE: Unpublished data from the U.S. Social Security Administration.

CASH INCOME ADEQUACY

Among a variety of measures that can be employed to assess the adequacy of incomes received by the aged, three absolute standards are used by the federal government for official purposes: the national poverty index, the "near-poor" index, and the hypothetical budgets for an urban elderly couple that are constructed by the U.S. Bureau of Labor Statistics (BLS).

The poverty index is based on a formula that considers the cost of food needed for a temporary subsistence diet (as determined by the Department of Agriculture) and the proportion of family income that is typically spent on food. Different indexes are developed to take into account factors such as family size, number of children in the family, age and sex of the family head, and farm and nonfarm residence. The thresholds are updated annually according to changes in the Consumer Price Index. In 1981, the poverty line was $5,470 for an aged couple and $4,350 for an aged individual.

Table 2.2
Poverty and Near-Poverty Rates* among Persons Sixty-five and Older, 1979

Group	Numbers (in thousands)	Percent in Poverty	Percent Poor and Near-Poor
Total	23,743	15.1	24.7
Male	9,783	11.0	18.5
Female	13,960	17.9	29.0
White	21,446	13.2	22.4
Male	8,803	9.5	16.3
Female	12,643	15.8	26.6
Black	2,020	35.5	49.2
Male	847	26.9	40.4
Female	1,173	41.7	55.5
Spanish origin	562	26.1	38.4
Male	259	22.8	—
Female	303	29.0	—

SOURCE: Unpublished U.S. Bureau of the Census data for 1979.

*In 1979, the national poverty line was $4,364 for an aged couple and $3,472 for an aged individual; the near-poor lines were $5,455 and $4,340, respectively.
Dash indicates figures not available

The poverty rate among the elderly population declined from 35 percent to 14 percent between 1959 and 1978 but rose noticeably in 1979 to 15.1 percent. In the same year the poverty rate for the entire population was 11.6 percent.

The near-poverty measure was developed to reflect a more adequate nutritional standard. It equals 125 percent of the poverty threshold for a given population. As is shown in table 2.2, near-poverty rates for the aged population are also high, indicating that substantial numbers of the elderly live on incomes only slightly above the official poverty level. Older women and minorities experience significantly higher rates of poverty.

The U.S. Bureau of Labor Statistics constructs three budgets for urban retired couples based on the prices of items on a hypothetical shopping list of goods and services. Prices are updated by changes in the Consumer Price Index for those goods and services. In 1979, there were approximately 6.1 million husband and wife couples with heads sixty-five and older whose incomes could be compared with the lower, intermediate, and higher standards of living described by the BLS budgets. One third of these couples could not meet the intermediate budget level, as indicated by table 2.3.

Table 2.3
Aged Couples with Incomes below Bureau of Labor Statistics Budgets for Retired Couples, 1979

BLS Hypothetical Budgets	Budget Levels	Number of Couples (in millions)	Percent of Couples with Incomes Below Standard
Higher budget	$12,669	3.8	62
Intermediate budget	8,562	2.2	36
Lower budget	6,023	1.1	18

SOURCE: U.S., Congress, Senate Special Committee on Aging, *Developments in Aging, 1980*, part 1 (Washington, D.C.: Government Printing Office, 1981), xvii.

IMPACT OF IN-KIND BENEFITS

As the foregoing discussion should make clear, interpretations of the rate of poverty among the aged can vary considerably, depending upon the absolute standards of income adequacy that are applied. Similarly, even if one holds standards of income adequacy constant, the rate of poverty will change if one adds to the cash income distribution among the aged the impact of other economic resources such as tax exclusions, intrafamily transfers, home equity, and in-kind benefits.

Among the studies that have attempted to assess the impact of these resources on the income adequacy of the elderly, perhaps the most widely cited has been a Congressional Budget Office (CBO) estimate that in 1977 the inclusion of in-kind benefits would reduce the rate of poverty among the elderly from 14 to 6 percent.[15] Indeed, this particular study has been widely quoted to support the journalistic assertions that the elderly are now relatively well off.

The CBO study and similar analyses of in-kind benefits are technically correct but somewhat misleading. For example, let us consider the fact that Medicare and Medicaid in-kind transfers comprise the bulk of non-money benefits included in this analysis, which calculates their value as if they were health insurance premium subsidies. The insurance value of these two programs accounted for 98 percent of all in-kind benefits attributed to older persons in 1978.[16] When the value of these two programs is examined in the context of an actual budget, the misleading aspects of the picture conveyed by the CBO analysis become apparent.

According to the budgetary components of the official poverty indexes, an elderly couple that had made it up to the poverty line in the year that the CBO conducted its analysis would have had fifty dollars per month per person for clothing, transportation, utilities, furniture, taxes, personal and property insurance, and medical and dental care. The average expenditures for medical and dental care are clearly assumed to be minimal. Yet, in the same year, out-of-pocket medical and dental expenses alone averaged over fifty dollars a month for each elderly person.[17] Thus, even with extensive Medicare and Medicaid benefits, many couples that had made it up to the poverty line, or even exceeded it, would have had little or nothing left for clothing, transportation, utilities, and all other items after paying their out-of-pocket health-care expenses. In short, receiving in-kind benefits from the government may change the category in which one is officially classified by government economists, but it does not necessarily lift one out of poverty in a functional sense.

HOW WELL OFF ARE THE ELDERLY?

Obviously, the income status of older Americans is most accurately understood in terms of disaggregated descriptions. Some older persons are extremely wealthy, others are economically comfortable, and still others are poor. An older black woman is more than four times likely than a white male to have an income below the poverty line. Whether society has a responsibility to better the economic status of those who are below the poverty line, the near-poor line, and/or the BLS budget standards is, of course, an issue that can only be resolved through the political process.

It can be stated, however, that the assumptions used to construct the poverty index (by which 15.1 percent of the elderly are classified as poor) do not accurately reflect the income needs of an older person.[18] A consequence of these inaccurate assumptions is that the poverty line imposes an exceedingly harsh measure of economic security. Consider the budget of an aged couple that had reached the poverty line in 1980 and therefore was not classified as poor. According to official assumptions, the couple would have had, for instance, sixteen dollars per person for food each week. Not surprisingly, many analysts and official reports have suggested that higher standards than the poverty line should be used for measuring the economic security of older persons. Indeed, the original creator of the poverty indexes, Molly Orshansky, recently estimated that 36 percent of the aged "have too little income of their own to live by themselves."[19]

It is clear that, wherever the poverty line is drawn precisely, millions of older persons are clustered just above it, and their condition is not substantially different from those aging who are under it. As Borzilleri has pointed out, an extra twenty-five dollars a week could remove about three million elderly out of poverty as officially defined.[20] This would make the official record look different but would hardly have a major impact on the living standards of the recipients.

COSTS

Scholars, journalists, and public officials have raised serious questions about the economic capacity of American society to maintain the burden of an aging population. Because this issue has emerged relatively recently, few scholarly analyses have addressed it directly. Nonetheless, two recent leading studies make it possible to draw some useful, though tentative, conclusions.

As indicated at the outset of this chapter, dramatic estimates have been made that 40 percent of the federal budget will be spent on the aged early in the next century, and 63 percent by the year 2025. These numbers do not rest on assumptions that policies will be changed to improve the income status of current and future cohorts of the elderly poor. Rather, they reflect assumptions of continuity in current policies, predictions of increased numbers of older persons, and estimates concerning such matters as the rate of increase in health-care costs, trends in inflation, rates of real economic growth, and other macroeconomic factors.

Numbers that express the percentage of federal expenditures devoted to a single function such as "benefits to the aged" or "defense" may be important political symbols. But they do not necessarily represent unsustainable economic burdens. The central question to be answered in this discussion is, Can the American economy afford to continue, well into the next century, the current policies through which it provides benefits to the elderly? Evidently it can, according to a recent study that has addressed this issue.

An analysis published in 1981 by economists Robert L. Clark and John Menefee has shown that maintenance of current benefits per older person in real terms (1978 dollars) through the year 2025 would require a smaller proportion of the gross national product (GNP) in the years ahead than it does at present, if the consumer price index is used as the measure of inflation for benefit levels.[21] They point out that the percent of GNP required to finance federal benefits for the aged in 1978 was 5 percent. Maintenance of benefits per person in real 1978 dollars, according to their analysis, would require 3.8 percent of GNP in the year 2000, 3.3 percent in 2010, and 3.8 percent in 2025.

To date, most of the public discussion of the economic implications of an aging population has been confined to policy issues concerned with maintaining the viability of existing governmental mechanisms that provide income benefits to the elderly through specific, established formulas. An additional issue, of course, is whether the American economy can sustain the costs of improved income adequacy for the elderly through any mix of economic resources that might be available to older persons.

Despite contemporary portrayals of the elderly as relatively well off, millions of older persons are poor as measured by any of several absolute standards that are widely recognized. The same will hold true for millions among the future cohorts of the aged unless private and public policy conditions change substantially.

If one considers the substantial array of economic resources available to the elderly briefly sketched earlier in this chapter, it should be apparent that a variety of public and private strategies could be pursued to enhance the income status of the aging. Expansion of opportunities for older persons to earn income through employment might be achieved through government and private sector strategies to eliminate age-based job discrimination, retrain and reeducate older workers, and restructure jobs to permit more flexible working arrangements. Government could create additional incentives to promote increased personal savings. Appealing strategies for unlocking home equity and other nonliquid assets can be developed. Public policy and/or collective bargaining could promote the expansion and inflation-indexing of private pensions and health insurance benefits. Successful policies to promote general economic productivity and growth could provide large bases of employment and taxation for sustaining public income transfers to the elderly through cash and in-kind benefits.

This plethora of possible strategies, however, obfuscates the issue of whether the American economy can sustain the costs of an improved level of income adequacy for the aged. A complex chain of assumptions must be fulfilled for each strategy to result in increased income for older persons, and the relationship among such strategies and their requisite assumptions is intricate. Moreover, most of these strategies cannot substantially solve the income problems of those subgroups within the aging population who are frequently without significant employment histories—the frail elderly, older women, and minorities.

One of the more useful approaches for considering the capacity of the American economy to provide income adequacy for the elderly was undertaken by the Technical Committee for the 1981 White House Conference on Aging (WHCOA), which addressed the "Implications for the Economy" of population aging. In the context of an overall study of "Economic Policy in an Aging Society," it examined the probable aggregate economic effects of an expanded public income transfer program that would be used as a direct measure for addressing income-adequacy problems of the elderly through the year 2005. While the WHCOA Committee recognized that other policy alternatives might have some impact on improving income adequacy for the aging, it explicitly observed that "only an income transfer program directly targeted on the poorest elderly can have a significant impact."[22]

In analyzing the economic impact of increased transfers that would guarantee adequate income for all older persons over the next twenty-five years, the committee chose a relatively high absolute standard of adequacy, an income consistent with the BLS Intermediate Budget for Retired Couples. In addition, it posited that such transfers would only be made to those below the BLS standard and would be financed by increased taxes rather than by a redistribution of tax revenues.

The WHCOA committee's analysis led to the finding that such a program of increased income transfer and taxation "would not have a significant effect on the overall economy."[23] To be sure, such a program would add to federal expenditures; the analysis indicated that nineteen billion dollars would be required to fund the program in 1981, but the amount needed would decline to twelve billion dollars (in current dollars) by 2005. Nonetheless, this technical committee found that an intermediate and ongoing direct guarantee of an adequate income to all older persons for the next twenty-five years would have no harmful effects on the American economy.

No definitive judgments can be made on the basis of either this WHCOA committee report or the analysis conducted by Clark and Menefee. They are among the first in what will undoubtedly be a spate of serious technical studies examining the implications of an aging population for the American economy. But they do provide early indications that the challenges of maintaining or improving the economic status of the elderly in the years ahead are primarily political, not economic.

NOTES

1. *U.S. News and World Report*, September 1, 1980, p. 500.

2. See, for example, Robert B. Hudson, "The 'Graying' of the Federal Budget and Its Consequences for Old-Age Policy," *Gerontologist* 18, pt. 1 (October 1978): 428–40.

3. U.S., Office of Management and Budget, *The Budget of the United Stated Government: Fiscal Year 1981* (Washington, D.C.: Government Printing Office, 1980).

4. Joseph A. Califano, Jr., "U.S. Policy for the Aging—A Commitment to Ourselves," *National Journal* 10 (1978):1576.

5. U.S., Congress, Senate, Special Committee on Aging, *Emerging Options for Work and Retirement Policy* (Washington, D.C.: Government Printing Office, 1980):24.

6. See, for example, Robert J. Samuelson, "Aging America—Who Will Shoulder the Growing Burden?" *National Journal* 10 (1978):1712-17.

7. *Forbes*, February 18, 1980, p. 51.

8. Public Law 95-216.

9. See U.S., President's Commission on Pension Policy, *Coming of Age: Toward a National Retirement Income Policy* (Washington, D.C.: Government Printing Office, 1981), pp. 21-26.

10. Louis Harris and Associates, Inc., *Study of American Attitudes Toward Pensions and Retirement*, commissioned by Johnson and Higgins (New York, February 1979).

11. See Martha Derthick, *Policymaking for Social Security* (Washington, D.C.: Brookings Institution, 1979).

12. Yosef Riemer and Robert H. Binstock, "Campaigning for 'the Senior Vote': A Case Study of Carter's 1976 Campaign," *Gerontologist* 18 (December 1978): 517-24.

13. The data presented in the following discussion of economic resources are combined from the following sources: President's Commission on Pension Policy, *Coming of Age: Toward a National Retirement Policy* and *Appendix* (Washington, D.C.: Government Printing Office, 1981); U.S., Office of Management and Budget, *The Budget of the United States Government: Fiscal Year 1981* (Washington, D.C.: Government Printing Office, 1981); and unpublished data from the U.S. Social Security Administration.

14. Marilyn Moon, *The Measurement of Economic Welfare: Its Application to the Aged Poor* (New York: Academic Press, 1977).

15. U.S., Congressional Budget Office, *Poverty Status of Families Under Alternative Definitions of Income*, Background Paper no. 17, rev. (Washington, D.C.: Government Printing Office, June 1977).

16. Thomas C. Borzilleri, "In-Kind Benefit Programs and Retirement Income Adequacy," *National Journal* 12 (1980):1821-25.

17. U.S., Congress, Senate, Special Committee on Aging, *Developments in Aging: 1978*, part 1 (Washington, D.C.: Government Printing Office, 1979), p. 42.

18. See U.S., Congress, House, Select Committee on Aging, *Poverty Among America's Aged, Hearing*, 95 Cong., 2nd sess., August 9, 1978; and U.S., President's Commission on Pension Policy, *An Interim Report* (Washington, D.C.: Government Printing Office, 1980).

19. U.S., Congress, House, Select Committee on Aging, *Poverty*, p. 203.

20. Borzilleri, "In-Kind Benefit Programs."

21. Robert L. Clark and John Menefee, "Federal Expenditures for the Elderly: Past and Future," *Gerontologist* 21 (1981):132-37.

22. U.S., White House Conference on Aging, Technical Committee on an Age-Integrated Society—Implications for the Economy, *Economic Policy in an Aging Society* (Washington, D.C.: White House Conference on Aging, 1981), p. 29.

23. Ibid., p. 2.

JENNIFER L. WARLICK

3

Aged Women in Poverty: A Problem Without a Solution?

Old age is a state of life usually approached with apprehension and ambivalence. Women have especially good cause to feel this way. Indeed, poverty statistics suggest that for a woman not to ponder her future economic circumstances with caution, and in some cases despair, is to defy the hard facts of economic reality. In 1978, one of every six women aged sixty-five years and over had an income below official poverty lines, and women were twice again as likely to experience poverty during old age than were their male counterparts.

Moreover, older women were overrepresented among the poor, both young and old. In 1978, aged females accounted for 6 percent of the total U.S. population but for 10 percent of the total poor; they comprised 59 percent of the aged population but 71 percent of the aged poor. And the facts darken as women consider their own peculiar fates. For example, the probability of living in poverty for black aged females was nearly 40 percent in 1978. Similarly, poverty was the rule for one of every five women living without a spouse, and the probability that any woman would be spouseless in old age was 63 percent (that is, three of every 5 women sixty-five years and over were either widowed, separated, divorced, or never married in 1978).[1]

It has been argued that such statistics exaggerate the true incidence of poverty because they are based on current income and thus ignore intrafamily and in-kind (for example, Medicare) transfers as well as net worth that could be converted to a cash flow to supplement low, current cash balances.[2] Use of alternative measures that account for these criticisms does not alter the fundamental conclusion that a substantial proportion of the aged, and in particular aged women, lives in dire poverty.[3] More frequently the argument is made that the true incidence of poverty among the aged is understated by these statistics, which are derived from an outmoded methodology dating back to 1963. In this case, shifting to a more realistic updated methodology just about doubles the number of aged poor.[4]

Efforts to count and identify the poor undeniably encounter many problems, and criticism of any chosen method is inevitable. But as we have noted, regardless of the measure employed, the number of aged persons living in poverty is regretfully high. Moreover, poverty among women is consistently greater than among men. This chapter investigates the special problems of women that explain this fact.

We begin by comparing the poverty status of aged men and women as measured by their pretransfer income, that is, the sum of earnings, interest, dividends, rents, private pensions, royalties, alimony, and contributions from family members. We then add the amount of government transfers (Social Security, Supplementary Security Income, civil service, military, railroad retirement and veterans' pensions, unemployment insurance, and worker's compensation) to pretransfer incomes and determine the effect of these transfers on the poverty status of aged men and women. We examine the extent to which government transfers act as an equalizer or neutralizer, eliminating variations in the incidence of pretransfer poverty by living arrangements, marital status, age, and race. We also observe those instances in which government transfers are a nonequalizer creating variations in posttransfer status where there were none according to the pretransfer measure of income. The data presented in tables 3.1 through 3.7 are based on a sample of 11,635 census families containing at least one member age sixty-five or over drawn from the 1979 Current Population Survey. Subsequently, we describe the policies under which transfers are made in an effort to determine the extent to which these policies are responsible for the disadvantaged economic position of aged females. In particular, we examine recent charges that the Social Security system treats women unfairly, thus contributing to their economic problems.[5] We conclude by considering whether, in the absence of policy change, current poverty trends among aged women will continue into the future, in view of the recent increases in labor force participation among women and projections regarding the marital, age, and sex distribution of the elderly. Is poverty among aged women a problem that will solve itself as women become less economically dependent upon men during the prime working years of life, or is it a problem without a solution?

PRETRANSFER POVERTY STATUS

The extent to which the aged population is dependent upon government for income support is vividly illustrated by an examination of pretransfer income and poverty status. The mean pretransfer income of families headed by or containing at least one aged person was not quite $6,500 in 1978, or 32 percent of the mean for nonaged families.[6] On average, pretransfer income accounts for only 58 percent of final or

posttransfer income.[7] With pretransfer incomes at these low absolute
and relative levels, it is not surprising to find that 60 percent of all aged
families have pretransfer incomes below the poverty line appropriate for
their family size and composition.[8]

As the first column of table 3.1 shows, aged families headed by women
experience substantially higher rates of pretransfer poverty than those
headed by men: 65 percent as against 54 percent. For the most part,
today's aged females spend the majority of their adult lives out of the
labor market as homemakers dependent upon their husbands for income
support. The lack of labor force experience affects pretransfer income
during old age in at least two ways. First, it diminishes the earnings
capacity of women relative to that of men; second, it results in less
frequent entitlement to private pensions among females in their own
right. (Married women may be entitled to private pensions as a husband's
dependent or survivor, although the rules of most private pensions
discourage this arrangement, as we shall see later in this chapter.) These
implications of less labor force experience are illustrated in table 3.2,
which shows mean pretransfer income and the absolute values and
relative importance of its components for aged nuclear families living
alone.[9] The average mean pretransfer income of aged families headed by
males is almost three times as large as that headed by females. Differences in the mean value of earnings and private pensions account for
almost 80 percent of this gap.

The incidence of pretransfer poverty varies with the race as well as the
sex of the head of aged families. When the categories are ranked according to greatest risk for poverty, we find black women at the top, the
incidence of poverty among this group exceeding that of its nearest
contender, aged black males, by ten percentage points. Nonblack aged
women have the third highest incidence of pretransfer poverty, followed
by nonblack aged males, nonblack nonaged males, and black nonaged
males. Further analysis shows that the effect of being black on the
probability of having pretransfer income below poverty lines is twice that
of being female: being black raises the mean probability by twelve percentage points, while being female increases it by six percentage points.[10]
Because the racial effect is so large, racial distinction will be maintained
throughout the remainder of this chapter.

LIVING ARRANGEMENTS

The incidence of pretransfer poverty shows substantial variation
when aged familes are categorized by type of living arrangement, as
shown in the first three columns of table 3.3. Census families consisting
of a single aged nuclear family (NF=CF) have substantially higher rates of
pretransfer poverty in every headship category than do census families
containing more than one nuclear family. Census families headed by an

Table 3.1
Pretransfer Poverty Status of Aged Families, 1978

	Percentage of Pretransfer Poor	Mean Pretransfer Income	Ratio of Pretransfer Income to Posttransfer Income	Ratio of Income of Pretransfer Poor to Poverty Line	Percent Distribution
Total aged families	60	$ 6,449	.58	.26	100
Sex of head of aged family					
Male	54	7,301	.57	.29	53
Female	66	5,370	.58	.22	47
Race/sex/age of head of aged family					
Nonblack male under 66*	35	11,638	.72	.32	2
Black male under 66*	27	8,827	.67	.35	<1
Nonblack male over 65	54	7,466	.58	.30	46
Black male over 65	71	4,450	.51	.22	4
Nonblack female over 65	65	5,575	.59	.23	43
Black female over 65	81	3,168	.50	.18	4

SOURCE: U.S. Bureau of Census, *1979 Current Population Survey* (Washington, D.C.: U.S. Government Printing Office).

*The categories of nonblack and black males less than sixty-six refer to aged couples in which the wife is sixty-six or older.

Table 3.2
Components of Pretransfer and Posttransfer Incomes for Aged Families Consisting of One Nuclear Family, 1978, by Race and Sex of Head

Income Component	All		Nonblack		Black	
	Male	*Female*	*Male*	*Female*	*Male*	*Female*
Mean Pretransfer income	$6,026	$2,124	$6,267	$2,274	$2,626	$500
Mean earnings	$2,911	$ 439	$2,966	$ 452	$2,085	$305
Mean capital income	$2,184	$1,360	$2,331	$1,471	$ 166	$146
Mean private pensions	$ 875	$ 274	$ 912	$ 296	$ 362	$ 38
Mean alimony and contributions	$ 55	$ 50	$ 58	$ 54	$ 12	$ 11
Ratio of earnings to pretransfer income	.48	.21	.47	.20	.79	.61
Ratio of capital income to pretransfer income	.36	.64	.37	.65	.06	.29
Ratio of private pensions to pretransfer income	.15	.13	.15	.13	.14	.08
Ratio of alimony and contributions to pretransfer income	.01	.02	.01	.02	.01	.02

SOURCE: U.S. Bureau of the Census, *1979 Current Population Survey* (Washington, D.C.: U.S. Government Printing Office).

Table 3.3
Variations in Pretransfer and Posttransfer Poverty Status for Aged Families, 1978, by Living Arrangement

	Percentage of Pretransfer Poor			Percentage of Pretransfer Poor Removed from Poverty			Percentage of Postransfer Poor		
	NF=CF[a]	HDOTH[b]	OTHHD[c]	NF=CF	HDOTH	OTHHD	NF=CF	HDOTH	OTHHD
Total aged families	68	39	27	73	79	84	19	8	4
Sex of head of aged family									
Male	60	33	29	83	79	80	10	7	6
Female	80	45	26	63	78	85	29	10	4
Race/sex/age of head of aged family									
Nonblack male under 66[d]	38	18	0	89	51	NA[e]	4	9	0
Black male under 66	41	0	0	70	NA	NA	12	0	0
Nonblack male over 65	59	31	28	84	85	86	9	5	4
Black male over 65	79	64	36	61	62	59	30	25	15
Nonblack female over 65	78	43	24	66	82	88	26	8	3
Black female over 65	98	62	43	34	59	73	64	26	12

SOURCE: U.S. Bureau of the Census, *1979 Current Population Survey* (Washington, D.C.: U.S. Government Printing Office).

[a] NF=CF: Aged families living alone; 77 percent of all families.
[b] HDOTH: Aged families heading larger census families; 12 percent of all families.
[c] OTHHD: Aged families living in larger census families headed by someone outside the aged family; 11 percent of all families.
[d] The categories of nonblack and black males less than sixty-five refer to aged couples in which the wife is sixty-six or older.
[e] NA: Not applicable.

aged person (HDOTH) have higher rates than aged nuclear families living in a census family headed by a nonaged individual (OTHHD). The most dramatic comparisons are between family types NF=CF and OTHHD. For all categories of headship, the incidence of pretransfer poverty declines by 60 percent as the focus shifts away from independent nuclear families and to those living in households headed by a nonaged person. The poverty status of nonblack aged families is most improved by shared living arrangements of this type, with the incidence of pretransfer poverty declining by 70 percent. These changes are not surprising when one considers that the mean pretransfer per capita income of aged nuclear families increases by 57 percent when they move into the households of younger relatives. This increase testifies, for the most part, to the greater earning power of the younger family members. In contrast, the mean per capita pretransfer income of HDOTH family types falls when the pretransfer income of younger persons who share the living facilities of their aged relatives is accounted for.

When nuclear families living alone are considered, the greater incidence of pretransfer poverty among families headed by aged women than among those headed by men becomes even more apparent: four of every five families headed by aged women experience pretransfer poverty, as against three of five male-headed families. Moreover, the risk differential between aged black males and aged nonblack females essentially disappears. Although the variation in rates of poverty between male and female heads of other family types is not as large, it is nevertheless substantial.

MARITAL STATUS

Table 3.4 shows that variation in the incidence of pretransfer poverty by marital status favors married couples living together. Aged persons who have never married experience the second lowest rates of pretransfer poverty, followed by widows, divorced persons, and married couples living apart. Further analysis reveals, however, that the apparent advantage that married couples enjoy over persons widowed and never married disappears when the influences of other determinants of the probability of living in poverty (such as age, sex of head, and educational attainment) are controlled for. In contrast, even after controlling for these factors, married couples living together have a lower probability of experiencing pretransfer poverty than either divorced or separated persons owing to their greater earnings from both labor and capital and to higher average private pensions. Per capita pretransfer income for married couples is 20 percent greater than the average for divorced or separated persons.

Examination of pretransfer poverty rates for men and women, within specific marital status categories, yields some surprises. Women who are

Table 3.4

Variations in Pretransfer and Posttransfer Poverty Status for Aged Families, 1978, by Marital Status

Marital Status	Percent Pretransfer Poor				
	Married, Spouse Present	Married Spouse Absent[a]	Widowed	Divorced	Never Married
Total of aged families	52	72	65	69	59
Sex of head of aged family					
Male	52	74	59	73	58
Female	NA[b]	71	66	66	60
Race/sex/age of head of aged family					
Nonblack male under 66[c]	35	NA	NA	NA	NA
Black male under 66[c]	27	NA	NA	NA	NA
Nonblack male over 65	52	66	57	75	56
Black male over 65	69	84	73	61	62
Nonblack female over 65	NA	65	65	64	58
Black female over 65	NA	90	80	83	88
Percent of all aged families	40	3	47	4	7
	Percent Pretransfer Poor Removed from Poverty by Transfers				
Total of aged families	86	54	68	63	74
Sex of head of aged family					
Male	86	65	76	76	70
Female	NA	45	66	56	76
Race/sex/age of head of aged family					
Nonblack make under 66[c]	87	NA	NA	NA	NA
Black male under 66[c]	70	NA	NA	NA	NA

Percent Pretransfer Poor Removed from Poverty by Transfers

Marital Status	Married, Spouse Present	Married Spouse Absent[a]	Widowed	Divorced	Never Married
Nonblack male over 65	87	77	77	76	76
Black male over 65	66	47	63	78	27
Nonblack female over 65	NA	48	69	57	77
Black female over 65	NA	35	41	37	60
Percent Posttransfer Poor					
Total of aged families	7	33	21	25	16
Sex of head of aged family					
Male	7	27	14	17	17
Female	NA	41	22	31	14
Race/sex/age of head of aged family					
Nonblack make under 66[c]	5	NA	NA	NA	NA
Black male under 66[c]	8	NA	NA	NA	NA
Nonblack male over 65	7	17	13	18	14
Black male over 65	24	46	27	13	45
Nonblack female over 65	NA	34	20	28	13
Black female over 65	NA	57	47	52	35

SOURCE: U.S. Bureau of the Census, 1979 *Current Population Survey* (Washington, D.C.: U.S. Government Printing Office).

[a] Includes separated persons.

[b] NA: Not applicable.

[c] The categories of nonblack and black males less than sixty-five refer to aged couples in which the wife is sixty-six or older.

widowed experience a higher incidence of pretransfer poverty than do their male counterparts, but divorced or separated men have higher rates of pretransfer poverty than divorced or separated women. There is no significant difference in the rates of pretransfer poverty between men and women who have never married.

Focusing solely on women, the primary variation across marital status is between women living with their spouses and those whose spouse is absent. There is surprisingly little variation across the remaining categories.[11] Consistent with the previous tables, table 3.4 shows that black aged females have the highest rates of pretransfer poverty in all marital status categories.

OTHER DEMOGRAPHIC CHARACTERISTICS

The incidence of pretransfer poverty appears to vary systematically with several additional demographic characteristics, including age, educational attainment, regional residence, and whether the head is of Spanish origin. As shown in table 3.5, the risk of pretransfer poverty increases with the age of the family head for every race–sex category, up to age eighty years and over, at which point there is a slight decline in all categories except black males. Additional years of formal education produce the opposite result, reducing the probability of pretransfer poverty by two percentage points for each additional year. Residing in the Southern or Western regions of the United States raises the probability of pretransfer poverty by five and six percentage points, respectively, relative to living in the Northeast. The probability of pretransfer poverty of families headed by persons of Spanish origin is dramatically lower than that of their white and black counterparts (twenty-one and thirty-three percentage points, respectively). This is an unexpected finding that warrants further investigation.[12]

GOVERNMENT TRANSFERS AND POVERTY

POSTTRANSFER POVERTY STATUS

The preceding section established that, in the absence of government transfers, the incomes of three-fifths of all families containing an aged person place them among the poor. Government transfers increase the pretransfer incomes of all aged families by 72 percent, bringing 74 percent of the pretransfer poor out of poverty, thereby reducing the poverty rate among the aged from 60 to 16 percent. Only 4 percent of all aged families do not receive government transfers, and the poverty rate among these families is 21 percent, compared with 16 percent among those who do receive such aid. Social Security retirement benefits are by far the most important type of transfer, accounting for 83 precent of all government transfers to the aged.[13] Benefits from the Supplementary

Table 3.5
Variations in Pretransfer and Posttransfer Poverty Status for Aged Families, 1978, by Age of Head

	Percent Pretransfer Poor				Percent of Pretransfer Poor Removed from Poverty by Transfers				Percent Posttransfer Poor			
	Under 66	66–71	72–79	80 and Over	Under 66	66–71	72–79	80 and Over	Under 66	66–71	72–79	80 and Over
Total of aged families	34	54	66	67	86	76	74	79	45	13	17	21
Sex of head of aged family												
Male	34	48	60	68	86	83	83	81	5	9	10	14
Female	NA*	61	70	66	NA	69	67	62	NA	19	24	26
Race/sex of head of aged family												
Nonblack male	35	46	59	67	87	85	85	83	5	7	9	11
Black male	27	65	75	78	70	60	66	49	8	26	25	39
Nonblack female	NA	59	69	65	NA	72	70	64	NA	16	21	24
Black female	NA	80	84	77	NA	48	40	32	NA	42	51	52

SOURCE: U.S. Bureau of the Census, 1979 *Current Population Survey* (Washington, D.C.: U.S. Government Printing Office).
*NA: Not applicable.

Security Income program, the primary welfare program for aged persons, account for an additional 4 percent. The remaining 13 percent is comprised of public employee retirement pensions (6 percent), veterans' pensions, unemployment insurance, worker's compensation benefits, and benefits from other welfare programs (General and Emergency Assistance, and Aid to Families with Dependent Children).

GOVERNMENT TRANSFERS AS A NEUTRALIZER

It was shown in table 3.1 that the incidence of pretransfer poverty is substantially higher (twelve percentage points) among families headed by aged women than among aged families headed by men. Turning to table 3.6, we see that, although the percentage of female-headed aged families that receive government transfers is nearly identical to that of male-headed families (indeed, exceeds the latter by two percentage points), the mean transfer for female-headed families ($3,297) is only 65 percent of the mean for male-headed families. Consequently, it is not surprising to find that transfers remove a higher percentage of male-headed aged families from poverty than female-headed families. It follows that the incidence of posttransfer poverty is greater for women than for men. Moreover, the risk of living in poverty associated with being female increases relative to its pretransfer poverty level: being female increases the probability of having posttransfer income less than the poverty line by eight percentage points, compared with the six percentage-point differential characterizing pretransfer poverty status. Alternately stated, whereas female-headed families were 22 percent more likely to experience pretransfer poverty than their male-headed counterparts, after government transfers they were 130 percent more likely than male headed families to live in poverty. Thus, it can hardly be said that government transfers eliminate or in any way neutralize the sex differential in the incidence of pretransfer poverty. Rather, they exacerbate this differential, worsening the economic circumstances of aged women relative to men.

As was true of pretransfer poverty status, when the categories of aged male and female heads are disaggregated by race and age, families headed by black females over sixty-five years old experience the highest rate of posttransfer poverty; almost one-half of all such families live in poverty. Families headed by aged black males rank second, with a poverty rate of 28 percent, followed by aged families headed by nonblack females (20 percent) and nonblack males. Younger males, regardless of race, are the least likely to be living in poverty. Although the proportion of blacks receiving transfers is similar to that of nonblacks, as was true in the case of women, the average transfer to blacks is smaller than that to nonblacks.

It was shown in table 3.3 that the incidence of pretransfer poverty was less for aged families that share living arrangements with other families,

Table 3.6
Government Transfers and the Posttransfer Poverty Status of Aged Families, 1978

	Percent Receiving Government Transfers	Mean Government Transfer	Percent of Pretransfer Poor Removed from Poverty by Transfers	Mean Posttransfer Income	Percent Posttransfer Poor
Total of aged families	96	$4,250	74	$11,107	16
Sex of head of aged family					
Male	95	5,117	82	12,788	10
Female	97	3,297	66	9,220	23
Race/sex/age of head of aged family					
Nonblack male under 66*	87	4,611	87	16,249	5
Black male under 66	88	4,260	70	13,087	8
Nonblack male over 65	96	5,501	84	12,967	8
Black male over 65	94	4,247	61	8,697	28
Nonblack female over 65	97	3,943	69	9,518	20
Black female over 65	96	3,115	41	6,283	48

SOURCE: U.S. Bureau of the Census, 1979 Current Population Survey (Washington, D.C.: U.S. Government Printing Office).
*The categories of nonblack and black males less than sixty-five refer to aged couples in which the wife is sixty-six or older.

particularly when the latter represent the larger census family. Although aged families living alone (NF=CF) receive larger transfers, on average, than families with other living arrangements ($4,508 as compared with $4,120 for aged families heading larger census families and $2,709 for aged families living in a census family headed by someone outside the aged family), these transfers remove a smaller percentage of these other households living alone from poverty (see table 3.3, columns 4 through 6). Consequently, the risk of living in posttransfer poverty for aged families living alone, relative to families with other living arrangements, is even greater than the relative risk of experiencing pretransfer poverty.

Transfers remove a higher percentage of male-headed families living alone from poverty than they do female-headed families of the same type and, in so doing, compound the relative economic disadvantage experienced by the latter. They are neutral with respect to male/female-headed aged families heading larger census families (HDOTH) and provide a slight advantage to female-headed families living in larger census families headed by some younger relative.

As measured by the percentage of pretransfer poor families (table 3.3, columns 4 through 6) who are removed from poverty, the effectiveness of government transfers is greatest among married couples living together. It follows that these couples have the lowest incidence of posttransfer poverty (table 3.3, columns 7 through 9) and that relative to them the risk of living in poverty is increased by government transfers for members of all marital statuses. As was true of pretransfer poverty status, persons who are separated from their spouses continue to experience the highest rate of poverty.

The distribution of transfer disfavors women, worsening their relative economic position in all categories except those who never married. Whereas women in the latter category experience a rate of pretransfer poverty marginally above that of men, they experience a posttransfer poverty rate slightly below that of their male counterparts. Divorced or separated women experience the greatest increase in the incidence of poverty relative to men as a result of government transfers.

The risk of pretransfer poverty rises with advancing age; falls with additional years of formal schooling; is greater among blacks than non-blacks, particularly among families headed by persons of Spanish origin; and is higher for families living in the Southern and Western regions of the United States relative to those living in the Northeastern and North-central regions. Government transfers maintain these relationships among the posttransfer poor with two exceptions. First, they place residents of the Northcentral region of the United States at a higher risk for posttransfer poverty relative to their counterparts in the Northeast. Second, they eliminate the lower risk of poverty for families headed by persons of Spanish origin, placing them on a par with nonblack families.

GOVERNMENT POLICIES TOWARD AGED WOMEN

The previous section has shown that government transfers are not neutral with respect to the economic status of aged men and women but, rather, are more effective in reducing the degree of pretransfer poverty among aged families headed by males. In this section we argue that this result is the logical outcome of the interaction of the distributions of male- and female-headed families across all possible marital statuses and of government programs that tailor the computation of transfers to the marital status of beneficiaries. We begin with an examination of the eligibility and benefit computation rules governing the Social Security Old Age and Survivors Insurance Program (OASI). We then examine the federal civil service and military retirement pension programs. We conclude by considering the distributional effects of the Supplementary Security Income (SSI) program. Under SSI, eligibility is universal for aged persons satisfying certain needs criteria (income and assets must not exceed specified limits), and only two marital statuses (couples living together and individuals) are recognized in the computation of benefits. Due to these characteristics, the antipoverty effectiveness of SSI is less biased sexually than that of the other programs and favors beneficiaries with the lowest pretransfer incomes. But, as we have seen, women are disportionately represented among the aged poor. It follows therefore that SSI's antipoverty effectiveness is greatest among women, thereby offsetting to some degree the reverse effects of OASI and government employee retirement programs.

SOCIAL SECURITY OLD AGE AND SURVIVORS INSURANCE

OASI pays benefits to retired workers who have worked in covered employment for a requisite number of years, and who had been required to pay a payroll tax on prior covered earnings, up to a specific taxable maximum. The size of the monthly benefit that a retired worker receives is based upon his or her average indexed monthly earnings (AIME) in covered employment.[14] A progressive benefit formula is then applied to the AIME to determine the amount of the benefit, known as the primary insurance amount (PIA), to which the worker is entitled. The benefit formula for persons attaining age sixty-five in 1981 replaces 90 percent of the first $211 of AIME, 32 percent of the next $1,063 of AIME, and 15 percent of any remaining amount of AIME. The benefit actually received may not equal the PIA for several reasons: Benefits are decreased if a worker retires before age sixty-five or if he or she earns an amount above specified limits ($5,500 in 1981). Benefits may exceed the PIA if the worker delays retirement beyond age sixty-five, is married, and/or has dependent children. That benefits are increased when a worker has dependents is a break with the original design of OASI, which intended that benefits would be paid only to retired workers. This original intent was quickly modified, however, to ensure income adequacy for the dependents of living and deceased workers. These modifications reflect the assumption that women are economically dependent upon their husbands, remaining at home to care for dependent children. Although this assumption is challenged by the recent dramatic rise in female labor-force participation, it is a good characterization of the level of a majority of today's OASI beneficiaries.

The current program provides a noncontributory benefit to the spouses (the vast majority of whom are women) of retired workers equal to one-half of the retired worker's benefits, providing that the spouse is not entitled to a larger benefit in her or his own right as a worker. For example, the wife of a retired worker entitled to a benefit of $400 per month would be eligible for a benefit of $200 per month if she had never worked in covered employment or had not worked a sufficient amount of time to receive benefits in her own right. If the wife were entitled to a retired workers benefit of $150 per month, on the basis of her own earnings, she would receive an additional $50 per month so that her total benefit would equal one-half ($200) of her husband's. A wife does not receive a spouse's benefit if her own retired worker's benefit is equal to or greater than 50 percent of her husband's benefit.

Widows of retired workers are eligible for survivors benefits equal to the amount that the deceased worker would have received if he were still living. If they are also entitled to benefits as workers, they receive the higher amount. Since 1977, widowers have been entitled to survivors benefits under provisions identical to those for widows. Prior to 1977, to be eligible for survivors benefits a widower was required to pass a dependency test by demonstrating that he had received at least one-half of his support from his wife in the twelve months preceding her death. The benefits of a widow or widower age sixty or over are not affected by remarriage. Prior to 1979, remarriage resulted in the termination of benefits if the remarried widow or widower became entitled to benefits as a dependent spouse equal to or greater than her or his survivor's benefit.

Divorced spouses of retired workers who do not remarry are entitled to a dependent's benefit equal to 50 percent of their exspouse's benefit provided that the marriage lasted ten years and the exspouse is, in fact, retired. Surviving divorced spouses may receive 100 percent of the deceased exspouse's benefit. Prior to 1979, the duration-of-marriage requirement was twenty years. Like widows and widowers, divorced wives who also receive benefits as workers receive the higher of the two amounts. Legally separated spouses of retired workers are entitled to dependents and survivors benefits similar to those available to divorced spouses.[15]

How do these computation rules interact with the distribution of aged females and males by marital status to produce a distribution of post-transfer income that finds female-headed families overrepresented among the poor? To answer this question we need first to identify the effects of Social Security transfers on the incidence of poverty among aged persons of different marital statuses. Consider an aged couple with one retired worker (if the other member of the couple did work, assume that his or her PIA is 50 percent or less of that of the primary earner) and an individual who has never married, both households having the same earnings record (and thus the same PIA). The retired couple will receive a benefit equal to 150 percent of the worker's PIA, while the never-married individual will receive 100 percent of the PIA. Thus, the couple receives a 50 percent bonus to meet the consumption needs of its additional member. But when we compare the respective poverty lines for an aged couple and a single person, we find that the ratio of the former to the latter is 1.25, implying that only a 25 percent bonus is required to maintain consumption parity between them. Assuming that pretransfer income as a percentage of the poverty line is the same for the couple and individual, the extra 25 percent bonus granted to the couple by OASI computation rules decreases their probability of having posttransfer income less than the poverty line, relative to the individual.

As an example, consider Ross and Virginia, a couple who have followed traditional sex roles throughout their lives. Virginia entered the labor force during the Depression years of the 1930s to supplement Ross's earnings but did not accumulate the quarters of coverage required to receive Social Security benefits as a worker. Ross was employed as an unskilled laborer at the prevailing wage for the majority of his work life and retired with average annual earnings of $5,300. Consequently, his annual PIA is $2,945. As a dependent spouse, Virginia will receive benefits of $1,472.50, half of Ross's benefits. Together they will receive total annual Social Security benefits of $4,417.50.

Now consider Frances, a never-married individual who, like Ross, worked for the minimum wage for most of her work life and is eligible at retirement for benefits equal to $2,945 annually. Because Frances has no dependents, this amount represents her total annual benefits from OASI. Assume further that Ross and Virginia receive $197 annually in interest on a small savings account, while Frances receives $158 from a similar source. This is the only nontransfer income either family receives and represents 5 percent of their respective poverty lines of $3,947 and $4,159. Adding their Social Security benefits to their pretransfer income ($4417 + $197) we find that Ross and Virginia have total posttransfer income of $4,614.50. Government transfers have raised their income above their appropriate poverty lines by 17 percent. Frances does not fare as well, however, with total posttransfer equal to $3,103 ($2,945 + $158),

$56 or 2 percent shy of the poverty line for aged individuals. If, however, Virginia had received a spouse's benefit equal to only 25 percent of Ross's benefit as implied by the ratio of the poverty lines, Ross's and Virginia's total annual income would have equaled $3,878 ([$2945 × 1.25] + $197). As in the case of Frances, this amount is 2 percent less than the appropriate poverty line, so that they too would have remained in poverty. Thus we see that the extra 25 percent bonus granted to Virginia as Ross's spouse favors couples relative to never-married individuals, shifting the relative incidence of poverty.

The same conclusion holds true for couples relative to widows and widowers who face the same poverty line as never-married individuals and who receive 100 percent of their deceased spouse's (retired worker's) PIA. The balance is shifted even more heavily in the direction of couples compared with divorced and separated persons who receive only 50 percent of the exspouse's PIA. It follows logically that the antipoverty effects of Social Security should be greatest among couples. Because never-married persons and surviving spouses receive 100 percent of a retired worker's PIA, the degree of poverty reduction in these two categories will be similar to each other and less than that for married couples, provided that they are characterized by equivalent distributions of pretransfer income and PIAs. Finally, Social Security benefits will have their smallest impact on separated and divorced persons, who are eligible for at most, if at all, 50 percent of their exspouse's PIA.

These conclusions are partially substantiated by the data presented in table 3.3.[16] Reviewing columns 4 through 6, it is clear that the greater antipoverty effects of transfers are felt by married couples. Widows and never-married persons are aided to a lesser (and similar) degree, while separated persons form a lower, third tier. Divorced persons fare better than our predictions would suggest, falling roughly halfway between the combined category of widows and never-married persons, on the one hand, and separated individuals, on the other. This result does not necessarily contradict our earlier assumption, since divorced men who receive 100 percent of their PIAs are included in this category in addition to dependent divorced spouses.

To understand why these transfers are more effective in reducing poverty among families headed by aged males rather than females, we need only to examine the distributions of male- and female-headed families across marital status categories. These distributions are shown in table 3.7. The most striking differences in the distributions occur within the categories of married persons (spouse present) and widows. The proportion of aged men living with a spouse is more than double that for women, while almost four times as many women as men either have been widowed or have never been married. The distribution of males and females across the remaining categories is almost identical. It follows then that, because the percentage of males living with spouses is so much greater than that of females, Social Security benefits are more effective in reducing poverty among families headed by males than by females (table 3.6, column 3).

This general conclusion applies to the specific marital status categories of widowed, separated, and divorced persons as well as to married couples. Because males are more likely to be entitled to a full worker's benefit regardless of their marital status, they are likely to experience a higher rate of poverty reduction and a lower incidence of poverty than divorced or separated women (see columns 4 through 9 of table 3.3). Widows experience a smaller reduction in poverty than widowers because they are older, on average, and their benefits are based on the less favorable earnings records of older, deceased husbands. The poverty effectiveness of Social Security transfers is greater for females than for males only among persons never married. This outcome most probably reflects a higher average PIA among never-married women. Previous research regarding the labor-force experiences of single persons suggests that the single status of men reflects some inherent instability, rendering them undesirable as both husbands and employees. Hence, their work histories are more sporadic, and their lifetime earnings are lower than their female counterparts'.[17]

Table 3.7
Percent Distribution of Aged Persons, 1978, by Sex and Marital Status

Marital Status	Male	Female
Married, spouse present	76	37
Married, spouse absent	3	2
Widowed	14	52
Divorced	3	3
Never Married	5	5

SOURCE: U.S.Bureau of the Census, 1979 Current Population Survey (Washington, D.C.: U.S. Government Printing Office).

Note: Percentages may not sum exactly to 100 due to rounding.

CIVIL SERVICE AND MILITARY RETIREMENT PROGRAMS

The provisions of the federal civil service and military service retirement plans, and thus the subsequent distribution of benefits from these programs, reinforce the effects of OASI on the economic status of aged women relative to aged men.[18] The federal civil service has its own retirement system, which replaces Social Security. Consequently, the spouses of federal civil employees are deprived of the most minimal protection afforded by the Social Security system unless they or their spouses have earned a separate Social Security benefit through work in covered employment outside the federal government. In contrast to the worker who qualifies for Social Security, a civil servant may elect to participate in a plan that does not provide survivors benefits simply by so requesting in writing. The spouse is not required to play a role in this decision. If a worker opts out of the survivors plan, benefits are paid to the couple during the time they are both alive but cease upon the worker's death. Moreover, the system provides an incentive to opt out by reducing a couple's benefit if the survivors plan is chosen. The prospects of a divorced wife of a civil servant are even bleaker; she has no rights whatsoever to his retirement income, regardless of the timing of the divorce or his subsequent marital status.

The position of dependent spouses of career military personnel—spouses who are predominantly women—is somewhat better than that of federal employees for three reasons. First, military personnel are covered by Social Security, and, consequently, their spouses (married, widowed, or divorced) are provided minimal protection. Second, although military personnel may elect not to participate in a plan providing survivors benefits, the system notifies the spouse of this choice. This is not the case under the federal civil service retirement program. Finally, under public law the surviving spouse (but not a divorced spouse) of a career serviceman is entitled to a minimum annual income of $2,100, regardless of the serviceman's decision regarding the survivor option. Like the divorced wives of federal employees, the divorced wives of military personnel have no rights to their spouses' retirement benefits. However, if the marriage lasted ten years the spouse is entitled to Social Security benefits.

It follows from these provisions that the federal civil service and military retirement programs favor married couples and never-married individuals, relative to widows and divorced wives, to a greater degree than does Social Security. Consequently, the effects of Social Security upon the relative economic status of women is reinforced by the inclusion of civil service and military pensions in the measure of government transfers.

SUPPLEMENTARY SECURITY INCOME PROGRAM

Implemented in 1974, the Supplementary Security Income Program replaced the states' Old Age Assistance programs as the primary source of public assistance to low-income aged persons. To be eligible for SSI, an aged couple or individual must have total countable income below specified limits. This includes all other types of government transfers (with the exception of state supplements to SSI) as well as the components of pretransfer income.[19] Thus, SSI is truly an income supplement available only when income from other sources is inadequate to ensure minimal consumption standards.[20] The maximum federal SSI benefit available to an aged couple is 1.5 times that available to a single individual. Thus, like

Social Security, SSI could, in principle, have greater antipoverty effectiveness among couples than individuals. Unlike Social Security, however, SSI makes no further distinctions among beneficiaries according to marital status.

Despite its potential for favoring couples over individuals and, hence, male-headed families over female-headed families, SSI in fact ameliorates to a small degree the imbalance initiated by OASI. SSI benefits remove an additional 5 percent of pretransfer poor female-headed families from poverty but only 1 additional percent of male-headed families. Its greatest impact among females occurs for divorced persons, reducing the incidence of poverty among the pretransfer poor by an additional 14 percent.

These outcomes are not surprising in light of the supplemental function of SSI. They simply reflect higher eligibility and participation rates among women than men, which result in part from the distribution of OASI benefits.[21]

THE ECONOMIC STATUS OF FUTURE COHORTS OF AGED FEMALES

The key determinants of the economic status of future cohorts of aged women include the extent to which they are entitled to retirement pensions from private and public retirement systems as workers, their earnings potential, and their distribution across marital status, age, and racial categories. The first two of these factors are commonly determined by labor-force experience. The continuity, duration, and industry of employment, as well as an individual's earnings history, are crucial determinants of one's eligibility for both private and public retirement pensions. These factors influence a person's ability to retain or obtain employment, allowing him or her to supplement pensions with earnings. Future entitlement to pension benefits also depends critically on the prevalence of private pension plans—and their provisions defining eligibility—and on their benefit computations as well as those for OASI.

A woman's marital status will continue to be important as long as the current benefit computation rules of OASI and government retirement plans prevail, but its significance will fade somewhat as larger percentages of females become entitled to retired worker's benefits in excess of 50 percent of their husband's benefits. Longevity is critical because the real value of most pension benefits diminishes through time relative to the earnings and pensions of younger cohorts because they are not normally indexed to increases in productivity.[22] Race is included among these determinants to reflect the fact that aged black females persistently experience the highest rates of poverty, even after accounting for the influence of other characteristics. Thus, to answer the question, Will poverty continue to be a problem among future cohorts of aged females?, we need to consider first the following questions:

- Will the labor-force experience of future cohorts of aged females be significantly different from that of today's aged females?
- What will be the prevalence of private pensions in the future? Will the eligibility and benefit computation rules of the future resemble those of today?
- Will the treatment of women under OASI change in the future? If so, what will be the shape of change?
- How will the distributions of aged females by marital status, age, and race differ in the future?

We consider each of these questions in turn.

LABOR-FORCE EXPERIENCE OF FUTURE COHORTS

One of the most dramatic changes in the composition of the American labor force in recent years regards increased participation by women. Female members of the labor force have increased both absolutely and relatively. Between 1947 and 1977, the number of female workers more than doubled from seventeen to forty million; the percentage of women sixteen years of age and over who were in the labor force rose from 32 to 48 percent. During those thirty years, three of every five new workers were women, their proportion of the total labor force rising from 28 to 40 percent. The long-run increase in participation rates affected all age groups, except women sixty-five years and over, whose participation has not changed significantly.[23] Moreover, taking the cohort of women born in the years 1886–95 as a reference point, each successive cohort has demonstrated a greater propensity for career development. A moderate proportion of the 1886–95 cohort worked prior to marriage and child-bearing, but family responsibilities signaled permanent departure from the labor force for the vast majority of these women. In contrast, the decline in labor-force participation associated with family formation and care of preschool children has diminished with successive cohorts such that for the cohorts of 1936–45 and later there is little perceptible change on labor-force participation rates from ages twenty to twenty-nine. Thereafter, when children are in school, requiring less home supervision, labor-force participation rates have been rising at increasing rates for successive cohorts.[24] And these trends are projected to continue into the future.

That the average continuity and duration of labor-force experience of successive cohorts is increasing implies that the proportion of cohorts who will be entitled to retirement benefits as workers in the future is also rising. Unfortunately, there is little evidence to suggest that such increases in duration and continuity have been accompanied by improvements in women's overall labor-market status. New entrants have been concentrated in jobs traditionally dominated by females (for example, clerical, health-care service), which are characterized by low wages and few fringe benefits. Consequently, the gap between the average earnings of males and females has actually widened.[25] However, as noted by Gordon, the differences in retirement benefits will be less than these earnings differentials due to the progressive benefit formula under OASI.[26] On balance then, all other factors held constant, it seems likely that the long-run increase in labor-force participation will lead to improvement of both the absolute and relative economic status of future cohorts of aged women.

PRIVATE PENSION PLANS

The impact of increased labor-force participation among women would be magnified if accompanied by a growth in the prevalence of private pension plans and/or liberalization of their dependency provisions. Although coverage under OASI extends to almost all kinds of employment, private pension coverage is concentrated in a few industries: communications and public utilities, mining, manufacturing, and finance, insurance, and real estate. In 1972, the percent of full-time employees with private pension coverage in these industries ranged from 82 percent in communications to 52 percent in finance. Coverage was provided to only 29 percent of the full-time employees of the service industry, an industry for which the proportion of female employees is traditionally high. Overall, approximately 44 percent of all full-time and part-time employees in private industry are covered by private pensions. The proportion of employees with coverage is higher for males than females: 52 percent for men compared with only 36 percent for women. The percentage of workers who ultimately receive private pensions is lower still. Data from the Social Security Administration's Retirement History Survey indicate that, in 1972, 72 percent of the men but only 55 percent of the women covered by private pensions and earning no money actually received private retirement pensions.[27]

If today's cohorts of working women are to benefit from the economic protection of private pensions during their retirement years, coverage must be extended to industries with heavy concentrations of female employees, which are precisely those industries where it is now low. The prospects for such growth are bleak, however. Growth in coverage has slowed significantly as the coverage of the employees of large, affluent corporations has become almost complete, leaving small employers (for instance, the small retailer, the local restaurant, repair services, real estate agencies) as the primary source of potential growth. The ability of these employers to bear the costs of providing private pensions was severely handicapped by the passage of the Employee Retirement Income Security Act (ERISA) in 1974. Intended to ensure the financial integrity of existing pension plans, the costs of complying with ERISA's complex regulations appear to have encouraged some smaller plans to go out of existence and have discouraged the formation of others.[28]

Improvement in the economic position of future cohorts of aged women could be achieved in the absence of such growth if the provisions of private pensions regulating dependent's benefits were revised. ERISA mandated for the first time that all pension plans offer joint and survivors benefits. But, like the federal civil service system, workers may opt out of a survivor benefits plan without notifying the spouse, the election of survivors benefits usually results in a reduction of benefits during the couple's lifetime, and divorced wives living in noncommunity-property states have no rights to benefits at all.[29] Many plans pay no benefits if the worker dies prior to retirement, and postretirement death benefits may take a variety of forms, including a fixed monthly payment over a six-month to five-year period, a lump-sum payment (which is usually a nominal or token amount), a percent of the worker's benefit (usually 50 percent), and the return of a worker's contributions plus interest.[30]

THE FUTURE TREATMENT OF WOMEN UNDER OASI

The issue of equal treatment by OASI of men and women in a world where traditional sex roles are changing is well recognized. The Social Security Administration created a special task force to study this issue; it was also taken up by the 1979 Social Security Advisory Board, a group of nongovernment experts, that convenes every fourth year, and the U.S. Commission on Civil Rights.[31] In addition, numerous academic researchers have become involved at their own initiative.[32] As a result, a number of plans that would revise current eligibility provisions and benefit computation rules have been proposed and analyzed. The most important of these include individually based benefits, homemaker credits, and earnings sharing. Under an individually based benefits system, workers alone would be eligible for benefits with no provisions for dependents or survivors of workers. Under the homemaker credits approach the value of nonmarket work within the home would be explicitly recognized through the award of homemaker credits. These would allow eligible dependents to receive Social Security benefits as workers. The earnings-sharing method would split equally between spouses the total Social Security claims accumulated by the couple during the marriage. If and when the marriage dissolved, each spouse would be left with an earnings record equal to one-half of the combined total. A common variation on both the individually based benefits and earnings-sharing approaches is to provide to all aged persons a fixed annual grant, in addition to their earnings-related benefits, to ensure that all receive a socially agreed upon minimum income.[33]

Analysis of the potential costs of the three major proposals shows that the individually based system is significantly less expensive than the current system, while both the homemaker credits and earnings-sharing proposals are slightly more expensive.[34] Combining the individually based benefits or the earnings-sharing system with a universal grant further increases their costs.[35] While the ultimate judgment regarding the desirability of any of these proposals should not be based on its cost alone, we focus on this factor because of its crucial role in political decisions. It is necessary to consider the likelihood of congressional approval of a Social Security system that would consume even more of society's resources than the system in operation today. In our opinion, the prospects that any of the proposals can win approval are dismal. The costs associated with the homemaker credits and earnings-sharing approaches seem prohibitive given the atmosphere of financial crisis currently enveloping OASI. The individually based benefits approach would reduce current costs but at the expense of dependents and survivors. To date, Congress has shown an unwillingness to enact legislation that would worsen the economic position of such a large segment of the aged population. Thus, in our view, speculation regarding the incident of poverty among future cohorts of aged women would best take place under the assumption that the future treatment of women under Social Security will closely resemble that of today.

PROJECTED TRENDS

In the absence of major reform of the Social Security and private pension systems, the economic status of future cohorts of aged women may be determined largely by their age, race, and marital composition for reasons explained earlier. What are the projections for each of these demographic characteristics? Is significant change anticipated?

The aged population has been getting older and is expected to continue to do so, at least until the year 2000. Thereafter, the average age is likely to decrease. For example, in 1976, 39 percent of the older population was in the age group seventy-five and over. This proportion is expected to rise to 45 percent by the year 2000 and then fall back to 39 percent by 2020. Rates of increase are expected to be greater for females than males, although not dramatically so.[36] In the present context, these projections imply a temporary worsening of the economic status of aged women to the year 2000 that will be reversed in the following two decades.

The question of the race composition of future cohorts of aged women is a question of future trends in life expectancy. Life expectation at birth of white females is well above that of black and other nonwhite females, although this difference fell dramatically between 1900 and 1976 from 16.1 to 4.7 years. The differences in life expectancy at age 65 have been much smaller historically, reaching a maximum of 1.3 years in 1968. More importantly, the sign of this differential has fluctuated through time, defying trend definition.[37] Considered jointly, these two data series could be construed to imply a slight increase in the proportion of future cohorts of aged females who are nonwhite. It would follow that the economic status of these cohorts might decline slightly. But these conclusions must be made in the absence of convincing data that the decline in the difference of life expectancy at birth will continue and that the difference at age 65 has stabilized.

The marital composition of future cohorts of aged women can be projected with least confidence. Certain facts are well established. For example, it is well known that a higher proportion of aged females than aged males are widowed. The higher proportion of widows among elderly women is explained by three factors. First, aged men experience higher mortality rates than aged females. Second, husbands are typically older than their wives by several years. Third, a higher proportion of widowers than widows remarry, taking their wives not only from the population of aged widows but also from the populations of women under sixty-five and divorced and single women over sixty-five.[38] But will this imbalance continue into the future? If current trends in mortality rates continue and are not offset by changes in the other two factors, about which less is known, it would appear likely. The male–female difference in life expectancy at age sixty-five has grown steadily since 1901, reaching 4.3 years by 1976. In that same year, the death rate of males sixty-five and over exceeded the corresponding rate for females by nearly 50 percent. Forty years ago, just as many males as females were reported at ages sixty-five and over; but there has been a steady decline in the proportion of men. There are currently only sixty-nine males for every one hundred females sixty-five and over. This trend is expected to continue, reaching sixty-five males per one hundred females in the year 2000. The sex ratio corresponds to an excess of 6.5 million aged women by the year 2000.[39]

Similarly, it is known that the divorce rate among couples aged sixty-five and over increased 35 percent between 1968 and 1975.[40] If continued, this trend suggests that higher proportions of aged females will be divorced in the future. But the divorce rate among younger couples, which appears to have stabilized, as well as the incidence of remarriage, must also be considered.

On balance, it is tempting to conclude that future cohorts of aged females will be characterized by larger proportions of widows and divorcees than at present. This conclusion must be viewed as tenuous at best, however, resting as it does on the fragmentary evidence presented above.

SUMMARY AND CONCLUSIONS

This chapter has attempted to document and explain the higher incidence of poverty among aged females relative to aged males. The first part of this task proved simple, since the aggregate of aged females are twice as likely as their male counterparts to have total cash income below poverty lines. That women are more likely than men to experience poverty during old age remains true even when the total female and male populations are disaggregated by living arrangements, marital status, and age. Only when race is introduced do we find a subgroup of males with a higher incidence of poverty than women.

Our explanation of why poverty is a particularly acute problem for aged women began with an examination of sex differentials in pretransfer income and the incidence of pretransfer poverty. Because most women currently old followed traditional sex roles, remaining at home to take care of dependent children, they have sporadic work histories, which reduce their earnings potential and disqualify them for private pensions as workers. Women who do work tend to be concentrated in job categories that are not covered by private pension plans. Payments of dependents and survivors benefits are spotty, as workers are allowed to opt out of such plans. Where they are paid, these benefits rarely amount to more than nominal sums. Consequently, females are characterized by higher rates of pretransfer poverty than males.

For the most part, government transfers exacerbate the pretransfer income and poverty differentials, primarily because Social Security, which accounts for 83 percent of all government transfers, differentiates between beneficiaries on the basis of marital status in a way that favors married couples over all other categories. Most men sixty-five and over are married and live with their wives (three of every four). Only one of every three women over sixty-five is married and living with a husband. Benefit computation rules under the federal civil service and military retirement systems resemble those of private pensions and generally reinforce the effects of Social Security.

Will the problems of acute absolute and relative poverty mark future cohorts of aged women? The answer to this question depends critically on future trends in the labor force, experience of women, growth in the coverage of private pensions, reform of Social Security and other retirement systems, and trends in the marital, age, and race composition of the population of aged women. On the basis of the information available regarding each of these factors, we reluctantly conclude that dramatic improvement is not likely in the foreseeable future. Although the rise in labor-force participation among females of all ages over the past thirty years has been dramatic, this phenomenon has not been accompanied by similar increases in the average job status of women vis-à-vis men or in the proportion of females entitled to private pensions as workers. The prospects for comprehensive reform of Social Security are bleak in today's atmosphere of concern over the financial soundness of the program. Such a focus has been stimulated, in part, by projections of a sharp rise in the ratio of elderly persons to persons of working age when the baby boom cohorts retire. Evidence regarding trends in the marital, age, and race composition is fragmentary, but that which does exist seems to point to a worsening of the economic status of women. Thus, we see little reason to be optimistic about the economic status of future cohorts of aged women. Improvements, if they come at all, will not occur naturally but must be the deliberate outcomes of policies designed explicitly to address the needs of aged females.

NOTES

1. The poverty statistics are from U.S., Bureau of the Census, "Characteristics of the Population Below the Poverty Level, 1978," *Current Population Reports*, series P-60, no. 124 (Washington, D.C.: Government Printing Office, 1980). In this chapter we have selected the traditional benchmark of sixty-five years to define the onset of old age and the aged population, even though we recognize that the chronological age at which the biological signals of old age occur varies significantly across individuals.

2. Marilyn L. Moon, *The Measurement of Economic Welfare: Its Application to the Aged Poor* (New York: Academic Press, 1977).

3. When Moon replaced a current income measure with a broader measure of economic welfare that includes net worth and intrafamily and in-kind transfers, she found that the percentage of all aged families living in poverty in 1966 as measured by goverment poverty lines fell from 41 to 14 percent. Families did not benefit uniformly from the inclusion of these resources in the meaning of economic well-being, however. Indeed, the percentage of families headed by females in the lowest quintile (20 percent) of the income distribution rose by 8 percent (ibid., pp. 68, 79).

4. The official poverty lines currently employed by the U.S. government to count the poor are based on poverty lines constructed in 1963 by estimating the cost of an adequate diet as recommended by the U.S. Department of Agriculture and then increasing this dollar amount to account for nonfood necessities (shelter and clothing). See Mollie Orshansky, "Counting the Poor: Another Look at the Poverty Profile," *Social Security Bulletin* 28 (1965): 3-29. The poverty lines employed today have been updated to reflect increases in the cost of living as measured by the Consumer Price Index (CPI), but the basic methodology remains unchanged. For example, recent changes in family spending patterns (percent spent on food versus shelter) have been ignored. Orshansky estimates that current poverty

lines would rise by 40 percent if the logic employed in the construction of the original poverty lines were applied to these new spending patterns. See U.S., Congress, House, Select Committee on Aging, *Poverty Among America's Aged, Statement Prepared by Mollie Orshansky*, 95th Cong., 2d sess., August 19, 1978, p. 57.

5. For example, see Richard V. Burkhauser, "Are Women Treated Fairly in Today's Social Security System?" *Gerontologist* 19 (June 1979): 242-49; Karen C. Holden, "The Inequitable Distribution of OASI Benefits Among Homemakers," *Gerontologist* 19 (1979): 250-56.

6. Pretransfer income is defined as the sum of wages and salaries, earnings from farm and nonfarm self-employment, interest, dividends, rents, royalties, income from annuities and private pensions, alimony and contributions, and monetary gifts from private sources. The measure of pretransfer income used is for the census family, that is, all persons living under the same roof and sharing living facilities who are related by blood or marriage. There may or may not be more than one nuclear family in a single census family. For example, an aged couple living with an adult child (older than seventeen years) comprises a single census family but two nuclear families. In measuring pretransfer income for the census family rather than its member nuclear families, we implicitly assume that nuclear families share the income available to them with the other nuclear families in their census family just as they share living facilities.

Sheldon Danziger generously provided that statistic of mean pretransfer income of aged families as a percent of mean pretransfer income of nonaged families.

7. Posttransfer income is defined for the census family as the sum of pretransfer income plus any income from government sources including Social Security or railroad retirement benefits; civil service, military, or veterans' pensions; Supplementary Security Income and other welfare benefits; unemployment insurance; worker's compensation; and other government cash transfers.

8. Official poverty lines used to measure the extent of poverty vary by the age and sex of family head, the number of children residing in the family, and the residence (farm or nonfarm) of the family. For example, the poverty line in 1978 for a single woman age sixty-five or greater living on a farm was $2,650, while that for a nonaged, nonfarm family of four (two adults and two children) was $6,610.

9. Aged families heading or living with larger census families were eliminated so that an accurate picture of the relative importance of the components of pretransfer income such as the earnings of aged persons could be obtained.

10. The probability of having pretransfer poverty less than the appropriate poverty line can be estimated with a statistical technique known as probit regression analysis. This technique also allows estimation of the effects of various demographic characteristics (independent variables) hypothesized to determine pretransfer poverty status.

11. Probit regression analysis reveals that, when the effects of other demographic variables are controlled for, being widowed or divorced raises the probability of pretransfer poverty among aged women by four and eight precentage points, respectively, relative to women who never marry. These results are significant at a 5 percent significance level.

12. The effects of educational attainment, regional residence, and being of Spanish origin were obtained with probit regression analysis.

13. Receipt of Social Security benefits cannot be distinguished from receipt of railroad retirement benefits in the 1979 Current Population Survey. Consequently, Social Security benefits as a percentage of total government transfers may be somewhat less than 83 percent. In fiscal year 1975–76, railroad retirement benefits were 6 percent of combined Social Security and railroad retirement benefits (U.S., Department of Health, Education, and Welfare, *Social Security Bulletin: Annual Statistical Supplement, 1976* (Washington, D.C.: Government Printing Office), p. 45, table 3.

14. Prior to the 1977 Social Security Amendments, the computation of average monthly earnings was based on the nominal earnings history of the retired worker. Current earnings for the years between 1951 and the year in which the worker reached sixty-five (year T) were summed and divided by the number of intervening months ([T - 1951] x 12). The 1977 amendments alter the computation by indexing earnings through age sixty to average earnings for the year in which the worker turned sixty. The new average is referred to as average indexed monthly earnings (AIME). Suppose nominal earnings for some past year are equal to $2,000. If average wages for all workers in covered employment have tripled between that year and the year the worker turns sixty, then earnings for that year are set equal to $6,000 for the computation of AIME. Earnings for years after the worker reaches sixty are included without indexing.

15. For more information regarding the provisions governing eligibility and benefit computation, see U.S., Department of Health, Education, and Welfare, *Social Security Handbook*, 6th ed. (Washington, D.C.: Government Printing Office, July 1978).

16. Table 3.3 does not strictly confirm our logic because it refers to the antipoverty effectiveness of total government transfers and not just OASI. When a similar table for OASI transfers alone was constructed, it revealed the same relationships between marital status categories as did table 3.3.

17. William G. Bowen and T. Aldrich Finegan, *The Economics of Labor Force Participation* (Princeton: Princeton University Press, 1969), pp. 43–44.

18. For details of these provisions, see 5 U.S.C., §8331-8348; P.L. 93-474; Stat. 1438; 42 U.S.C. § 410 (1) 1; 10 U.S.C. § 1447-1455; P.O. 92-425 § 4; and U.S., Congress, House, Select Committee on Aging, *Pension Problems of Older Women*, 94th Cong., 1st sess. (October 21, 1975), pp. 31–34.

19. Not all income is counted when determining SSI benefits. The first sixty-five dollars of monthly earnings are totally disregarded, but the benefit entitlement is reduced by fifty cents for each additional dollar of earnings. Similarly, the first twenty dollars of nonemployment income (for example, Social Security) is disregarded, but nonemployment income greater than this amount offsets benefits dollar for dollar. For more details regarding the eligibility requirements of SSI, see U.S., Department of Health, Education, and Welfare, *Social Security Handbook*, ch. 2.

20. The maximum federal SSI annual benefits for a couple and an individual are approximately 84 and 70 percent of their respective poverty lines. Thus it can be argued that even SSI does not meet the goal of ensuring adequate income.

21. In 1978, approximately 30 percent of aged females but only 25 percent of aged males were eligible for SSI. Similarly 70 percent of current SSI aged participants are female (U.S., Department of Health and Human Services, *Supplemental Security Income, Quarterly Statistics* [Washington, D.C.: Government Printing Office, June 1981]).

22. Social Security benefits are increased annually to reflect increases in the cost of living; that is, they are indexed to compensate for decreased real purchasing power resulting from inflation. In years when increases in prices are lower than increases in wages, the real income of Social Security beneficiaries will fall relative to the working population. Moreover, young cohorts of retirees will receive higher benefits than older retirees with similar relative incomes during their work lives (for example, consider two retirees fifteen years apart in age, both of whom earned the median wage throughout their work lives) because the former will have benefited from increases in real wages not available to the latter.

23. E. J. Burtt, *Labor in the American Economy* (New York: St. Martin's Press, 1979), pp. 22-25.

24. Karl E. Taeuber and James A. Sweet, "Family and Work: The Social Life Cycle of Women," in *Women and the American Economy: A Look to the 1980s* (Englewood Cliffs, N.J.: Prentice-Hall, 1976), pp. 31-60.

25. Nancy S. Barrett, "Women in the Job Market: Occupations, Earnings, and Career Opportunities," in *The Subtle Revolution: Women at Work,* ed. Ralph E. Smith (Washington, D.C.: Urban Institute, 1979), pp. 32-36.

26. Nancy M. Gordon, "Institutional Responses: The Social Security System," in *The Subtle Revolution: Women at Work,* ed. Ralph E. Smith (Washington, D.C.: Urban Institute, 1979), pp. 223-55.

27. James H. Schulz, "Private Pensions and Women," in *Women in Midlife: Security and Fulfillment (Part I): A Compendium of Papers,* U.S., Congress, House, Select Committee on Aging, 95th Cong., 2d sess. (Washington, D.C.: Government Printing Office, December 1978), pp. 205-20.

28. Ibid., 211-13.

29. U.S., Congress, House, Select Committee on Aging, *Pension Problems of Older Women,* 94th Cong., 1st sess., October 21, 1975.

30. Schulz, "Private Pensions," pp. 215-17.

31. See U.S., Department of Health, Education, and Welfare, *Report of the HEW Task Force on the Treatment of Women Under Social Security* (Washington, D.C.: Government Printing Office, 1978); U.S., Department of Health, Education, and Welfare, *Social Security and the Changing Roles of Men and Women* (Washington, D.C.: Government Printing Office, 1979); U.S., Department of Health, Education, and Welfare, *Social Security Financing and Benefits: Reports of the 1979 Advisory Council on Social Security* (Washington, D.C.: Government Printing Office, 1979); and Nancy M. Gordon, *The Treatment of Women Under Social Security* (Washington, D.C.: U.S. Commission on Civil Rights, 1978).

32. R. R. Campbell, *Social Security: Promise and Reality* (Stanford: Hoover Institute Press, 1977); R. R. Campbell, "The Problems of Fairness," in *The Crisis in Social Security: Problems and Prospects,* ed. Michael J. Boskin, (San Francisco: Institute for Contemporary Studies, 1977); R. M. Flowers, *Women and Social Security: An Institutional Dilemma* (Washington, D.C.: American Enterprise Institute for Public Policy

Research, 1977); J. D. Brown, *Essays on Social Security* (Princeton: Princeton University Press, 1977); Alice H. Munnell, "The Future of Social Security," *New England Economic Review* (July–August, 1976).

33. See, for example, A. H. Munnell and L. Stiglin, "Women and a Two Tier Social Security System," and J. L. Warlick, D.E. Berry, and I. Garfinkel, "The Distributional Efforts of the Double Decker Alternative to Eliminating Dependency in Social Security," both in *A Challenge to Social Security: The Changing Roles of Men and Women in American Society,* ed. R. Burkhauser and K. Holden (New York: Academic Press, 1982).

34. Gordon, "Institutional Responses."

35. See Munnell and Stiglin, "Women and a Two Tier Social Security System"; Warlick, Berry, and Garfinkel, "Distributional Efforts."

36. U.S., Bureau of the Census, "Prospective Trends in the Size and Structure of the Elderly Population, Impact on Mortality Trends, and Some Implications," by J. S. Siegel, *Current Population Reports,* series P-23, no. 78 (Washington, D.C.: Government Printing Office, 1979), p. 10.

37. Ibid., p. 12.

38. U.S., Bureau of the Census, "Demographic Aspects of Aging and the Older Population in the United States," *Current Population Reports,* series P-23, no. 59 (Washington, D.C.: Government Printing Office, 1976), pp. 12–14.

39. Ibid., p. 14.

40. U.S., Bureau of the Census, "The Future of the American Family," by P. C. Glick, *Current Population Reports,* series P-23, no. 78 (Washington, D.C.: Government Printing Office, 1979), p. 3.

JACQUELYNE JOHNSON JACKSON

4

The Politicalization of Aged Blacks

The current paucity of available data about the politicalization of aged blacks and the recent shifts in federal policy affecting blacks, as well as those affecting the aged, mitigate against any comprehensive exploration of that politicalization at this time.[1] But, with that caveat in mind, three basic issues related to the politics of growing old and remaining black in the United States, now and in the foreseeable future, are explored tentatively and cautiously in this chapter.

The first issue deals with certain political implications of racial differences between aged blacks and whites, where the aged are defined as those over sixty-five years. The major foci are demographic differences and the feasibility of equating ageism with racism, insofar as that equation affects aged blacks.

The second issue examines on their four corners alone the extent to which the Older Americans Act Amendments of 1981[2] and the *Summary Reports of the Committee Chairmen, the 1981 White House Conference on Aging*[3] recognize aged blacks as a distinct minority group or as aged members of a distinct minority group. Is there a tendency for federal legislators, aging specialists, and deliberators about aging policies to co-join highly disparate minority groups as if they were homogeneous? What provisions, if any, are made for the equal protection of aged blacks as members of a suspect class under the Constitution? Are such provisions legally necessary?

The third issue deals briefly with the "pushes and pulls" to which many aged blacks are increasingly subjected as various single-issue organizations vie to number them among their political constituents and to speak for them. Various single-issue organizations now clamor in different degrees to speak for aged blacks or to garner their votes. They include organizations that focus principally on their blackness or their ageness, as well as other organizations attempting to divide them further politically by focusing on their womanhood or poverty level, or any combination thereof combined with blackness or ageness.

"Who speaks for aged blacks?" is an important, political question. Given the cultural and socioeconomic variations among aged blacks that influence their political preferences, the most appropriate answer in the long run may well be that aged blacks best speak in different tongues for themselves. Such a possibility is critical to any evaluation of the politicalization of aged blacks now and in the future.

This exploration is limited to native-born blacks, except where survey data are undifferentiated by place of birth. However, almost all aged blacks are native born, and a hefty majority yet live in the state in which they were born. The exploration is based partially on empirical data from primary or secondary surveys and observations. A few unstructured or informal interviews were conducted with several black public officials and with several white officers of local organizations of the elderly with some black members, such as a local chapter of the National Council of Senior Citizens in a Southern city.

Certain value judgments of the author also influenced the outcome of this chapter. Insofar as aged blacks were concerned, the most critical value judgment related to the equating of ageism with racism. Racism is far more important in affecting the conditions under which blacks age than is ageism. The application of the concept of multiple jeopardy[4] to aged blacks does not presuppose that ageism's negative impact on their well-being is more grave than that of racism. The social conditions of the aged, including their life styles, are affected substantially by those same conditions in their younger years. The aged are, after all, products of their youth.

Given the great significance of the topic of the politicalization of aged blacks for public policies affecting them as they age as blacks and when they are aged and remain black, as well as the insufficiency of current data for handling this topic comprehensively, the conclusions proferred herein may feasibly be treated as hypotheses for needed research. In fact, it is hoped that researches will subject these hypotheses to local and national investigations involving representative samples of black and white aged.[5]

AGED BLACKS AND WHITES

Perhaps the most pervasive political issue in ethnogerontology relating to aged blacks is the political implications of racial differences between them and aged whites. This issue is highly controversial for many reasons, three of which should be noted now. One reason involves the confusion between the classification of blacks as an ethnic group and as a minority group. The confusion is not merely semantic. A second reason is the undue influence of ethnocentrism on gerontologic or geriatric considerations of the existence and significance of racial differences. A third

and compelling reason is that vested interests of black and white gerontologists and geriatricians affect profoundly their attitudes and behaviors regarding the distribution of power and funds for aging research,
training, and services and, indeed, for federal policies specifically geared
to the aged. Not surprisingly, political competition between blacks and
whites over control of aging policies and funds for or about issues
relating to blacks is intense. Most often, whites win.

ETHNIC OR MINORITY GROUP

The confusion between classifying blacks as an ethnic or as a minority
group is political because different political considerations emerge from
either classification. Currently on the political scene, blacks are classified
as an ethnic group, so that they can be co-joined with other ethnic
groups, although they are spoken of as members of minority groups. The
pluralization of minority groups here is deliberate, emphasizing the fact
that they are rarely considered as a single minority group.

Sociologically, the term *ethnic* was traditionally defined as "having to do
with the ethnos; characterized by unity of both race and nationality."[6]
Ethnos, in turn, referred to "a group bound together and identified by ties
and traits of both race and nationality."[7] *Ethnic groups* were "the logical
product of human evolution under conditions of relative isolation and
segregation."[8] In contrast, a *minority group* represented "a subgroup within
a larger group (ordinarily a society), bound together by some special ties
of its own, usually race or nationality, but sometimes religion or other
cultural affiliations."[9] *Culture,* a term also often confused politically with
ethnicity and minority groups, "includes all that is learned through
intercommunication. It covers all language, traditions, customs, and
institutions."[10]

Aged blacks who are native born of native-born parentage and grand-
parentage in the United States are collectively unified by race. To the
extent that nationalistic unification exists in the United States, aged
blacks share such nationalism in varying degrees with similar native-
born citizens of native-born parentage and grand-parentage of other
races. Blacks are not unified by religion because there is no "black religion." They are also not uniquely bound by other cultural affiliations. In
short, blacks are not an ethnic group. Aged blacks, as other blacks, hold
membership in the minority group of blacks, a group bound by race. The
majority group, in this majority–minority relationship, is white. The
majority group of whites includes Hispanics racially classified as white
and socially considered, by race, to be white. Some Hispanics, of course,
are racially classified as black, raising interesting questions that go
beyond the scope of this chapter about their political affiliation with
blacks or with Hispanics. These questions become especially important
when the political goals of blacks and Hispanics are diverse.

In my judgment, the best view of blacks and whites in any political consideration of the aged is that of a majority–minority relationship, or of a power relationship, because racism is a more important domestic problem than is ageism.

Political comparisons of black and white aged differ from scientific comparisons of them because the purpose is different. This differentiation is often overlooked by aging specialists acting in the political arena. One suspicion is that the oversight is frequently deliberate. Political comparisons are most useful when they rely on categorical comparisons undistinguished by traits other than age and, to a lesser extent, sex. The reasoning behind this view is that individual or subgroups of blacks benefit best politically when political gains are sought in the name of the black minority group, even though it is clear from the outset that the accrued gains will be disproportionately distributed, often to blacks of higher socioeconomic status.

Political advocates for aged blacks typically argue that substantial differences of kind, and not of degree, distinguish aged blacks and whites. Careful examination of the differences to which they allude, however, shows that they are merely ones of degree and not of kind. For example, these advocates cite the differential rates of poverty of aged blacks and whites, where poverty rates are always much higher for blacks than whites.[11] They rarely, if ever, refer to structural inequities concretely. When they evoke racism as the cause of the differences, a frequent ploy, they treat racism as if it were a homogeneous concept not in need of specific definition. It is enough for these advocates simply to state that racism per se is the cause of all past and current differences between blacks and whites in the United States. However, invoking racism as *the* cause provides no explanation for the vast variation between subgroups of aged blacks, some of whom have socioeconomic statuses that poor aged whites would envy. According to those advocates, whose views are important because they dominate the lobbying efforts on the federal level for aged blacks, the appropriate remedies for aged blacks must involve equitable, compensatory, and preferential treatment. No one supportive of the Constitution would quarrel with equitable treatment, but the specific form, if any at all, of compensatory and preferential treatment leads to political discourses ultimately involving federal questions of a legal nature. Unfortunately, the legal sufficiency of the pleas of these advocates has not been of major concern to them.

One can well argue against the inadequacies of the bulk of the advocates for aged blacks. But the need for their kinds of generalizations should also be presented. That need may be illustrated briefly by the historical fact that the racial doctrine of "separate, but equal," the holding of *Plessy* v. *Ferguson,* 163 U.S. 537 (1896), was only overturned technically as it applied to education in *Brown* v. *Board of Education of Topeka, Kansas, et al.,* 347 U.S. 483 (1954). The doctrine of "separate, but equal" was subsequently overturned technically in a series of cases related to "public beaches and bathhouses, municipal golf courses, buses, parks, public parks and golf courses, athletic contests, airport restaurants, courtroom seating, and municipal auditoriums" during the next few years following *Brown*.[12] The doctrine related to transportation was overturned technically in *Gayle* v. *Browder*, 352 U.S. 903 (1956). That case arose from the Montgomery bus protest in Alabama, led by Martin Luther King, Jr. The Civil Rights Act of 1964, mandating racial desegregation of public places, among other concerns, prompted sanctions against educational and economic institutions denying equal rights to blacks. The Voting Rights Act of 1965, which forbade the denial of voting rights to blacks solely on the basis of race, clearly promoted black voting and the development of a black voting bloc in some voting districts. One outcome was the massive increase in the number of black public officials, especially in the South. Another and a very important outcome was the increase in the number of white public officials who had to exhibit some concern about blacks in order to be elected.

In 1982, all aged blacks were born before 1917, at least thirty-nine years before the U.S. Supreme Court outlawed racial segregation on a technical basis, forty-seven years before public places could no longer deny them entry solely on the basis of race, and forty-eight years before the federal government intervened to guarantee them their voting rights. Any presumption, then, that aged blacks now or in the immediate future, were not affected by racial segregation or its consequences is clearly unfounded. Thus, the typical advocate for aged blacks, lacking in legal sophistication, is, nevertheless, standing on solid ground in invoking the negative effects of racial segregation on their current well-being. What is missing, however, is the relationship between that background and its rational connection to contemporary pleas for compensatory or preferential treatment.

Given the legacies of slavery and racial segregation, one critical question in need of examination is that of the substantial differences by race between aged blacks and whites, as well as the political implications of those differences for policy determinations.

The major sources of data employed by typical advocates for aged blacks to demonstrate those differences and to make a reasonable case for differential treatment of aged blacks and whites on the basis of those differences are demographic data collected by the U.S. Bureau of the Census and historical recountings of the legacies of slavery and racial segregation against blacks.

DEMOGRAPHIC DIFFERENCES

The only 1980 demographic data available when this chapter was written were provisional data about size, age, and sex of blacks and whites. Over time, the absolute socioeconomic position of aged blacks and whites improved, but their relative positions in comparison to each other remained unchanged. That is, the socioeconomic position of aged blacks as a group remained inferior to that of aged whites. A similar pattern will probably emerge from the detailed 1980 census data. Thus, the absence of those data does not prevent assessments of the demographic differences by race. Further, two useful references provide detailed demographic comparisons of aged blacks and whites before 1980.[13] The limited discussion below focuses on size, age, sex, and location; socioeconomic conditions; marital and household composition; and health.

Size, age, sex, and location. An obvious difference among whites, blacks, and other races is population size. Table 4.1 contains 1980 provisional data about the size, age, and sex of the total population and the populations of whites, blacks, and other races in the United States in 1980. More than four-fifths of the total population were white. Slightly less than 12 percent were black. Other races were about 5 percent. The white proportion declined recently, with no appreciable rise among blacks. Other races rose.

Table 4.1 shows that whites are older than blacks or other races. The proportion of persons under five years was larger among blacks and other races than among whites. But about two-thirds of each group were between fifteen and sixty-four years of age. The proportion of aged persons was much higher among whites (12.2 percent) than blacks (7.9 percent) and other races (4.4 percent). Aside from white control of politics, the greater and earlier visibility of aged people among whites helps to account for the earlier and more sustained public interest of whites than blacks in the conditions of the aged.

The differences by sex distribution varied by degree and not by kind. Female excessiveness, or more females than males, characterized blacks and whites, but not other races. It was highest among blacks. Males dominated each population under five years. More males than females are born into all human populations. Between fifteen and sixty-four years, the sex ratio (the number of males per every one hundred females) was roughly equal for other races (99.9) and whites (97.6) but below parity for blacks (87.5). Female excessiveness was much greater among the aged than among younger adults. The 1980 sex ratios of the aged were 84.8 for other races, 68.2 for blacks, and 67.2 for whites. The black–white similarity was much closer than that between their younger counterparts. The larger aged sex ratio of other races, with the exception of American Indians or Alaskan natives (who are included among other races), was due principally to male excessiveness among immigrants.

Table 4.2 shows the 1980 age and sex distribution of the aged population in the United States by race. Compared with the racial distribution of the 1980 total population, a larger proportion of the aged population was

Table 4.1
Age and Sex Distribution of the U.S. Population, 1980, by Race

Characteristic	Total	percent	White	percent	Black	percent	Other Races	percent
Number, total population	226,504,825		188,340,790		26,488,218		11,675,817	
of total population		100.0		83.2		11.7		5.1
female within population		51.4		51.3		52.7		49.9
Number under 5 years of age	51,282,460		40,122,497		7,598,770		3,561,193	
within population		22.6		21.3		28.7		30.5
female within population		48.9		48.7		49.6		49.1
Number 15–64 years of age	149,678,232		125,274,260		16,803,622		7,600,350	
within population		66.1		66.5		63.4		65.1
female within population		50.9		50.6		53.3		50.0
Number over 64 years of age	25,544,133		22,944,033		2,085,826		514,274	
within population		11.3		12.2		7.9		4.4
female within population		59.7		59.8		59.4		54.1

SOURCE: U.S. Bureau of the Census, *Census '80: Projects for Students* (Washington, D.C.: Government Printing Office, 1981), p. 39.

Table 4.2
Age and Sex Distribution of the Elderly U.S. Population, 1980, by Race

Characteristic	Total	percent	White	percent	Black	percent	Other Races	percent
Number over 65 years of age	25,544,133		22,944,033		2,085,826		514,274	
of total population		100.0		89.8		8.2		2.0
Number 65–69 years of age	8,780,844		7,811,071		776,597		193,176	
within population		34.4		34.0		37.2		37.6
female within population		55.6		55.4		57.3		53.7
Number 70–74 years of age	6,796,742		6,094,178		563,377		139,187	
within population		26.6		26.6		27.0		27.1
female within population		58.0		58.1		58.4		51.9
Number 75–79 years of age	4,792,597		4,309,286		387,231		96,080	
within population		18.8		21.0		18.6		18.7
female within population		61.4		61.7		60.6		53.7
Number 80–84 years of age	2,934,229		2,684,793		199,760		49,676	
within population		11.5		11.7		9.6		9.7
female within population		65.3		65.6		62.5		57.8
Number over 84 years of age	2,239,721		2,044,705		158,861		36,155	
within population		8.8		8.9		7.6		7.0
female within population		69.6		70.0		66.6		60.9

SOURCE: U.S., Bureau of the Census, Census '80: Projects for Students (Washington, D.C.: Government Printing Office, 1981), p. 39.

white, and smaller proportions were black and other races. Each population group experienced numerical increases over time, but the relative proportions of aged blacks and whites during the past decade tended to remain constant. A major change in the proportion of aged blacks within the population of the aged is not anticipated within the next several decades.

The aged white population is older than the aged black or the aged of other races. But in 1980, slightly more than one-third of each group was under seventy years, and more than one-half were under seventy-five years. The greater age of whites in the aged population is also reflected in the population of all ages. The 1980 median age for the latter population was 30.0 years. The median age was slightly higher for whites (31.3) and somewhat lower for remaining groups: 28.6 years for Asians and Pacific Islanders; 24.9 for blacks; 23.0 for American Indians, Eskimos, and Aleuts; and 22.8 for persons not elsewhere classified. A separate calculation for persons of Spanish origin showed a median age of 23.2 years.[14]

Except for other races under seventy-four years, female excessiveness among the aged rosed consistently with age. Due largely to sex differentials in longevity, females are now the dominant sex among the aged, including aged blacks, but this was not always so. In 1930, for example, the aged black sex ratio was 103.5. Except for causes of death specific to females, such as maternal mortality and diabetes mellitus, the black female death rates are lower than those of their male counterparts.

Greater geographical restriction typified aged blacks than whites in and before 1980. Most aged blacks live in the South, true also of a slight majority of blacks of all ages. Compared with aged whites, aged blacks were far more likely to be metropolitan dwellers, mainly in central cities. They were also more likely to live in poorer census tracts, where they were at greater risk for inadequate public services (for instance, garbage collection, transportation, and street cleaning). The rates for crimes against persons were also higher in the areas where they tended to live.

SOCIOECONOMIC CONDITIONS

The socioeconomic condition of the aged, as measured solely by their educational, income, and employment levels, is lower for blacks than whites when the data are undifferentiated by sex. A similar pattern characterizes younger blacks and whites. In 1980, more than twice as many aged whites (42.8 percent) than aged blacks (17.7 percent) had completed at least high school, and almost three times as many whites (9.0 percent) than blacks (3.2 percent) had completed college. But most of the aged, including whites, it should be noted, were not high school graduates in 1980. Comparable data for Hispanic aged were 18 percent for at least high school graduation and 4.7 percent for college graduates, rates that were only slightly higher than those of aged blacks.

Measured by the median of total money income for families (which does not include non-money or in-kind contributions), black–white income gaps widened between 1970 and 1980, where the 1980 data were based on the current population surveys and not on the 1980 census. The 1970 black and white median incomes of $7,442 and $10,236, respectively, rose to $12,674 and $21,904, respectively, in 1980. The 1970 black–white ratio of 72.7 percent fell to 57.9 percent in 1980. This widening may well be explained by such factors as the greater proportion of black and white female-headed families and the much smaller proportion of black than white dual-earning couples in high-income employment.

The poverty rate of aged blacks and whites fell dramatically between 1959 and 1980, from 55.1 to 38.1 percent for blacks and from 33.1 to 13.6 percent for whites. Even so, proportionately more aged blacks were in poverty in 1980 than were aged whites in 1959. In 1980, the proportion of related children under eighteen years of age in poor families approximated the aged poverty rate: 42.1 percent for blacks and 13.4 percent for whites. Poverty is obviously neither unique to nor more pronounced among black or white aged than among related children in families, a fact often ignored by advocates for the aged.

Aged females, typically poorer than aged males, are generally more dependent on Social Security or welfare payments and less likely to have private pensions in their own names or on their own right. Black females are more impoverished at any age than are white females. Poverty is greatest among aged black females residing as unrelated individuals when measures of total income only are used as the gauge. However, they may not be the aged black females most affected adversely by shifting economic conditions, such as growing inflation, because they are more likely to be eligible for and to receive subsidized services, such as food stamps, Medicaid, and housing.

Most aged blacks and whites are not gainfully employed, nor do most of them desire full-time, gainful employment. Among those retired from gainful employment, racial differences by voluntary or forced retirement are insignificant.[15] Labor-force participation rates for the aged are somewhat higher among black than white females and somewhat lower among black than white males. Unemployment rates of the aged, as unemployment rates of the nonaged, remain higher among blacks than whites.

Marital and household composition. The presence of a spouse is less likely among black than white aged but more likely for aged black males than for aged white females. Widowhood is more prevalent among aged blacks, and it was more likely to have occurred at an earlier age (often before old age) for blacks. Remarriage of the aged is more probable among whites than blacks and, within each sex group, among males than females. The current marital statuses of nonaged blacks and whites suggest strongly that racial gaps will widen considerably for future cohorts of aged blacks and whites. Today, for example, most black women of all ages do not have a spouse present, whereas most white women do. The trend of decreasing presence of spouse is not explicable by welfare regulations related to the "man-in-the-house" rule.

The widespread sterotype of most aged blacks living in extended families and, thus, under the same roof with relatives of different generations, is decidedly false. Most aged blacks either live only with their spouses or alone. Almost one-half of aged black women now live alone, a pattern less characteristic of aged white women.

Future cohorts of aged blacks will have experienced greater socialization in living alone prior to becoming aged. That is, they will enter old age having already lived alone, in some instances for many years. Consequently, they should be familiar with the advantages and disadvantages of single living. But there are at least two kinds of problems that may confront them when they are old that did not confront them in earlier years. One is decreased interaction with other people outside their homes. For example, many people who live alone in their younger years are also gainfully employed and often surrounded by other people for more than one-third of the typical day. When they retire, however, contact with other people gained through employment is lost or diminished. Further, when they experience increasing physical decrements associated with aging, they may eventually find themselves unable to undertake adequate physical care of themselves and their homes. To this extent, they will become increasingly dependent on others, whether relatives, friends, or outsiders, such as agency personnel.

Although home ownership by the aged is higher among whites, most aged people, including blacks, live in owner-occupied dwellings. Residence as owners or renters among the aged in age-segregated housing or communities is higher among whites than blacks but generally rare among both groups. Residence in federally subsidized housing for the elderly is also rare among the aged, although higher among blacks than whites. The current decline in black home ownership, particularly among black women, may well lead to different types of housing needs of aged blacks in the future, unless public policies foster increased home ownership among nonaged blacks now.

The shaky data about racial differences in institutionalization of the aged (only about 5 percent of whom are institutionalized at any given time) typically show higher institutionalization among whites. These comparisons are rarely controlled for age and never controlled for socioeconomic differences or for differences in presence of kin willing and able to provide home services to the afflicted individual. The increased aging of the black aged population will probably necessitate greater use of institutionalized facilities for the aged in the future.

Health. Comparative findings of the overall health statuses of aged blacks and whites are inconclusive. Some studies report black inferiority, others white inferiority, and still others no significant differences by race.[16] The variations in the reported findings are caused by methodological and temporal factors. Morbidity data about aged blacks are quite scant, as are, to a lesser extent, those about aged whites. Available morbidity data on the national level often show racial differences, largely because they are not controlled or are insufficiently controlled by socioeconomic variables. Some of the differences favor whites, while others favor blacks. For example, aged black males tend to have better hearing than do aged white males.[17]

A recurring issue about the comparative health statuses of aged blacks and whites concerns the racial crossover in mortality, with the usual assumption being that, among the aged, the black mortality rate is lower. A recent study of the age-adjusted death rates of aged blacks and whites in the United States for the period 1964–78 showed, however, that for all causes of death, blacks were more likely than whites to die in any given year. Among those over eighty years of age, the crude death rate was lower for blacks than whites of either sex. Of interest was the narrowing of the racial differences among those 80–84 years of age and the widening of such differences among those over eighty-five years of age.[18]

HISTORICAL DIFFERENCES

Historical differences by race have been described amply in many tomes. To the best of my knowledge, none of them, however, have focused explicitly on historical differences between specific cohorts of black aged, or between specific cohorts of black and white aged. Sociologists also have not explored this topic in any depth. Frazier did analyze the changing role of "Granny" before and after Emancipation by concentrating largely on the inverse relationship between Granny's power and that of the father as his role as the chief economic provider for the family grew.[19]

Many historical differences between aged blacks and whites can be inferred readily by their differential status of citizenship, but what is needed is a comprehensive analysis of those historical differences over time, focusing on the consequences of those differences for the aged. Racial attitudes and behaviors of cohorts of blacks and whites should be studied to determine the impact of those attitudes and behaviors on perception of problems of the aged and on racially desegregated participation in federally supported facilities for the aged, where direct interaction between the races cannot be avoided. Rosow's proposition that ethnically homogeneous settings are more conducive to elderly participation in such settings should be investigated carefully.[20] The extent to which Mead's conception of historical discontinuity between the generations is an explanation of generational gaps[21] should also be considered. While Mead tended to view World War II as a significant landmark separating the generations, additional landmarks should be explored for blacks. Currently, it seems reasonable to hypothesize that blacks and whites who are reared under conditions of racial segregation tend to differ from those who were reared after racial segregation became constitutionally impermissible.

Whatever approach is taken to an investigation of the significance of historical differences between aged blacks and whites, no comprehensive political analysis of those differences can ignore the political feasibility of equating ageism with racism as that equation may affect blacks.

Robert Butler, a psychiatrist long active in the field of aging and the first director of the National Institute of Aging, coined the term *ageism*. Beattie construed the term to mean "... social practices including prejudices and stereotypes which are negative in their appraisal of older persons and their role in the society."[22] Most widespread in industrialized societies, ageism "...discounts the value of older persons and subtly raises barriers to the availability of resources and services required by them. It exludes the aging from continuing participation and contributions to social life."[23] Both Butler and Beattie accepted ageism as a given in the United States. But they did not provide empirical data to substantiate conclusively the existence of ageism. They also failed to distinguish between negative appraisals that were "true-negative" and "false-negative." A meaningful distinction is that "true-negative" stereotypes are realistic, whereas "false-negative" ones are unrealistic. In this conception, "true-negative" stereotypes could not be considered as prejudicial. Ageism is not equatable to racism.

Daniels and Kitano define racism to mean "very simply the belief that one or more races have innate superiority over other races."[24] Correctly emphasizing the variety of definitions of racism, Daniels and Kitano further stressed that any definition of racism must include several or more of the following quoted points:

1. There is little validity in the doctrine of racial equality; some races are demonstrably superior to others.
2. Races can be graded in terms of superiority. The Caucasian is presumed to be superior, and history is used to validate this claim. Caucasians have constantly shown their physical and mental superiority.
3. Nations and people who have interbred with the nonwhite races do not progress, and countries controlled by nonwhites do not progress.
4. Amalgamation means the wiping out of the superior Caucasian race, a process which leads to the eventual decline of a civilization.[25]

Unlike the case of race, it can be demonstrated that some age groups are superior to other age groups, depending upon the task at hand. For example, physical coordination and performance ability on selected tasks are handled less adequately by the very old than by young adults. A ninety-year-old white male, seven feet tall, who played professional basketball sixty years ago, is unlikely to be as an efficient basketball player today as Ralph Sampson, a black member of the University of Virginia's basketball team in 1982. The difference between their basketball proficiency is not race. It is age, and whatever other individual variations they may exhibit in their playing skills.

Even Caucasian aged have not constantly demonstrated their physical and mental superiority over nonaged Caucasian adults, nor is such a demonstration likely. Further, postmenopausal Caucasian women do not interbreed with younger Caucasians, and such interbreeding of old Caucasian men is very rare, although not impossible. Even where that interbreeding may occur, one cannot find any argument that it leads to a declining civilization. Finally, amalgamation between the nonaged and the aged is impossible.

For these and other reasons, then, the equation of these two concepts appears unfounded. In a related context, Streib rejected a conception of the aged as a minority group by distinguishing between the use of that concept as a technical or as an "image-producing" one. He noted, "most people are 'victims' of their own biology—not 'victims' of society."[26] Victims of racism are societal victims; victims of purported ageism are not societal victims. The Holy Bible reminds us that those born of women are born to die. Between birth and death, aging is the inevitable progression toward death. In other words, as opposed to race, age involves increasing deterioration of the body, with the final result being death. Surely aging advocates of ageism are well aware of the fundamental distinctions between ageism and racism.

Perhaps those aging specialists who invoke the concept of ageism as equatable with racism use it polemically. Given the federal recognition of racism as a domestic problem, they seek to raise ageism to that level. One example of its polemical use may be seen in Claude Pepper's unfounded attack on William Raspberry. Pepper, the octogenarian chairman of the U.S. House of Representative's Select Committee on Aging and, in 1982, the oldest representative in the House, accused Raspberry, a black columnist for the *Washington Post*, of hypocrisy in ignoring the similarities of blacks and the aged.[27]

If ageism is equatable to racism—an unreasonable proposition—its proponents must offer empirical data to support that equation and must demonstrate that public policies are needed to eradicate ageism. To date, they have failed to do so. Whether they can provide valid data in the future is doubtful. The need, for example, for federal assistance with health costs is not unique to the aged. Otherwise, Medicaid, a federal-state program providing assistance in paying the health-care costs of the poor, regardless of age, would not be needed. What is questionable is whether Medicare, a federal program providing certain health-care costs only on the basis of age (that is, being over sixty-five years) or disability is needed. Because a large proportion of the aged are not poor, questions must be raised about their greater need for assistance with health-care costs than needs that may arise among younger persons. An argument that the health costs of the aged are higher than those of younger persons is not a sufficient response. On the average, their health costs are higher, but their costs related to childrearing and home mortgages, for example, are considerably lower or nonexistent. Public policies may well consider programs based on need requirements, as opposed to age requirements. Certainly, they should not consider programs based on age alone, except in the case of retirement programs.

When the topic is aged blacks, some consideration must be given to the multiple jeopardies affecting them not only when they are old but also when they were younger. Aged blacks may be victimized for being old and black, but they were also victimized for being young and black. The important political question for aged blacks in the future is not the ascendency of ageism over racism but of the reduction of racism to permit them to prepare, when they are young, for their later years.

Far too often today, even advocates for aged blacks concentrate solely, or almost so, on those who are already old. They forget that those who are now old and poor, for example, were once generally young and poor. The emphasis on providing services to black aged because they are now black and old should never override the need to seek political action to make certain that future cohorts of aged blacks will not be poverty-stricken, a point to which we will return in a brief discussion of transforming Social Security into social insurance.

POLITICAL IMPLICATIONS

The overall power, prestige, and status of aged blacks remain inferior to that of aged whites. But the racially stratified society in which contemporary aged blacks and whites have grown old also witnessed and continues to witness increased physical and social distances among blacks, as well as among whites, of different socioeconomic backgrounds, and some reduction in those distances between blacks and whites of similar socioeconomic backgrounds, exclusive of race. Race is a variable that influences heavily but does not determine solely one's social class membership in the contemporary United States.[28]

The political implications of the demographic and historical differences between aged blacks and whites must be considered against the legal backdrop of blacks as a racially suspect class,[29] entitled to equal protection under the Fourteenth Amendment to the U.S. Constitution (or, in Washington, D.C., under the Fifth Amendment).

It seems clear that statistical recitation of demographic differences between aged blacks and whites is not sufficient to justify differential treatment on the basis of race, unless those differences can be demonstrated to have been caused by racial discrimination. Moreover, the racially conservative U.S. Supreme Court under Warren E. Burger, unlike that Court under Earl Warren, has focused increasingly not on the results of racial discrimination for a test of constitutionality, but on whether racial discrimination was intended. A recent example of the use of the test of intent, as opposed to a test of results, was seen in *City of Mobile* v. *Bolden*, 100 S.Ct. 1490 (1980), where the Court held that an at-large electoral system, as opposed to a ward system, did not violate black voting rights. Plaintiffs now bear a much greater burden in proving racially discriminatory intent than racially discriminatory results.

The problem then becomes one of demonstrating that particular public policies related to the aged are not racially neutral, a problem that cannot be legally justified, for example, in considering Social Security. However, it may be possible to demonstrate the lack of racial neutrality in the distribution of certain funds for aging research, training, and services.

Advocates for aged blacks may fare better politically if they concentrate their efforts on the reduction of racism confronting blacks throughout their lives than if they simply concentrate on the specific problems of blacks who are already old. They also should consider the shortcomings of various systems servicing the elderly and attempt to modify them for the aged. For example, the economic difficulties experienced by many aged blacks could be reduced substantially if Social Security were transformed into a true social insurance program. Ferrara has shown that the returns could be highly beneficial. Using a reasonable set of economic assumptions, he presented an example of an average-income worker, beginning work when he graduated from college at age twenty-two and earning an average income throughout his working life.

Social Security would pay this average-income worker $8,172 per year, or 40% of his preretirement income, if he retired single at age sixty-five. It would pay him $12,258 per year, or 60% of his preretirement income, if he retired with a spouse, falling to $8,172 a year after one spouse died.

Under the private system assuming a 6% real rate of return, this worker could retire at age sixty-five with a private retirement fund of $488,008. This fund could pay him perpetual interest of $29,281 per year, 143% of his preretirement income. This would be about three and one-half times what social security would pay a single worker and about two and one-half times what it would pay a worker with a nonworking spouse, all while allowing the worker to leave about $0.5 million to his children.[30]

Perhaps, then, a major political implication of the racial differences between aged blacks and whites is the need to concentrate on ways of reducing those differences, beginning in the economic sphere.

AGING LEGISLATION AND RECOMMENDATIONS

In this section, the politics of remaining black and growing old are considered via an examination of the "four corners" of the 1981 Older Americans Act (OAA) and the Summary Recommendations of the 1981 White House Conference on Aging (WHCOA). The WHCOA recommendations are important because Congress mandated itself to consider those recommendations. No provision of OAA and no WHCOA recommendation was specific to blacks, but some were explicit about the larger category of minorities.

OLDER AMERICANS ACT

As noted above, OAA and its predecessors have never contained a specific provision about blacks, despite the efforts of various individuals or groups over time to have such legislation enacted. To the best of my knowledge, no bill to provide preferential treatment for aged blacks per se has ever been introduced into the Congress. Legislation specific to minorities deals either with racial and ethnic minorities or with economic minorities. The only whites included under racial and ethnic minorities are Hispanic whites. The majority of the economic minorities, or the aged poor, are white. The economic minorities are typically classified as being below the federally defined poverty level, or up to 125 percent of that level.

Why do federal legislators and many aging professionals typically co-join highly disparate minorities? Convenience seems to be the most plausible answer; those legislators and professionals are typically aware of the considerable historical and sociocultural differences within and between these groups. Yet, minorities of racial and ethnic groups are now broadly classified federally as American Indians or Alaskan natives, Asians or Pacific Islanders, blacks not of Hispanic origin, and Hispanics.

This broad classification simply ignores the diversity even among blacks. For example, blacks not of Hispanic origin include native-born blacks whose great-great-great-great-grandparents were native born, blacks who immigrated to the United States some years ago from various countries, and blacks who only immigrated quite recently, some of whom are illegal aliens. They also include blacks with many cultural differences. Green isolated nine different culture areas for blacks in the United States, including six separate areas in the South. These Southern areas were classified as Tidewater-Piedmont, Lower Atlantic Coastal Plains, Lowland Southern, Southern Louisiana and Environs, Upland or Border

South, and Mountain South or Appalachia. Sociocultural variations characterized each area. By religion, Episcopalians and Presbyterians were more pronounced in the Tidewater-Piedmont area than among the remaining areas. Catholicism was more pronounced in the Southern Louisiana and Environs area than among the remaining areas.[31] These cultural differences were not, of course, limited to religion. They include a host of differences, including diet, linguistic idioms, and political participation.

Co-joining disparate minorities for political convenience may well be unfair to the co-joined groups. For example, the aged Black not of Hispanic origin who requires bilingual service providers is extremely rare. This is not an argument against inclusion of such provisions in OAA for applicable groups. But the interpretation of the need for bilingual service providers, for example, is often extended to at least an implicit requirement that minority aged should be served by minority service deliverers. The underlying rationale is that service providers from the same cultural background and fluent in the native language and English are more competent than others in service delivery. That argument is typically valid for immigrant aged and, no doubt, for American Indians living as tribal members.

But the argument is invalid for most aged blacks. The dramatic shift from overt to covert racial discrimination confronting aged blacks is not eradicated merely by changing the color of the service provider. Black service providers are often salaried employees functioning as "middlemen" and not as policymakers. They generally conform to agency policies, principally because they place higher priority on maintaining their employment than they do upon changing agency policies in order to promote the greater well-being of their clients. This is not a fault peculiar to those salaried blacks, however. It is a characteristic they share with most salaried employees regardless of race.

One element typically missing from OAA is a need to train both black and white professionals who can deliver services to both black and white aged. Implicit within OAA is the age-old notion in social services that whites may deliver services to anyone but that blacks should be restricted to blacks.

OAA may also be approached critically by considering the need, if any, for black-specific legislation. It was noted earlier that political comparisons of aged blacks and whites require comparisons made without the benefit of controlled variables, such as socioeconomic status. Comparisons controlled for socioeconomic status generally lead to a conclusion that greater weight should be attached to socioeconomic status than to race as a differentiating variable. That conclusion leads to a feasible argument that federal programs for the aged, other than Social Security, should be based on need and not on race, or, for that matter, on age. That is, the need for race-specific legislation for aged blacks has not been demonstrated, nor is it likely that it could be demonstrated under current conditions.

The politicalization of aged blacks and advocates for aged blacks has not produced black-specific legislation in OAA and it is not likely to do so in the immediate or distant future. Such legislation would not lead to any significant improvements in the well-being of current and future aged blacks. Instead, it would hamper that well-being.

The minority-specific provisions of OAA do apply to some aged blacks, such as rural or poor aged blacks, but they do not apply across the board to all aged blacks. Thus, it may be concluded that OAA does address the needs of some aged blacks by including applicable blacks in other groups. The confusion comes about when the legislation enjoins minorities on a categorical grouping, but actually treats not so much their racial background as specific subgroups within racial groupings. The legislation could be improved by explicit provisions prohibiting discrimination that is unconstitutional within the programs and heavy sanctions against those who, while using OAA monies, so discriminate. For instance, if a state agency on aging practiced racial discrimination in distributing funds to agencies within its state, then it would forfeit any rights to federal funds for the aged allocated to its state for a period of five years. Otherwise, the remaining provisions would clearly identify specific subgroups of the aged in need of services, including poor aged.

WHCOA RECOMMENDATIONS

The United States has held three White House conferences on aging, each a decade apart. The racial impact of the 1961 black delegates, barely a handful, on the conference was practically, if not entirely, nil. It stands in sharp contrast to the 1971 conference, which was affected by black participation, due largely, if not entirely, to the efforts of the ad hoc group of the National Caucus on the Black Aged. NCBA originated primarily through the combined efforts of the late Hobart C. Jackson and Robert Kastenbaum. Jackson was then the chief administrator of what is now the Stephen Smith Geriatric Center in Philadelphia. Kastenbaum, one of the pioneering psychologists in aging in the United States, was then a faculty member at Wayne State University. The membership of the small ad hoc group was biracial. Jackson was black; Kastenbaum was white. This author was also a member of the original ad hoc group.

The work of that ad hoc group led to, among other things, a substantial increase in the proposed number of black delegates to the 1971 WHCOA, and to the conference officials eventually establishing special sessions for four specific minority groups, to be held for only four hours midway in the conference. Of parenthetical interest, perhaps, is the fact that the conference officials scheduled the Special Session on Aging Blacks in the Lincoln Room and the counterpart session on American Indians in the Thoroughbred Room of the Washington Hilton Hotel. The other two groups focused on Hispanics and Asians. One specific outcome of the session on blacks was its official report containing specific policy proposals.[32]

Unlike the 1971 WHCOA, the 1981 WHCOA built in from the outside relatively ample provisions for minority representation. However, for reasons unexplored in this chapter, the overall impact of black delegates on that conference was far less substantial than was the case in 1971.[33]

The present concern is not with the 1961 and 1971 WHCOAs but with the 1981 WHCOA recommendations specifically related to minority groups. Presentation of the applicable recommendations, extracted from the summary report of the fourteen different committees, seems appropriate here, primarily because a verbatim report permits any interested reader to assess them by his or her own criteria. The extracted recommendations are quoted directly below in the order presented in the summary report, along with an indication as to the specific committee from which they emerged.

Committee on Public Sector Roles and Structures

1. Federal and state governments and their political subdivisions shall plan, finance, and facilitate implementation of a continuum of services to meet the needs of the elderly including both those who live in the community and those who are institutionalized, tailored to individual needs and delivered without regard to race, religion, sex, national origin, physical or mental disability, or source of payment.

2. All public programs for the elderly be monitored by all levels of government to ensure: (1) protection of the rights and benefits of all elderly minorities and (2) the proportionate representation and participation of minority elderly in policy and program planning, and service delivery. The elderly and the minority elderly should be specified as a targeted group.

3. The Department of HHS [Health and Human Services], AOA [Administration on Aging], State, and area agencies in cooperation with minority aging organizations develop a national policy for insuring minority representation at all levels of aging planning, policy making and service delivery.

4. The federal government continue to exert a leadership role in improving life quality for the elderly through the establishment of minimal standards, and the assurance of equity in treatment and service for all older Americans regardless of income, race, sex and physical or mental condition.

5. The legislative division of the federal government should assure its senior citizens that funds it distributes under the Older Americans Act and other related federal funds be allocated to States, tribes, and territories, not just on a population basis but also in consideration of economic variables such as cost of living, degree of poverty, energy requirements, minority population and rurality.

6. Establish outreach system to eliminate language barriers for minority elderly. The Federal Government should establish policy for all minority groups to set age eligibility for Medicare, SSI and OAA according to demonstrated life expectancy.

7. Older persons be involved in the planning and delivery of their own social services and that special attention be accorded to the unique heritage, language and life styles of older persons.

Committee on Private Sector Roles, Structures and Opportunities

8. The private sector should promote job training and counseling for older Americans who wish to hold jobs or volunteer, especially for minorities, the handicapped, those in rural areas, and women.

Committee on Older Americans as a Continuing Resource

9. The right to freedom from discrimination because of age, race, sex, creed, or marital status.

Committee on Educational and Training Opportunities

10. [Its preamble will read that] education . . . is a necessity for a society struggling to achieve a fuller measure of social justice for all Americans irrespective of age, race, sex, economic status, color, handicap, territorial residence, or national origin.

11. [Supplemental statements, meaning lack of majority approval, were not detailed, but there was an indication that six of them] addressed the needs of special interest groups—rural, Native Americans, transportation, and peer counseling. Eight Statements suggest specific training and educational programs, including development of . . . minority and bilingual professionals to serve the elderly.

12. [Under additional views, a category for recommendations receiving almost no support, there was a focus] on special group needs of Native Americans, residents of territories and trusts-minorities, and the visually impaired.

Committee on Concerns of Older Women: Growing Number, Special Needs

13. A group of 10 recommendations on the quality of life encompassed cooperative public/private intergenerational programs. . . . [one of which was] that minority elderly be served by multilingual programs which will provide education and training, attitudinal training, and inclusion in planning and policy making.

Committee on Research

14. A joint effort between the research community and the many diverse cultural, racial and ethnic minority groups to insure that the knowledge base adequately reflects the unique situation of older people in these groups.

Committee on Health Care and Services

15. A national health care policy for aged native Americans.
16. Greater sensitivity to ethnic and cultural differences in the delivery of health care services to the elderly.

Committee on Implications for the Economy of an Aging Population

17. We should reduce or eliminate all restrictions on older workers with particular reference to mandatory retirement, age, sex, or race discrimination, and the lack of sufficient or adequate incentives.

18. Federal, state, and local government should set an example by hiring the elderly and minorities.

19. [Supplemental statement.] At least 20% voted that the Special Task Force [on Social Security] to be appointed by the President, Speaker of the House, and Senate Majority Leader should be directed to study and make recommendations as to whether the disparity in life expectancy between Blacks and other minorities and persons in the majority population justify different Social Security age eligibility requirements and/or different payroll tax rates that reflect the disparity in mortality rates.

Committee on Family and Community Support Systems

20. [Supplemental statement.] National policy should serve to encourage and strengthen American Indian and Alaskan native family networks to preserve cultural strengths and diversities.

21. Cultural, bi-cultural, and bilingual programs [in the public and private sector] should be expanded.

Committee on Promotion and Maintenance of Wellness

22. [Additional view.] Nutrition programs for the elderly include special services for minority populations.

Committee on Conditions for Continuing Community Participation

23. [With respect to transportation] Escort and bilingual services be provided where needed.

24. [With respect to multipurpose senior centers] Assuring that all services and programs are free from physical and language barriers.

25. [Supplemental view.] Since the life span of many members of minority groups is significantly lower than the population at large, a life expectancy scale for such groups should be used to calculate program eligibility.

Committee on Housing Alternatives

26. Federal legislation specify that Indians be included in all sections of proposed housing legislation.

27. The Indian elderly should have the opportunity for suitable housing appropriately constructed in a manner and location of their choice which they can reasonably afford.

28. Housing options and opportunities available to older Americans should also apply to elderly residents of the Virgin Islands, Guam, American Samoa and Puerto Rico.

Committee on Options for Long-Term Care

29. Access to [long-term care] service should be available without regard to race, creed or color. However, individuals should retain the right to express cultural, fraternal and/or ethnic heritage.

These twenty-nine recommendations culled from the summary report may be evaluated by focusing on their treatment of blacks as a minority group and of minorities as a target group.

The first focus is easily dismissed because none of those recommendations were expressly directed to blacks as a specific group. As in the OAA, the only minority group expressly recognized was American Indians.[34] The collective perception of the conferees was not one of older or aged blacks as a specific or unique group meriting preferential attention. They were presumably treated as minorities.

Focusing on minorities as a targeted group reveals occasional recognition by the conferees of majority-minority differences of the aged or of the efforts of minority conferees to establish those differences, for whatever reasons. Incidentally, the reference to blacks in recommendation 19 above was not to blacks per se but to "blacks and other minorities." Of the twenty-nine extracted recommendations, five were totally or largely specific to American Indians. Most often, the recommendations treated minorities homogeneously. When this was not the case, differentiation was usually made on a linguistic basis.

Contradiction was apparent in the Committee on Public Sector Roles and Structures (see recommendations 1 and 2) about whether governmental units providing elderly services or monitoring aged programs should consider race. The issue of when and where race should be considered needed clarification. "Without regard to race" is not the same mandate as "with regard to race."

Most of the recommendations specific to minorities concentrated on governmental action, or action in the public sector. An appropriate focus, to be sure, these recommendations were typically quite vague and ambiguous. It is not known if the lack of concreteness was due to inchoate preparedness of the minority delegates or a need for compromise for passage of the recommendations in sessions dominated by a racial majority. Illustrative of this criticism is recommendation 2. What is the implementative meaning of that recommendation? When policy refers to acts of the Congress, does it imply that a representative proportion of minority elderly should be members of the Congress? The electoral process now in force clearly mitigates against that conclusion. What are the criteria for determining proportionate representation? Suppose further that a total of ten minority elderly equaled proportionate representation, however defined, on the Federal Council on Aging. Does this mean that one representative each would be selected from American Indians, Alaskan natives, blacks not of Hispanic origin, blacks of Hispanic origin, Cubans, Puerto Ricans, Mexican-Americans, Vietnamese, Chinese-Americans, and Koreans? If so, what about Japanese-Americans, Haitian-Americans, and so on? Also, what about the fact that blacks not of Hispanic origin constitute well over eight out of every ten minority elderly in the United States? If blacks were then given nine of the ten available spots, which group would have the remaining spot? Is there a political problem? Indeed, there is.

The very nature of that political problem underscores the federal tendency to group conveniently various minority groups on the basis of racial, ethnic, or linguistic background within the larger category of simply minority groups. It will be noted that the hypothetical situation presented did not even begin to consider the economic minorities or the cultural subdivisions of native-born blacks.

Those promulgating recommendation 18 overlooked the fact that the critical problem with federal employment of blacks, at least, is not that they are not hired. In fact, they tend to be somewhat overrepresented by their proportion within the population. The program is the level at which they are hired. A recommendation here, thus, should have been more realistic in identifying carefully the particular problems of black employment in the federal government.

Recommendations 6, 19, and 25 sought differential age-eligibility requirements for minority participation in age-related programs on the basis of differences between the minorities and the majority in their life expectancies. Sophisticated legal and scientific research did not undergird those recommendations. One drawback was the failure to recognize the rapid turnover of the aged minority population. Characteristics of earlier cohorts of black aged, for example, do not necessarily repeat themselves in later cohorts.

I made the original proposal to modify age-eligibility requirements to reflect racial differences in life expectancy at the 1968 annual meeting of the Gerontological Society in Denver, Colorado. It was later adopted by both the ad hoc group of NCBA and the Special Session on Aging and Aged Blacks at the 1971 WHCOA.[35] It was also adopted in varying form by other groups.

The previous justification for my proposal was that many blacks were being shortchanged by Social Security. An extremely large proportion died before they ever became eligible for benefits. Their dependents also were often ineligible. Many of the older children did not meet the age requirements, or, if they did, they were not enrolled in school after eighteen years of age. The surviving spouses also often died before they became eligible to receive benefits. Some of those actually eligible did not receive benefits because they could not prove their age to the satisfaction of Social Security representatives charged with the responsibility of certifying them as eligible recipients. Fortunately, a number of these kinds of problems have decreased significantly over the years.

Life-expectancy values, computed for groups and not for individuals, may not be appropriate in setting age-eligibility requirements. In fact, it is probably unconstitutional. Thus, greater consideration should be given not to "beating a dead horse," as it were, but to a constitutionally permissible program that would benefit black payees of the Social Security payroll tax. Such a consideration should have led the minority and majority conferees who proposed racial distinctions in age-eligibility requirements to more inventive proposals. If, for example, they had read Ferrara's work on transforming Social Security into a true social insurance program,[36] they could well have proposed the elimination of welfare aspects from the current system. One postulation is that those delegates were insufficiently aware of the future aged and overly concerned about the present aged (often themselves). This is not to contend, of course, that no consideration should be focused on the present aged, but that any consideration of the present aged should also involve a consideration of future aged, as well as the effects on the future aged of the present system of intergenerational distribution of funds through Social Security. One reason for taking this position is that federal aging policies frequently outlive the aged group upon whom they were based, as well as many of the legislators who voted for them.

In general, insufficient consideration was given to minorities who will be aged in the future, in terms of concentrating on an improvement in the conditions under which they age so that they will be better off when they are old. This kind of band-aid approach fails to recognize that the conditions and life styles of the aged are heavily influenced by their earlier conditions and life styles. Recommendations to extend employment opportunities as a source of income for aged minorities should, at the very least, have been accompanied by recommendations to improve employment conditions for currently aging, but not old, minorities today. No focus whatsoever was placed upon the high unemployment rates of young black adults. The issue of the negative impact of the employment of illegal aliens on black adults in the secondary labor market was not mentioned in a single recommendation.[37] The political reality, however, is that the current increase in economic competition within the marketplace has implications for certain black subsets of the future aged.

The shortfalls in the recommendations related to minorities also point to other problems of the elderly that are not age related. One example is the recommendation (not cited above, because it was not expressly specific to minorities) advocating harsh sanctions against juveniles committing crimes against elderly persons. The question is not whether such sanctions are equitable or justified but rather whether they ought to have been advocated for nonelderly persons as well. Is the raping of a woman who is sixty-six years old more violent a crime than the raping of a woman who is fifty-nine years old?

It may well be hypothesized that blacks involved in the political processes affecting OAA and WHCOA in 1981 were not sufficiently politicalized to identify clearly the needs of aged blacks, now and in the future, which could have been ameliorated through political mechanisms. They were typically ineffective in promoting needed legislation, which would not and should not have been color-specific. For example, what was the stance of the National Center and Caucus on the Black Aged, on illegal immigration to the United States? The answer is that NCCBA remained silent on this important issue. Because those groups who presumably speak for aged blacks—usually groups that are called upon by the congressional committees on aging—remain notably silent when the issues may involve confrontation (perhaps because they are also dependent heavily on federal funding for their well-being), it becomes important to ask the critical question of who, indeed, should speak for aged blacks.

WHO SPEAKS FOR AGED BLACKS?

When Warren asked *Who Speaks for the Negro?*[38] he concluded correctly that there was no single voice. The same conclusion applies to the question, Who speaks for aged blacks? This answer is valid despite the tendency of congressional committees focused on the aged to seek testimony about aged blacks largely from the National Center and Caucus on Black Aged (NCCBA) and from blacks who are in salaried positions, supported entirely or largely by federal funds, where they are charged with the responsibility of helping to deliver services to the aged.

NCBA, previously mentioned as a biracial organization at its inception, differed from NCCBA in many ways, several of which are worth noting now. NCBA never presumed to speak for aged blacks, nor did it attempt to build a constituency of aged blacks. Its primary purposes dealt with developing cogent descriptions and analyses of varying conditions of contemporary blacks who were already old, and still a group, or who were continuing to age, but not yet old. The results could be used to advocate for legislative, administrative, and other changes that could improve the quality of life for aged blacks. NCBA was also concerned about those blacks who were not yet old but who were growing old. A primary function here was one of education and demonstration. Also, those who labored initially to develop NCBA generally contributed their own energies, time, and monies to the organization, and they, themselves, were typically not dependent on federal funding for their own livelihood.

In contrast, NCCBA contains none of the founding members of NCBA. A large percentage of its board and most of its staff are heavily dependent on public funding for their own economic well-being. Perhaps to protect their own vested interests, or for other reasons, they tend to paint a negative picture of aged blacks. The perpetuation of negative stereotypes does not promote the politicalization of aged blacks. In all probability, most aged blacks remain unaware of NCCBA's existence.

Most blacks over sixty-five years of age do not consider themselves as a specific minority group on the basis of their race and age, nor do they consider themselves as members of a minority group on the basis of age. Many aged black women also do not perceive themselves as members of a minority group based on sex. If confronted with a forced choice between racism, sexism, and ageism as being most detrimental to them in their old age, a majority of aged blacks polled separately by sex would probably give the greatest weight to racism. This, of course, is an hypothesis that could and should be tested.

Research is also needed on the voting attitudes and behaviors of aged blacks. When confronted with conflicting choices, do they tend to vote more often on the basis of "blackness" or "ageness?" Do they tend to vote more often for experienced or inexperienced candidates for public office? Do they vote largely on the basis of issues or on the personalities of candidates? Are their voting patterns more similar to those of other aged people in their localities, or do they approximate more nearly those of younger blacks?

What little is currently known about the voting patterns of aged blacks is based on data collected by the U.S. Bureau of the Census. Voting data for the 1980 presidential and congressional elections were not available by race and age at the time of this writing. The available data for the civilian noninstitutionalized population of voting age showed that, in the 1980 presidential election, 60.9 percent of whites, 50.5 percent of blacks *and* other races, and 29.9 percent of people of Spanish origin reported that they voted.[39]

In the 1976 presidential election, among those sixty-five to seventy-four years of age, the percentage reporting that they voted was highest among white males (72.5), followed by white females (64.0), black males (58.1), black females (56.1), Hispanic males (47.2), and Hispanic females (29.0). Among those over seventy-five years of age, the voting rates were somewhat lower, and black males were more likely to have reported voting than were white females: white men (63.9), black men (58.1), white women (50.8), black women (45.3), Hispanic men (18.3), and Hispanic women (10.7). In general, the aged majority was more likely to have reported voting, but some variations in the race–sex patterns by age do occur.[40] Older blacks, as older whites, were somewhat more likely to vote than were their younger counterparts.

The fact that a majority of aged blacks now tend to vote may have helped to promote greater interest in them by nonblack organizations. A growing number of national organizations on aging and on women seek increasingly to include applicable blacks under their scope. The organizational motives for doing so may vary considerably. These organizations, however, tend to concentrate their political efforts on ageism or sexism and not on racism. Some of these organizations seek to include blacks in order to improve their chances for federal funding. They may also wish to cultivate an image of being concerned about blacks. Some years ago, the National Council on Aging, which has concentrated some of its efforts on older blacks, attempted to do so on at least one occasion by competing directly and unfairly with NCBA.[41] White research applicants to the National Institute on Aging and the Administration of Aging are much more likely now to include the black population in their proposed samples because it may increase their chances of funding.[42]

The political "pushes and pulls" to which aged blacks are being increasingly subjected come from two major directions. Local, state, and national black political organizations *and* aging organizations pursue them. When these groups do not conflict on political issues, including endorsement of candidates, the potential problems remain hidden. But what will happen, as asked earlier, if conflict occurs?

Impressionistic judgments based on a few interviews I held with several local black politicians and several leaders of local organizations for the aged produced mixed results. The politicians argued that aged blacks active in aged organizations would be more likely to follow the political dicta of those organizations, largely because their regular participation on a social basis would have led them to form greater attachments to such organizations. For example, a local organization on the aged that contains a relatively large proportion of blacks tended to meet frequently, with most meetings including a social hour with refreshments. The black political organizations in the area did not have such meetings. Further, the membership overlap between the black political organization and the organization for the aged under consideration was slim—one person, himself a former elected official. Another difficulty could be that the black organization tended to seek out the black elderly when they wanted them to vote in prescribed ways.

In contrast, the chief official of the local aged organization, himself white, argued that aged blacks would vote primarily on the basis of their race. A retired labor union official, he believed that race was far more important than age and that the oppressed group of blacks should always vote "black." In fact, he was influential in directing the voting behavior of his constituents; his voting recommendations, to date, have coincided with those of the local black organization. The attitudes of the leader become an important variable, but it is also doubtful that a biracial organization on the aged could attract as members aged blacks whose votes it could control unless some focus was also placed on race.

Subsets of aged blacks are also subjected to other "pushes and pulls." Older black women are increasingly sought by women's organizations, including the Older Women's League. Organizations focused on the poor, such as the North Carolina Senior Citizens' Federation, also seek them. Some differentiation by socioeconomic status may also be evident in an examination of the demographic characteristics of black members of the Gray Panthers, as well as active members of the National Association of Retired Federal Employees. Aged blacks attracted to these kinds of groups tend to be retired professionals. Generally middle-class throughout their lives, they are also more likely to have had a history of participation in formal organizations outside of the church during most of their adult years. A useful research study could describe and analyze the differences between aged black participants and nonparticipants in various organizations for the aged. One focus of such a study could concentrate on factors influencing the political attitudes and behaviors of older blacks.

Who, then, speaks for aged blacks? Currently, no one really does, and it is unlikely that there will be a single individual or organization doing so in the future. No single individual or organization speaks for blacks of all ages, but the Congressional Black Caucus (CBC) is attempting to become that voice through implementation of its "Black Leadership Family Program for the Survival and Progression of the Black Nation,"[43] the preamble to which states, "The current circumstances dictate that the Plan operate in the form of participants accepting directives from their leadership."[44] The three purposes of the Plan are (1) the development of basic rules by which blacks can live, (2) the establishment of a Black Defense Fund, and (3) the promulgation of instructions to implement the Plan.[45] The success of the Plan is dependent on black compliance through financial contributions and adherence to the instructions.

A portion of the Plan is specific to black elderly. They are to be protected, as are youth, and, during the month of April, blacks are to contribute at least one dollar to senior citizens organizations. Also, senior citizens were assigned a mission, with executory instructions, as quoted directly below:

Operation Instructions
Receiving Organization: Senior Citizens

Mission

Your primary responsibility is to provide guidance, expertise and inspiration to all segments of the Black Nation to insure that the Black Nation's decisions, actions and programs benefit from your rich knowledge and experience.

Execution

a.   You shall maintain close contact and membership with organizations in your fields of interest and expertise, and actively participate with them in their goals and objectives toward developing the Black Nation.

b. Research and develop genealogical data in support of class action suits for reparations.

c. Provide media and CBC [Congressional Black Caucus] Regional Coordinator with information on violations of procedures and practices established for the benefit and rights of the elderly.

d. Operate as resource persons for informing your elected officials and your CBC Coordinator of specific unmet needs and requirements of the elderly.

e. Report to your CBC Coordinator the names and positions of individuals involved in anti-Black activities.

f. Generate a positive awareness of the role of Black defense organizations in the Black Nation.

g. Support development of the youth through:
    1. active participation in re-directing gang members;
    2. initiation of and participation in school tutorial programs;
    3. offering your services as foster grandparents;
    4. serving as advisors to local Black Junior Achievement companies.

h. Actively participate in all directed, organized economic selective patronage and picketing activities directed at those who oppose the goals and objectives of the Black Nation.

i. You are to organize and implement voter registration and get-out-to-vote drives, and assist in the registration and absentee balloting of shut-ins.

j. Spearhead community fundraisers in support of the Black Defense Fund.

k. Promote and advocate the "Rules for Black Unity and Survival."

l. Make the Black media your primary source for accurate, reliable and complete information regarding the issues affecting any segment of the Black Nation.

m. Serve as volunteers in letter writing and mailing and telephone bank campaigns in support of issues affecting any segment of the Black Nation.[46]

The Plan, dictatorial or totalitarian in nature, presumably seeks to establish a nation within a nation, a political impossibility. It directs aged blacks away from participation in biracial organizations and toward organizational efforts to promote the "Black Nation." If the Plan were implemented as outlined, black senior citizens organizations would receive $12.5 million during the first operational year, presumably in 1982.[47] Finally, no consideration is given to the possibility of intergenerational conflicts, such as over the issue of Social Security; instead, black unity is stressed throughout. It is unlikely that the implementation of this plan will effect any considerable politicalization of aged blacks. It is also unlikely that the Congressional Black Caucus will become a major spokesman for aged blacks, primarily because it has not yet developed the necessary expertise and coalition ties to function effectively within that role. This is not to contend, however, that such a role could not evolve.

CONCLUSIONS

This chapter about the politicalization of aged blacks has explored the three major issues of the political implications of racial differences between aged blacks and whites, the adequacy of the Older Americans Act Amendments of 1981 and the *Summary Reports of the Committee Chairmen, the 1981 White House Conference on Aging* in recognizing aged blacks as a distinct group, and the diversity of political "pushes and pulls" to which aged blacks are being increasingly subjected.

In addition to the lack of data needed to explore adequately these topics, the major conclusions reached were that demographic differences between aged blacks and whites are politically important, that OAA and WHCOA did not recognize aged blacks as a distinct group, and that the political attitudes and behaviors of aged blacks are not homogeneous. However, it is probable that aged blacks are more concerned about racism than about ageism.

Much research is needed on the topic of the politicalization of aged blacks. The suggested research included empirical studies of their voting attitudes and behaviors, where comparisons could be made between them and younger blacks, as well as between the black and nonblack aged. Further, analyses distinguishing between aged black participants and nonparticipants in various organizations focused on the aged could be helpful, as would studies of the weighted influence of political groups who have aged blacks as their constituents. Finally, it was argued that those who purport to speak for aged blacks should base their political pronouncements on actual data from representative samples of aging and aged blacks. That is, greater recognition must be given to the relatively rapid turnover of the aged black population, mandating thereby more concentration on aged blacks in the future.

NOTES

1. Although the editors requested a chapter on minorities and not on blacks alone, I modified the topic after much cogitation and many false drafting starts. The difficulty experienced in attempting to develop a reasonable and readable chapter on minorities may be attributed to such factors as the significant historical and sociocultural differences among minorities in the United States, the continuing paucity of relevant data about them (especially nonblack minorities), and inadequate space to do justice to each group. It could also be argued convincingly that the increasing tendency of editors or authors of gerontological books to include *a* chapter on minorities may be meritorious in recognizing the existence of aged minorities and in boosting, perhaps, sales or use of a given work. But it could also be argued convincingly that such treatment of minorities typically fails to provide the reader with a meaningful discussion of aging related to any given minority, as well as to the collectivity of minorities, which is a questionable collectivity at best. These two conflicts could be defined as "shallow convenience"

and "in-depth concentration." Application of the "shallow convenience" model proved impossible for this author.

2. U.S., Congress, House, *Older Americans Act Amendments of 1981*, 97th Cong., 1st sess., Report no. 97-386.

3. *Summary Reports of the Committee Chairmen, the 1981 White House Conference on Aging* (mimeographed) (Washington, D.C., 1981).

4. The concept of "multiple jeopardy" was expanded from the initial application of the concept of "double jeopardy" to aged blacks. That concept arose in a report of a study by the Detroit Urban League and was cited as follows in *Double Jeopardy: The Older Negro in America Today* (New York: National Urban League, 1964), when Hobart C. Jackson, a founder of the National Caucus on the Black Aged, was chairman of the National Urban League's Health and Welfare Subcommittee on Aging:

Today's aged Negro is different from today's aged white because he *is* Negro . . . and this alone should be enough basis for differential treatment. For he has, indeed, been placed in double jeopardy: first, by being Negro and second by being aged. Age merely compounded those hardships accrued to him as a result of being a Negro.

"Multiple jeopardy" goes beyond "double jeopardy" by recognizing the additive factors that jeopardize the well-being of aged black subgroups. For example, I introduced the concept of "quadruple jeopardy" in 1971 to refer specifically to poor, aged, black women. The jeopardizing circumstances there are poverty, old age, black, and female. It might also be noted that the use of the concept of "double jeopardy" by the Detroit Urban League was specific to blacks and not to other minorities. Current literature often misinterprets this. For example, Vern L. Bengtson, et al., in "The Impact of Social Structure on Aging Individuals" (in *Handbook of the Psychology of Aging*, ed. James E. Birren and K. Warner Schaie [New York: Van Nostrand Reinhold, 1977]), misconstrued the concept by writing,

The National Urban League (1964) introduced the concept of "double jeopardy" to describe the situation of minority aged as one of additive disadvantage: minority aged face not only the problems associated with being old, and often poor, but also the accumulated problems of a lifetime of membership in a minority group. (p. 338)

The misconstruction is important in the present context, in that Bengtson and his colleagues extended the concept to minorities without sufficient consideration of the applicability of the concept to each minority group, and, indeed, without providing a definition of the groups included under the category of "minority aged."

5. In addition to the fact that most empirical investigations of aged blacks do not yet contain representative samples, attention should be focused on the fact that the massive study of the mental health of blacks, substantially funded by the National Institute on Aging, is headed by James Jackson as principal investigator. Jackson, a black psychologist at the University of Michigan, was funded after the National Institute on Aging had begun to encourage white researchers collecting empirical data through surveys or interviews to include blacks among their

samples. The interesting political question here is why Jackson's study does not include any whites.

6. Henry P. Fairchild, ed., *Dictionary of Sociology* (Ames, Iowa: Littlefield, Adams, 1959), p. 109.

7. Ibid.

8. Ibid.

9. Ibid., p. 134.

10. Ibid., p. 80.

11. Advocatory citation of the differential rates of poverty by race is not inappropriate if the focus is placed on the extant differentials of younger blacks and whites and if recommendations are made anew to reduce those differentials. The problem with the mere recitation of the differences is that they are not only already well known but expected in light of the differential income histories of surviving blacks and whites reaching old age. The point here is that political use of these kinds of data must go beyond a mere recitation of what is already known.

12. John E. Nowak, et. al., *Handbook on Constitutional Law* (St. Paul, Minnesota: West Publishing Co., 1978), p. 561.

13. See Robert Hill, "A Demographic Profile of the Black Elderly," *Aging* nos. 287-288 (1978): 2-9; and Jacquelyne J. Jackson, *Minorities and Aging* (Belmont, Cal.: Wadsworth, 1980).

14. U.S., Bureau of the Census, *Population Profile of the United States: 1980*, Current Population Reports, series P-20, no. 363 (Washington, D.C.: Government Printing Office, 1981).

15. Jackson, *Minorities and Aging*, p. 31.

16. For a limited and contrasting discussion of this issue, see Richard C. Crandall, *Gerontology: A Behavioral Science Approach* (Reading, Mass.: Addison-Wesley, 1980), and Jacquelyne J. Jackson and Bertram E. Walls, "Myths and Realities About Aged Blacks," in *Readings in Gerontology*, ed. M. R. Brown, 2nd ed. (St. Louis: C.V. Mosby, 1978).

17. Jacquelyne J. Jackson, "Special Health Problems of Aged Blacks," *Aging* nos. 287-288 (1978): 15-20.

18. Jacquelyne J. Jackson, "Mortality Patterns of Aged Blacks and Whites, United States, 1964-1978," *The Black Scholar* 13 (Winter 1982): 36-48.

19. E. Franklin Frazier, *The Negro Family in the United States* (Chicago: University of Chicago Press, 1939).

20. Irving Rosow, "Status and Role Change Through the Life Span," in *Handbook of Aging and the Social Sciences*, ed. Robert H. Binstock and Ethel Shanas (New York: Van Nostrand Reinhold, 1976), pp. 457-82.

21. Margaret Mead, *Culture and Commitment: A Study of the Generation Gap* (New York: Doubleday, 1970).

22. Walter M. Beattie, Jr., "Aging and the Social Services," in Binstock and Shanas, *Handbook*, p. 627.

23. Ibid.

24. Roger Daniels and Harry H. L. Kitano, *American Racism: Exploration of the Nature of Prejudice* (Englewood Cliffs, N.J.: Prentice-Hall, 1970), p. 2.

25. Ibid., p. 3.

26. Gordon Streib, "Social Stratification and Aging," in Binstock and Shanas, *Handbook*, p. 169. Also, for an interesting discussion of legal definitions of age, see

100   Aging and Public Policy

Leonard D. Cain, "Aging and the Law," in Binstock and Shanas, *Handbook*, pp. 342–68.

27. Claude Pepper, "Please, Raspberry, No More Fairy Tales," *Washington Post*, December 26, 1981, p. A17. In taking exception to William Raspberry's (a black columnist for the *Washington Post*) position on mandatory retirement in that "older workers would prefer the predictability of mandatory retirement," Pepper wrote,

Raspberry, of all people, should be aware of the fallacy in this argument. Racism, like ageism, is predictable, but that hardly makes it defensible. An essential commitment to the rights of individuals to be free from bias because of their race, color, creed, national origin or religion not only is fundamentally guaranteed by our Constitution and federal laws, but also has been the driving force behind the civil rights movement. *Ageism, of which mandatory retirement is a part, is as odious as racism and sexism. Raspberry's argument that an older worker should be willing to give up his job to a younger worker is analogous to arguing that a black man should be willing to give up his job to a white man at some future date, in exchange for job security now.* Such a proposal is paternalistic and nonsensical. [Emphasis added.]

An effective rebuttal to Pepper's characterization of Raspberry's proposal as "paternalistic and nonsensical" is that Pepper's analogy is unreasonable and also nonsensical. It should be noted that Pepper did not include age in the list of biases from which individuals are protected by the Constitution and federal laws. The elements necessary to prove ageism differ from those necessary to prove racism in a very fundamental way. Consider if the denial of a temporary job shoveling snow during a heavy snow storm to a physically fit (for his age), twenty-two-year-old, black male is the same as denying such a job to a physically fit (for his age), eighty-seven-year-old, white male, when the job requires outdoor work in below-zero temperatures. From a political standpoint, however, efforts to equate ageism with racism are feasible, because there is then no need to justify why ageism should become a significant domestic problem; it would become one by mere association with racism.

28. For a provocative discussion of the effects of race and social class on contemporary blacks, see William J. Wilson, *The Declining Significance of Race* (Chicago: University of Chicago Press, 1978).

29. The three suspect classes under the U.S. Constitution are those of race, nationality, and alienage. In *Korematsu* v. *United States*, 323 U.S. 214 (1944), the U.S. Supreme Court developed three items for analytical classifications of race or nationality. "First, these classifications were 'suspect' which meant, at a minimum, that they were likely to be based on an impermissible purpose. Second, these classifications were to be subject to independent judicial review—'rigid scrutiny.' Third, the classification would be invalid if based on racial antagonism and upheld only if they were based on 'public necessity.' From this opinion came the concepts of 'strict judicial scrutiny' and the requirement that some restrictions on liberty must be necessary to promote 'compelling' or 'overriding' interests" (Novak, *Handbook on Constitutional Law*, p. 557). Also it may be useful to stress that "Classifications in federal law which accord separate treatment to members of American Indian tribes are not racial classifications for purposes of equal protection. The relationship between the [U.S.] Constitution and American Indians is unique" (ibid., p. 588).

30. Peter J. Ferrara, *Social Security: The Inherent Contradiction* (San Francisco: Cato Institute, 1980), pp. 143–44.

31. Vera M. Green, "Levels of Diversity Among U.S. Blacks," in *Diversity in the Non-Farm Rural Population*, ed. Paul L. Wall (Tuskegee Institute, Ala.: Division of Behavioral Science Research, Carver Research Foundation, Tuskegee Institute, 1981), pp. 38–41.

32. See the *Report of the Special Session on Aging and Aged Blacks, the 1971 White House Conference on Aging* (Washington, D.C.: Government Printing Office, 1972).

33. This proposition can be approached in at least two ways. One is by comparing the recommendations of the two conferences that were specific to blacks and to minority groups. The other is to consider the fact that Congress is mandated to consider the 1981 recommendations, whereas it was not so mandated for the 1971 recommendations.

34. A personal conversation between the author and a legislative aide to a congressman involved in the reauthorization of the 1981 OAA disclosed that the act as a bill was not subjected to much lobbying. The Asian group on aging did not lobby at all. Minimal lobbying took place by the black and Hispanic organizations on aging. The most significant lobbying on behalf of a minority group was for Indians, undertaken not by the Indian organization on aging, but by the National Council of American Indians. That lobbying resulted in the removal of a chronological limitation for older Indians. Much of the lobbying support for the Indians came from Thomas Petri (Wisconsin) and Pat Williams (Montana) of the House of Representatives. Also, the North Carolina Senior Citizens Federation, Inc., whose founder and director is black, lobbied for senior opportunities and activities allowable under Title III, where the major concern was with provisions for the poor over sixty years of age, regardless of race.

35. See Jackson, *Minorities and Aging*, pp. 81–88.

36. See Ferrara, *Social Security*.

37. For a discussion of this issue, see Jacquelyne J. Jackson, "Illegal Aliens: Big Threat to Black Workers," *Ebony*, 34 (1979): 33–36, 38, 40.

38. Robert Penn Warren, *Who Speaks for the Negro?* (New York: Random House, 1965).

39. U.S., Bureau of the Census, *Population Profile*, p. 27.

40. Jackson, *Minorities and Aging*, pp. 147–50.

41. One specific incident relates to disseminating a bibliography on aged blacks. NCBA, then an ad hoc group, often met in the offices of the National Council on Aging, in Washington, D.C. When I was preparing a manuscript on "The Blacklands of Gerontology" for publication in *Aging and Human Development*, the most complete gerontological bibliography pertaining to aged blacks to date then, a request was made to have access to that bibliography for limited distribution to the group prior to its publication. I complied with the NCOA director's offer to duplicate my bibliography for limited distribution. A few months later, the bibliography appeared in a publication of the Senate Special Committee on Aging, as a product of NCOA.

42. Personal knowledge based on participation as a member of a reviewing committee of a federal agency funding aging research and from shared comments, on an informal basis, from a number of blacks and whites involved in

gerontology. Interestingly, the one recommendation from the 1981 WHCOA specific to minorities ignored the development of minority researchers.

43. *The Black Leadership Family Program for the Survival and Progress of the Black Nation* (Washington, D.C.: Congressional Black Caucus, November, 1981).

44. Ibid., p. iii.

45. Ibid., p. iv.

46. Ibid., p. 16.

47. Ibid., p. vii.

PAUL K. H. KIM

5

Public Policies for the Rural Elderly

Historically, the word *rural* has been defined in a bewildering variety of ways by academicians, politicians, and public officials. Sociologists define the term on the basis of categories such as population counts of occupational and sociocultural variables,[1] or on the basis of an index of rurality, including population proximity and population density.[2] While politicians view rurality in terms of political units, bureaucrats see it in terms of tax bases. Government officials define *rural* by the number of people living in an area who will be affected by their public programs. In 1900, a rural area was defined as one with a population of fewer than 4,000 people. Ten years later, in 1910, this figure was reduced to 2,500. In 1930, an occupational criterion was added to the farm–nonfarm continuum. Later, in 1960, the Standard Metropolitan Statistical Area (SMSA) concept was introduced, a rural or nonmetropolitan area (non-SMSA) being a specified geographical or governmental unit populated with fewer than 50,000 people. Some of the definitions used by public agencies today are as follows:

Bureau of the Census: According to the 1970 census definition, the urban population is comprised of all persons in (a) places of 2,500 inhabitants or more incorporated as cities, villages, boroughs, and towns, but excluding persons living in the rural portions of "extended cities" (places with relatively low population density in one or more parts of their area); (b) unincorporated places of 2,500 inhabitants or more; and (c) other territory, incorporated or unincorporated, included in urbanized areas. All other persons are lumped into the rural category.

Office of Management and Budget (OMB): The OMB measures for defining *rural* include Standard Metropolitan Statistical Areas (SMSA) and Standard Consolidated Statistical Areas (SCSA). Metropolitan/nonmetropolitan areas serve as the basis for definitions of *rural*.

Farmers Home Administration: The FHA uses three definitions depending upon the purpose of the program: uses U.S. Bureau of the Census's 2,500 population for water and sewer projects: uses 10,000 population for community development loans; uses 50,000 population for business and industrial programs. In the federal housing program, a gap existed between home loan programs in the FHA and the

Department of Housing and Urban Development (HUD). An interagency agreement that uses a ceiling of 15,000 people for rural areas has been established to resolve the problem.

Rural America: Rural America relies on the U.S. Bureau of the Census definition of a "nonurbanized" area. It can include an area with an SMSA.

Administration on Aging: The 1978 Older Americans Act Amendments do not define *rural*. There is no agreement within the AOA on a definition, and the AOA may leave it up to the individual states. As of January 1979, the following was suggested:

"Rural areas" will consist of planning and service areas (PSAs) that meet at least two of the following criteria: (1) The proportion of the total population of the PSA residing in urban areas as defined by the Bureau of the Census is less than 50 percent, according to the most recent decennial census; (2) the total population density of each county in the PSA is less than 100 persons per square mile; and (3) there is no more than one minor civil division or urban place of 20,000 or more inhabitants in a single county in the PSA.

U.S. Senate Bill S.670: Rural Development Policy and Coordination Act of 1979: All territory of a state that (1) is not within the boundary of any SMSA, as designed by the OMB, and (2) in addition, all territory within any such SMSA that is also within counties, parishes, towns, and townships having a population density of less than 200 persons per square mile is considered rural.[3]

Green Thumb, Inc., an employment program for the rural elderly funded by the Department of Labor through the Farmers Union, defines *rural* as

(1) All territory outside the boundaries of an SMSA as determined by the OMB, except cities of 50,000 population or more. (2) All territory within boundaries of SMSAs that meet one of the following criteria: (a) open country (unbuilt-up and subdivided lands not within the incorporated limits of a town, village, or city); (b) any village, town, or small city of up to 10,000 population. Should there be a question concerning the rurality of any area, the state director shall prepare and submit to the executive vice-president for decision, via regional representatives, a detailed description of the territory involved, including demographic and geographic data and the need for designating the proposed area as rural.[4]

In view of the general use of the SMSA/non-SMSA dichotomy in defining urban/rural areas, the terms *nonmetropolitan* and *rural* will be used interchangeably in this chapter to indicate areas populated with fewer than 50,000 people. This definition is the most inclusive of those reviewed above, and it is currently employed by the Administration on Aging.[5]

RURAL AMERICA AND THE ELDERLY

Although rural America long has been known as the backbone of this country, industrialization and technological developments in the early twentieth century gave birth to "urbanized" America. The outmigration from rural into urban areas was staggering during the period 1900-70. The proportion of rural people in the country (58.1 percent in 1900) declined steadily, with the result that less than one-third of the total population was living in nonmetropolitan areas by 1970—approximately a 4 percent loss during each decade since 1900 (see table 5.1).

Table 5.1
U.S. Population in SMSAs and non-SMSAs, 1900–1970

Year	SMSAs (percent)	non-SMSAs (percent)
1900	41.9	58.1
1910	45.7	54.3
1920	49.7	50.3
1930	54.3	45.7
1940	55.1	44.9
1950	59.2	40.8
1960	63.0	37.0
1970	68.7	31.3

SOURCE: Irene B. Taeuber, "The Changing Distribution of the Population in the United States in the Twentieth Century," in Commission on Population Growth and the American Future, *Population Distribution and Policy*, ed. Sara Mills Mazie, vol. 5 (Washington, D.C.: Government Printing Office, 1972), p. 78, table 19; G. F. DeJong and R. R. Sell, "Population Redistribution, Migration, and Residential Preference," *Annals of the American Academy of Political and Social Science* 429 (January 1977): 130–44; Ecosometrics, Inc., *Review of Reported Differences Between the Rural and Urban Elderly: Status, Needs, Services, and Service Costs* (Bethesda, Md., 1981), p. 35.

However, during the 1970s a reverse trend began. For example, between 1970 and 1974, metropolitan areas gained about 460,000 people, while nonmetropolitan areas gained 1,609,000. This represented percentage net migration of 0.3 percent and 3.0 percent and a growth rate of 3.4 percent and 5.6 percent for metropolitan and nonmetropolitan areas, respectively.[6] America still has a disproportionate population distribution today since about one-third of the population lives in more than one-half of the land territory of the country. Of the nation's 3,135 counties, 2,210 (70 percent) have fewer than 50,000 persons, and 32 states (64 percent) have fewer than 100 persons per sqare mile.[7] Furthermore, of 81,248 local governmental bodies, 62 percent were serving fewer than 1,000 people.[8]

The elderly population (age sixty-five and over) in rural areas has been increasing at a faster rate than that in urban areas, particularly since 1970. There were about 7 and 14 million rural and urban elderly in 1970, respectively, and by 1977 these numbers had increased to 8.3 and 15.8 million, representing an increase of 19.8 percent for rural and 12.2 percent for urban areas.[9] Such growth during the 1970s includes both a national increase, and elderly inmigration into nonmetropolitan areas.[10] From 1970 to 1975, 12 percent of the SMSA elderly moved to non-SMSA areas, while only 4 percent of the non-SMSA elderly migrated to SMSA areas.[11] By 1978, more than one-half of the elderly population in twenty-one states, and 30 percent or more in an additional eleven states, were living in rural areas.[12] In that year the rural elderly accounted for 37 to 40 percent of the nation's total aged population. Approximately 12 percent of the nonmetropolitan population and 9.7 percent of the metropolitan population were older people. Growth rates of metropolitan and nonmetropolitan elderly populations between 1970 and 1977 in each state are given in table 5.2.

Table 5.2
Elderly Population Growth Rates, by State, 1977

Regions and State	State Rate	Metropolitan (percent)	Nonmetropolitan (percent)
Region I			
Connecticut	18.0	18.0	18.2
Maine	14.0	11.8	15.0
Massachusetts	8.9	7.3	47.1
New Hampshire	19.6	20.6	18.8
Rhode Island	13.7	12.7	28.3
Vermont	13.9	0.0	13.9
Region II			
New Jersey	16.3	12.1	61.7
New York	6.5	5.9	11.2
Region III			
Delaware	22.3	20.2	26.3
District of Columbia	2.4	2.4	0.0
Maryland	20.7	20.9	20.0
Pennsylvania	13.1	12.8	14.3
Virginia	23.7	23.9	23.4
West Virginia	12.9	14.4	12.1
Region IV			
Alabama	22.7	24.4	20.4
Florida	46.9	45.6	55.9
Georgia	25.2	27.5	23.2
Kentucky	13.4	14.9	12.4
Mississippi	19.5	32.1	16.8
North Carolina	28.9	30.2	28.0
South Carolina	30.8	34.2	28.2
Tennessee	21.8	22.8	20.3
Region V			
Illinois	9.3	9.5	8.7
Indiana	12.5	14.1	9.4
Michigan	13.4	11.4	20.9

Table 5.2 (continued)
Elderly Population Growth Rates, by State, 1977

Regions and State	State Rate	Metropolitan (percent)	Nonmetropolitan (percent)
Minnesota	11.7	10.6	13.0
Ohio	11.5	12.1	9.3
Wisconsin	13.6	13.3	14.1
Region VI			
Arkansas	20.7	22.0	20.0
Louisiana	18.9	21.1	15.7
New Mexico	40.5	49.0	37.1
Oklahoma	16.9	21.8	13.2
Texas	24.4	27.6	18.5
Region VII			
Iowa	6.9	8.9	6.1
Kansas	10.4	16.0	7.7
Missouri	11.1	11.1	11.1
Nebraska	9.2	10.6	8.6
Region VIII			
Colorado	20.3	21.9	15.8
Montana	15.5	22.3	13.8
North Dakota	15.8	16.3	15.6
South Dakota	9.5	16.2	8.0
Utah	27.5	26.6	30.1
Wyoming	15.9	0.0	15.9
Region IX			
Arizona	56.8	57.1	55.7
California	21.8	21.0	31.6
Hawaii	43.7	45.5	39.2
Nevada	66.5	71.5	50.7
Region X			
Alaska	39.0	60.2	32.0
Idaho	25.0	29.1	24.3
Oregon	22.3	18.4	28.5
Washington	21.0	20.0	23.1
U.S. total	17.7	17.5	17.9

SOURCE: U.S., Department of Health and Human Services, Administration on Aging, *The Elderly Population: Estimates by County–1977*, Publication no. (OHDS) 80-20248 (Washington, D.C.: Government Printing Office, 1980).

PROBLEMS OF THE ELDERLY

Despite some recent theories ascribing differences in rural–urban populations to the presence of a single value system[13] or to mass attitudes,[14] pluralism in rural America has been widely recognized and discussed in the literature. Rural mentalities have been described by analysts with such terms as *relative prejudice, ethnocentrism, isolation, intolerance, distrust, religious, ascetic, work-oriented, puritanical,* and *uninformed.*[15] Other observers use terms such as *independent, progressive, prosperous,* and living *naturally* or *mutually.*[16] Values held by rural elderly are discussed in terms of insularity, independence, isolation, xenophobia, and individualism.[17] The rural elderly have also been described as placing an especially high premium on the values of independence, ambition, freedom, accomplishment, logical pragmatism, conservatism, integrity, and responsibility.[18]

Elderly persons in rural areas, however, have the same problems as those in urban areas: physical and mental health, housing, transportation, income, employment, social services, education, nutrition, and spiritual well-being. They share equally the discomforts associated with aging, both physiological and mental limitations and societal prejudices against them. Both rural and urban people have their own individual mentalities and styles of life that they have developed through years of experience. The only difference between the problems facing rural and urban elderly people is the degree or severity of problems and the means available for alleviating them. The rural elderly experience old-age problems more severely than do their urban counterparts primarily because of geographic isolation, inferior and reduced public service programs, and perhaps, to a lesser extent, their own values. The most crucial problems facing the rural elderly have been documented in numerous studies.[19]

INCOME SECURITY NEEDS

The incidence of poverty is disproportionately higher among the rural than among the urban elderly. In terms of median incomes in 1975, the metropolitan elderly received $5,375. Their nonmetropolitan counterparts received $4,440 per year, representing a difference of 21.1 percent. Stated differently, the urban elderly had 3.9 percent more, and the rural elderly had 14.2 percent less, than the national median income of $5,174.[20] Forty-four percent of the nation's elderly poor live in rural areas. Sixty-one percent of all rural elderly had 1977 incomes below $2,000, and 81 percent below $4,000; 5.5 percent had no Social Security benefits, and 3 percent had no income at all.[21] In 1978, 17.2 percent of the rural elderly lived below the poverty level, while 10.4 percent of their urban counterparts did so. Income conditions were worse among the elderly aged seventy-two and over; 22.1 percent of the rural elderly and 12.6 percent of their urban counterparts had incomes below the poverty level.[22]

Similar poverty data are reported for elderly people living in boom towns, a phenomenon of modern times. Elderly people in boom towns make up 25 percent of their populations, 14 percent higher than the average nationally.[23] Yet the elderly in such areas do not benefit from new economic developments. They suffer instead from an increasing cost of living and rising property taxes. They have difficulty purchasing essential goods and services on their low fixed incomes, with the vast majority experiencing severe economic deprivation.

Other types of income-related problems facing the rural elderly were emphasized during a 1979 conference on rural aging held in Des Moines, Iowa. Items included in the discussions were disincentives for older people to work; problems due to loss of public benefits; limited job opportunities; deficient efforts aimed at securing older people jobs by public agencies charged with their income development; the disproportionate share of taxes paid by the rural elderly; and eligibility guidelines for federal and state programs that discriminate against persons having agricultural income.[24]

PHYSICAL AND MENTAL HEALTH NEEDS

The physical and mental health problems of the elderly are related closely to their income needs. Availability of, accessibility to, and affordability of medical and mental health services are three crucial factors affecting the overall health conditions of the rural elderly.[25] Half of the rural elderly are reported to be in poor health, with 87 percent of them restricted in their movements.[26] Fifty-eight percent of all rural people take medication regularly at the advice of one, two, or more doctors.[27]

Health problems of the rural elderly are exacerbated by the conditions prevailing in rural areas. While 25 percent of the nation's people live in medically underserved areas, 60 percent of such medically underserved areas are rural. Ninety-five percent of the nation's 1,500 medically underserved counties are nonmetropolitan counties.[28] Only 12 percent of the nation's physicians and 18 percent of its registered nurses work in rural areas, and there are no physicians at all in 135 counties. Eighty-four percent of the areas lacking adequate health manpower are rural counties. This health manpower shortage is expected to continue for some years.[29] Furthermore, health facilities in rural areas are smaller, older, and less likely to be accredited.[30]

About 4 percent of the occupants of mental health facilities are older people.[31] Types of mental health problems are alike in rural and urban areas. However, since more unfavorable mental outlooks and greater helplessness and despair are reported in rural locations, there is a need for more services there. A U.S. Goverment Accounting Office report shows that rural elderly are in worse condition in terms of health, security, loneliness, and outlook on life; they also are less able to carry out their daily activities than urban elderly. Moreover, seventy-five percent of the rural elderly need help and do not receive any.[32] In boom town areas, the cost of health care is not affordable by the vast majority of the elderly, and health services are particularly difficult to obtain since existing ones are scarce and must be shared by younger people coming into the community.[33] Thus, the rural elderly generally rely heavily on self-care and home remedies.[34]

HOUSING NEEDS

Approximately 3,250,000 nonmetropolitan homes make up 60 percent of the nation's substandard housing; 25 percent of the inadequate homes are occupied by elderly persons. In 1970, 21 percent of rural older people's dwellings lacked all or some plumbing facilities, as against only 4.3 percent of those for the urban elderly.

A still more gloomy housing situation is seen in the boom towns in rural America. Most of these houses are older than the national average and are inadequately insulated. Consequently, their elderly occupants have to spend more money for home repairs and fuel. They must also contend with the hazards of hypothermia, pneumonia, and other viruses if they cannot afford to keep the temperature sufficiently high. Given the poverty and near poverty of so many of the rural elderly and the large increases in fuel costs during the past few years, they often spend over 50 percent of their total income just on winter heating. From 1975 to 1981, the increase in Social Security and Supplementary Security Income has been only 42.7 and 24 percent, respectively. This is far lower than the growth of fuel costs over the same time. Fuel oil, for example, increased by 136.3 percent; natural gas was up 126.7 percent; and electricity jumped 73.5 percent. High utility costs and repair bills, along with rising property taxes, tend to be beyond the financial capabilities of the growing percentage of the rural elderly, most of whom own their own homes. Renters face additional burdens.

In 1980, the New York Senate Standing Committee on Aging summarized the housing situation in rural America as follows:

Of the 2.7 million housing units in the country without complete plumbing, 1.7 million (63 percent) are located in rural areas. There are 30 million U.S. citizens who live in housing that is overcrowded and/or lacks complete plumbing; 46 percent of these people live in rural areas. In 1970, twelve out of every one hundred households in nonmetropolitan areas lacked some form of sanitary facilities, compared with only three out of every hundred in metropolitan areas. Four out of five nonmetropolitan households without full plumbing facilities had incomes in 1969 of less than $6,000, and more than half had deep-poverty incomes of less than $3,000. Elderly households (those with heads aged sixty-five and older) comprised 23 percent of all nonmetropolitan households, but they made up almost one third of the houses lacking plumbing. Over two-thirds of the rural elderly own their own homes, most of which were built prior to 1950.[35]

TRANSPORTATION NEEDS

Automobile ownership is almost a requirement of modern life in rural areas due to the paucity of public transportation. Rural older people are often left alone without transportation during most of the day when family members, friends, or neighbors work. Large numbers do not have a driver's license or cannot afford the price of a car or even the gasoline to run one. Nearly 49 percent of the rural elderly have some kind of transportation problem and experience considerable difficulty in shopping for groceries or obtaining medical and other essential services.[36]

Those who do own their own automobiles are experiencing another transportation-related problem. Not only must they cope with difficult traffic problems, but they also run into limited and inconvenient parking spaces where the goods and services are available. These factors discourage them from driving, yet walking where they want to go is not easy because of distance as well as the traffic they encounter.[37]

The transportation committee of the National Strategy Conference on Rural Aging identified several additional issues related to rural transportation. Although these issues are not always experienced by everyone, they should be considered when discussing the transportation needs of the rural elderly. They include safety, cost of insurance, and lack of coordination among rural transit systems.

PUBLIC POLICY AND THE RURAL ELDERLY

Public policies should be conceived, developed, and implemented to alleviate social problems, one of which is the plight of the nation's older people in both metropolitan and nonmetropolitan areas. However, for a variety of reasons that will be discussed below, rural programs have been discriminated against and are, therefore, less effective than urban ones. Inequitable federal spending and appropriation formulas, program regulations, and the "generality" of policy statements contribute to staggering and self-perpetuating problems for the rural elderly.

INEQUITABLE FEDERAL OUTLAYS

Hendler and Reid have reviewed federal outlays in 1978 for selected public programs, twenty-one programs administered under seven different executive departments and independent federal agencies.[38] Although one-third of the U.S. population lives in nonmetropolitan areas where problems are more severe and costlier to implement, a disproportionately low federal outlay was allocated to these localities (see table 5.3).

Table 5.3
Federal Outlays for Selected Programs, 1978

Program	Percent of Monies Spent	
	Metropolitan	*Nonmetropolitan*
AOA:		
Model Projects	92.6	7.4
Senior Centers	88.6	11.4
Training	90.4	9.6
DOL:		
CETA-ETA	91.3	8.7
DHEW (DHHS):		
Rehabilitation Service and Facilities	90.0	10.0
VA:		
Domiciliary	46.8	53.2
State Domiciliary Care	85.2	14.8
State Nursing Home Care	80.4	19.6
ACTION:		
Foster Grandparents Program	73.0	27.0
Senior Companion Program*	69.7	30.3
RSVP*	61.1	38.9
CSA:		
Older Persons Opportunity and Services*	60.0	40.0

SOURCE: Charles Hendler and J. Reid, *Federal Outlays in Fiscal 1978: A Comparison of Metropolitan and Nonmetropolitan Areas* (Washington, D.C.: Department of Agriculture, 1980).

Note: Asterisk indicates programs equitably supported by appropriate entitlement acts.

All but three of these elderly programs are inequitably supported by appropriate entitlement acts (see table 5.3), at least with regard to 1978 population patterns. Nevertheless, under the present administration's efforts at fiscal curtailment of social programs, the Community Services Administration (CSA), which recognizes the inequities for the rural elderly, is being considered for termination, and the Senior Companion Program was proposed a cut of $1.67 million.[39] CETA programs, which have provided salaries for manpower services to the elderly, have been eliminated in the name of "block grants," whose future is unknown.

In 1975, according to President Carter's report to Congress, federal outlays for family planning, child care, training programs, food stamps, Medicare, and Medicaid were, on a per capita basis, much higher in the metropolitan areas—about one hundred dollars more than in nonmetropolitan localities. Less than one-third of food stamp money was spent in rural areas, where the incidence of poverty was higher. The Department of Labor spent 11.7 percent of its budget for rural older people's employment programs; CSA's community economic development, legal services, and community action programs spent only 24.5, 29.9, and 7.9 percent of their budgets, respectively, on the rural elderly.

As indicated earlier, from one-half to two-thirds of the rural elderly are living on incomes barely above the poverty line. However, Social Service beneficiaries living in rural areas receive 10 percent lower benefits than do their urban counterparts—$176 as against $203 per month in 1976.[40] Moreover, the rural elderly with lower incomes spend proportionately more money on food, transportation, clothing, personal care, and medical care than do their urban counterparts.[41] Despite the fact that food and heating costs are higher in rural areas, the Office of Management and Budget's poverty guideline is 14.2 to 15.1 percent lower for rural residents. In 1980, the poverty guideline for one-person families was set at $3,250 for those in farming areas and $3,790 for nonfarm areas; for two-person families age sixty-five and over, it was $4,280 and $5,010 for farm and nonfarm areas, respectively.

Federal outlays for health care have been particularly inequitable for the rural elderly. Nearly 32 percent of Medicare recipients live in rural areas, while only 28.6 percent of Medicare Hospital Insurance and 27 percent of Medicare Supplemental Insurance goes to them.[42] Although 50 to 60 percent of the nation's poor and medically underserved people live in rural areas, they receive only 25 percent of the federal spending on Medicare, Medicaid, and Supplemental Medical Insurance.[43]

While CSA health payments are somewhat better, 25 percent went to the rural population; Health Services Administration (HSA) and grant projects spent less than one-fourth of their budgets in rural areas (24.1, 25.6, and 9.9 percent, respectively). In 1976, federal public health expenditures were reported to average $130 per rural person and $165 per urban person, representing 21 percent less for the former.[44]

The lack of mental health facilities in rural areas is compounded by inadequate facilities and by understaffing.[45] The National Institute for Mental Health (NIMH) reports these rural and urban comparison figures: only 17.5 percent of mental health services in rural areas are adequate, as compared with 49 percent in urban areas; 62 percent of the rural services need major structural modification, as compared with only 28.5 percent of those in urban areas. In city slum areas, 8,566 staff hours and 1,149 psychiatrist hours per 100,000 people were budgeted, while only 2,678 staff hours (68 percent fewer) and 72 psychiatrist hours (93 percent fewer) were budgeted for the same number of people in rural areas.[46] Expenditures for various mental health programs are contained in table 5.4.

Housing expenses are closely related to the income of older persons. Due to the high costs of other living necessities, rural elderly with lower

Table 5.4
Percent of Federal Budget Spent in Rural Areas, 1975

Program	Percent Expenditure
Hospital improvement	37.9
Training	8.7
Children's services	20.8
Community mental health services	26.8
Narcotic addiction rehabilitation	4.7
Alcohol demonstration programs	28.5
Community service programs	0.0
Demonstration programs	0.0
Special programs for the aging	10.6

SOURCE: U.S. Congress, House, *Rural Development: Seventh Annual Report* of the *President to Congress on Governmental Services to Rural America*, 95th Cong., 1st sess., 1977.

incomes should spend less money on housing. Unfortunately, public response to the issue is extremely meager, in that 81.6 percent of federal housing outlays went to metropolitan areas, while only 18.6 percent went to rural areas.[47] On a per capita basis, the rural resident received 41.2 percent less; namely, $50 for the rural individual versus $85 for the urban dweller. Although the Farmers Home Administration and the Department of the Interior spent higher proportions of their housing funds in rural areas (70 and 76.7 percent, respectively), the Department of Housing and Urban Development and the Veterans Administration spent only 9 and 18 percent, respectively, even with their far bigger budgets. Yet, most recently, under the Reagan administration's efforts toward a balanced national budget, the FHA budget is being cut by $103 million (or 11.5 percent), while funding for HUD's section 202 housing programs for the elderly may remain at last year's level.[48]

There are several public programs designed to mitigate the transportation needs of the rural elderly. These include the Federal Aid Highway Act, the Urban Mass Transportation Administration (UMTA), the Surface Transportation Assistance Act, Title III of the Older Americans Act, Titles XIX and XX of the Social Security Act, and the Vocational Rehabilitation Act. Despite these programs, why does rural transportation for the elderly still remain critical? Rural America suggests that (1) there is no public agency for rural public transportation equivalent to UMTA; (2) less than 1 percent of UMTA's outlays go to rural areas; and (3) in 1976, less than a quarter of the $550 million of public transportation monies went to rural areas.[49] Non-UMTA rural allocations are dwarfed by UMTA's $2 billion annual public transportation budget.[50] Moreover, $0.5 billion in UMTA's budget was not spent, since no guidelines or application procedures for the nonurban portion of their program were ever issued; eligibility was limited to public bodies; and the total capital funds were insufficient for rural areas. Thus, allocated dollars for transportation were not spent, despite the needs of the rural elderly. Exacerbating the problem was the bankruptcy of 235 private transportation companies between 1959 and 1970. Most of these were in rural areas.[51]

PUBLIC FUNDS AND APPROPRIATION FORMULAS

Public funds for human services are generally appropriated on the basis of social, economic, demographic, and/or political characteristics of the population. Some are based on social problem indexes such as crime rates, traffic accidents, environmental hazards, health and vital statistics; some on the degree of economic poverty; some on racial or age composition; and some on local tax bases such as revenue sharing. Two examples of public appropriation formulas merit our discussion.

The Administration on Aging under the Older Americans Act, uses what may be called an "equality formula," which provides a single rule for distribution of its funds. This formula counts the number of older persons in state and/or planning and service areas. The state or PSA that has more older people receives larger amounts of federal funds than one with a smaller number, regardless of population characteristics. This has led to inequities since many aspects of rural areas (vast territory, isolation, differential degrees of rural status and so on) are not included in the formula. Due to the low funding levels, rural states and PSAs, whose service activities cost three times more than those in urban areas, have been unable to stretch their dollars to provide the results obtained in urban areas.[52] In fact, out of those states that are primarily rural, only Colorado "uses a rural designation as a weighted factor in the allocation formula for disbursement of aging funds."[53] Problems of inequitable funding nationally and expensive rural programs are compounded by limited local resources and fewer professionally trained staff in rural communities.

Fortunately, in 1978, both houses of Congress amended the Older Americans Act to provide that rural programs, particularly Titles III and V, should receive no less than 105 percent of the funds appropriated for the previous year. It is also provided that rural-related research and training activities should be among the higher priorities prescribed. Problems for implementation are related to the sources of the 5 percent extra funding, however. The act contains the term *waive*, which implies that any state that believes its appropriation is favorable to rural programs might not be mandated to budget the extra 5 percent. With no extra funding source, and with this vague implication in the amendment, rural elderly programs may remain the same as they have always been.

Another way of distributing public funds is through the "catchment area" concept, which has been used by the NIMH Community Mental Health Programs. Each catchment area serves approximately 75,000 people and encompasses an average territory of 17,000 square miles having a range from less than 5,000 to 69,000 square miles, permitting several catchment areas to exist in one metropolitan unit.[54] On the other hand, one rural catchment area can cover many counties. Such a population-based unit, with appropriations based on it, favors people and programs in metropolitan areas.

PROGRAM REGULATIONS AND RIGIDITY

The U.S. government is being criticized by the present administration as an overregulatory one that is too costly to taxpayers and needs curtailment. In 1980, approximately eighty-seven thousand pages of federal regulations were published, four times the amount published one decade ago. They cost Americans 1.2 billion hours of work, at an expense in excess of one hundred billion dollars.[55] Needless to say, many of these regulations affect programs designed to serve older Americans, including the rural elderly, specifying such factors as service eligibility, quality of services, and reporting systems. Most of them, if not all, are monitored by federal staffs that have limited flexibility. These officials are required to do no more, or less, than what is written.

The adverse impacts of such rigid regulations are numerous. The Title XX bus regulations under the Social Security Act, for example, provide transportation only to those elderly who are eligible (by having a specified income level), while the Title III transportation program is open to all elderly persons. These dual regulations not only duplicate services but also waste funds. An older person living in a rural area with an income above the poverty level may be forced to let an empty Title XX bus go by for a Title III bus. Another example relates to the quality of professional service providers. Since rural agencies, in most instances, are staffed with "underqualified" workers, their services are not reimbursable by third parties, including the federal government. Community mental health services provided by psychiatrists, registered nurses, and MSW social workers are third-party reimbursable. But most rural agencies do not even have these specialists. Thus, rural programs are less effective. Similarly, rural housing projects suffer from a lack of high-quality staff. It is reported that there is no authority to initiate countywide rural housing programs and that welfare programs and other federal, state, and local housing policies and programs are uncoordinated. Due to restrictions on qualifications, limited available staff, and an outdated emphasis on FHA loans in New York, that state has returned large sums of uncontributed dollars to the federal government. These funds were utilized instead by other states that had more adaptable rural housing funding mechanisms.[56]

A further example of misguided control can be seen in regulations for "local matching." Available federal funds are distributed to state and local municipal governments and agencies only when these service providers provide their matching share as legally specified, in most cases by a 75 percent federal and 25 percent local funding rule. This kind of regulation disqualifies many rural areas due to their inability to raise their share of the costs.

GENERALITY OR NONSPECIFICITY OF PUBLIC POLICY

Most public policies are written without specifying the meaning of such terms as *rural elderly* or *older persons*. Regulations are written about research on aging, gerontology manpower training, and aging services, neglecting the use of the word *rural* altogether. CETA regulations mandate the provision of jobs to the "unemployed" without specifying an age factor. These generalities have resulted in disproportionate funding under CETA favoring urban areas and younger adults. Similarly, as indicated earlier, only 7.4 percent of the AOA's model projects, 11.4 percent of senior centers, and 9.6 percent of training funds in 1978 were used for nonmetropolitan-oriented programs. Despite enforcement under the Age Discrimination in Employment Act (ADEA), spending violations amounting to $6.6 million were found, together with 434 violations involving actual refusals to hire older workers.[57] The Commission of Human Rights found age discrimination in federally funded programs such as Community Mental Health Centers, legal services, and employment and training services.[58] In part, such mismanagement of entitlement acts that are written in "general" terms could stem from narrow interpretations of public laws, from public biases, or from both. It seems that program planners and administrators take it for granted that preventive health care and educational development funds were originally allocated for children and youth and that generic formula grants such as employment programs should be used only for young male workers. Only 2.8 percent of CETA funds in 1976 were spent on workers above the age of fifty-five; and similar low expenditures were made under Titles II and IV—5.1 and 4.9 percent, respectively.[59]

TOWARD AN EQUITABLE POLICY FOR THE RURAL ELDERLY

However various the definitions of *rural* or *nonmetropolitan* may be, this country is experiencing a reverse population trend in the 1970s—inmigration to nonmetropolitan areas—and a renaissance of rural America is at hand. Through this turnabout, a long forgotten population, the rural elderly, is being rediscovered; more is being learned about them despite sporadic and limited studies; and their problems, long neglected in the minds of the public, are being recognized as one of our top priorities. Neveretheless, the problems facing these rural elderly are still staggering and are exacerbated by discriminatory public policies.

In order to better serve older persons in rural America, I propose the following recommendations:

Unified definition of rural. A definition of *rurality* should be developed and used uniformly both in research and policymaking processes. A unified definition, based on such characteristics as number of people residing in an area, population density, and occupational and cultural characteristics, should then be transformed into a quantified measure of rurality, that is, an indication of the degree of rurality of an area in a continuum of rural/nonmetropolitan to urban/metropolitan.

No definition will be completely satisfactory, but the one proposed would be better than the ones used in the past, which have contributed to confusion. A nationwide effort, such as the decennial census-taking activity, should be made every five years in order to redesignate all areas of the nation in terms of their rural–urban specificity.

Rurality in appropriation formula. However relative and temporal, a rural-urban formula should be included in federal guidelines for all programs. For example, unless the federal government mandates each state to review carefully the needs of its rural communities, the new block grant programs will not only become urban-centered but will also perpetuate existing inequities and problems experienced by the rural elderly.

Specificity and flexibility. All government regulations for social programs should use precise terms rather than general language. For example, they should clearly state how many or what proportion of clients are or should be age sixty or over and specify whether they reside in rural or urban areas. Otherwise, public laws will be arbitrary and confusing. Flexibility should also be encouraged if regulations are to be effective in rural areas having unique values and distinct socioeconomic qualities. For example, cost–benefit measures and efficiency studies of rural agencies should not be compared with urban ones. Third-party reimbursement standards should be modified to be rural appropriate, with cross-coordination of programs funded by various entitlement acts. It is undesirable to impose rural-appropriate service delivery models on urban programs. Likewise, urban-oriented models that have been imposed on rural programs are not in fact transferable.

Research on rural aging. A very small proportion of the gerontological literature deals with rural elderly, much of it focusing on the rural aged as a part of the total elderly population. Such a paucity of studies on the subject has led policymakers and program planners to address the problems of the rural elderly with only limited insights. Actions based on inadequate knowledge must be suspect. To serve the rural elderly adequately, there must be more information about them. This must be obtained through enhanced research activities.

Manpower training. There are many gerontologists holding certificates based on short-term training programs, sometimes even on poorly defined academic degree programs in gerontology. The Administration on Aging now recognizes manpower needs not in a general sense but rather in specific gerontological areas (manpower to serve specific elderly populations having long-term care needs, housing and nutrition needs, the handicapped, low-income minorities, and so forth). Furthermore, professionals are being trained with urban-centered knowledge and skills and thus are ill prepared for rural services. Rural manpower training must be supported with a specified amount of funds under particular programs. Continuing education and in-service training for rural professionals should be given the highest priority. In addition, a systematically designed rural gerontology training program should be developed and implemented in rural-based colleges. The process of human aging may be universal, but patterns, degrees of problems, and coping strategies between the rural and urban elderly are different and call for differential training.

Monitoring rural services. The nation's rural problems have not resulted from a lack of legislation overall but rather from such things as conflicting programs and vague definitions. Some laws have overly broad specifications (such as rural or urban, young or old, men or women) that have resulted in a bias toward particular groups, including youth, urban residents, and males. In order to alleviate unintended processes of public laws, a rural monitoring system is proposed. An existing agency or office, such as the Human Rights Commission, Select Committees on Aging of the Congress, or the Office of Management and Budget, would be given a mandate to examine systematically the equity and prudence of public programs as they affect the rural elderly.

In conclusion, the rural elderly require greater attention than they currently receive. Through more responsible and creative efforts, including research, training, and advocacy, we can provide a better quality of life for older people who live in and who have moved to rural America.

NOTES

1. Robert C. Bealer, Fern K. Willits, and William P. Kuvlesky, "The Meaning of 'Rurality' in American Society: Some Implications of Alternative Definitions," *Rural Sociology* (1965): 255–66; Fern K. Willits and Robert C. Bealer, "An Evaluation of a Composite Definition of 'Rurality,'" *Rural Sociology* (1967): 165–77; and Paul G. Windley and Rick J. Scheidt, "The Well-Being of Older Persons in Small Rural Towns: A Town Panel Approach," *Educational Gerontology* (1980): 355–74.

2. Leo F. Schnore, "The Rural–Urban Variables: An Urbanite's Perspective," *Rural Sociology* 31 (1966): 131–43; B. J. Smith and D. W. Parvin, Jr., "Comparative Levels of Rurality" University of Georgia, Faculty Series no. FS74-2, 1974, and B. J. Smith and D. W. Parvin, Jr., "Defining and Measuring Rurality," *Southern Journal of Agricultural Economics* (July 1973): 109–13.

3. Marilyn M. Wiles, *Old Age and Ruralism. A Case of Double Jeopardy* (Albany. New York Senate Research Service, 1980), pp. 47-48, table 13.

4. Green Thumb, Inc., of the Farmers Union, *Procedural Manual of the Green Thumb, Inc.* (Washington, D.C.: Green Thumb, 1979).

5. Ecosometrics, Inc., *Review of Reported Differences Between the Rural and Urban Elderly: Status, Needs, Services and Service Costs* (Bethesada, Md.: Ecosometrics, 1981), p. 9.

6. Calvin L. Beale and G. V. Fugitt, "The New Pattern of Nonmetropolitan Population Change," in *Social Demography*, ed. K. E. Taruber, L. L. Bumpass, and J. A. Sweet (New York: Academic Press, 1978).

7. G. Richard Ambrosius, ed., *National Rural Strategy Conference to Improve Service Delivery to the Rural Elderly* (Spencer: Iowa Lake Area Agency on Aging, 1979); U.S., Department of Agriculture, Farmers Home Administration, *Improving Services for the Rural Elderly* (Washington, D.C.: USDA–FHA, 1980).

8. Rural America, Inc., *Platform for Rural America* (Washington, D.C.: Rural America, 1977).

9. Ecosometrics, Inc., *Review*, p. 21.

10. Ibid, p. 45.

11. Ibid., p. 48.

12. U.S., Department of Health and Human Services, Administration on Aging, *The Elderly Population: Estimates by County—1977*, DHHS Publication no. (OHDS) 80-20248 (Washington, D.C.: 1980).

13. Edward Gross and George Donohue, "Organizational Diversity: The Rural System as an Ideal Model," in *Benefits and Burdens of Rural Development*, ed. Iowa State University Center for Agricultural and Economic Development (Ames: Iowa State University Press, 1972), pp. 241–53.

14. N. D. Glenn and L. Hill, Jr., "Rural–Urban Differences in Attitudes and Behavior in the United States," *Annals of the American Academy of Political and Social Sciences* (1977): 36–50.

15. Norval D. Glenn and Jon P. Alston, "Rural–Urban Differences in Reported Attitudes and Behavior," *Southwestern Social Science Quarterly* 47 (1967), as cited in Ecosometrics, Inc., *Review*.

16. W. Rohrer and L. Douglas, *The Agrarian Transition in America* (New York: Bobbs-Merrill, 1969).

17. A. J. Auerbach, "The Elderly in Rural and Urban Areas," in *Social Work in Rural Communities*, ed. Leon H. Ginsberg (New York: Council on Social Work Education, 1976).

18. M.A. White, "Values of Elderly Differ in Rural Settings," *Generations* (Fall 1977): 6–7.

19. The needs of the rural elderly are partially reprinted from Paul K. H. Kim, "The Low Income Rural Elderly: Under-Served Victims of Public Inequity," in *Policy Issues for the Elderly Poor*, ed. Community Service Administration (Washington, D.C.: Government Printing Office, 1981).

20. Robert A. Bulund, N. L. LeRay, and C. O. Crawford, *Older American Households and Their Housing 1975: A Metro–Monmetro Comparison* (University Park: Pennsylvania State University Press, January 1980).

21. Rural America, Inc., *Platform*.

22. U.S., Department of Commerce, Bureau of the Census, *Social and Economic Characteristics of the Older Population: 1978,* Current Population Reports, Special Studies series P-23, no. 85 (Washington, D.C.: U.S. Government Printing Office, 1977).

23. Sharon S. Larson, "The Elderly: Victims of the Energy Venture," in *The Boom Town: Problems and Promises in the Energy Vortex,* ed. Joseph Davenport III and Judith Ann Davenport (Laramie: University of Wyoming Press, 1980).

24. Ambrosius, *National Rural Strategy.*

25. E. Grant Youmans and D. K. Larson, *Health Status and Need: A Study of Older People in Powell County, Kentucky* (Lexington: University of Kentucky Press, 1977); Vira Kivett and J. P. Scott, *The Rural By-Passed Elderly: Perspectives on Status and Needs,* Technical Bulletin 260 (Greensboro: University of North Carolina, 1979).

26. Rural America, Inc., *Rural America Fact Sheet: The Elderly,* RAF no. 5, (Washington, D.C.: Rural America, 1978).

27. John R. Ballantine and Paul K. H. Kim, "Rural Elderly and Drug Use" (paper presented at the Gerontological Society Scientific Meeting, Washington, D.C., 1979).

28. Rural America, Inc., *Platform.*

29. U.S., Department of Health, Education, and Welfare, Public Health Services, *Manpower: A Change in Course,* DHEW Publication no. (HRA) 79-41 (Washington, D.C.: DHEW, 1979).

30. "Another Myth Bites the Dust: Rural Living Isn't the Healthiest," *Courier-Journal* (Louisville), July 6, 1980.

31. U.S., House, Select Committee on Aging, *National Conference on Mental Health and the Elderly,* no. 76-186 (Washington, D.C.: Government Printing Office, 1979).

32. U.S., General Accounting Office, *A Report to the Chairman and the Ranking Minority Members* (Washington, D.C.: Senate Special Committee on Aging, 1980).

33. Larson, "Elderly."

34. Ambrosius, *National Rural Strategy.*

35. Wiles, *Old Age and Ruralism,* p. 173.

36. Kimley-Horn and Associates, Inc., "Planning and Development Program for Mass Transportation Services and Facilities for the Elderly and Handicapped in the State of Georgia, Summary Report," April 1975.

37. Larson, "Elderly."

38. Charles I. Hendler and J. Norman Reid, *Federal Outlays in Fiscal 1978: A Comparison of Metropolitan and Nonmentropolitan Areas,* Rural Development Research no. 25 (Washington, D.C.: U. S. Department of Agriculture, 1980).

39. Claude Pepper, Chairman of the U.S. House Select Committee on Aging, Memorandum to the Committee Members, "Impact of Proposed 1982 Budget on the Elderly," March 13, 1981.

40. Rural America, *Fact Sheet.*

41. U.S., Department of Labor, Bureau of Labor Statistics, *Three Budgets for a Retired Couple* (Washington, D.C.: U. S. Department of Labor, 1975).

42. U.S., Congress, House, *Rural Development: Seventh Annual Report of the President to Congress on Government Services to Rural America,* 95th Cong., 1st Sess., House Document no. 95-51 (Washington, D.C.: Government Printing Office, 1977).

43. Rural America, *Platform*; Rural America, Inc., *Toward a Health Platform for Rural America* (Washington, D.C.: Rural America, 1977).

44. "Another Myth Bites the Dust."

45. Ibid.

46. U.S., Department of Health, Education, and Welfare, National Institute for Mental Health, *A New Day in Rural Mental Health Services* (Washington, D.C.: Government Printing Office, 1978).

47. U.S., Congress, House, *Rural Development*.

48. Pepper, "Impact."

49. Rural America, *Platform*.

50. Rural America, *Fact Sheet*, p. 4.

51. Rural America, *Platform*.

52. U.S., Congress, Senate, Special Committee on Aging, Memorandum, no. 32 (n.d.).

53. Wiles, *Old Age and Ruralism*, p. 47.

54. James W. Flax, et. al., eds., "Mental Health and Rural America: An Overview," *Community Mental Health Review* 3 (September/December 1978): p. 7.

55. Republican National Committee, *First Monday; A Special Report*. (Washington, D.C.: Republican National Committee, May 1981).

56. Wiles, *Old Age and Ruralism*, 186–88.

57. William J. McAuley, "Preceived Aged Discrimination in Hiring: Demographic and Economic Correlates," *Industrial Gerontology* (Winter 1977): 21–28.

58. U.S. Commission on Civil Rights, *Age Discrimination Study* (Washington, D.C.: U.S. Commission on Civil Rights, 1977).

59. M. Shram, F. Sanford, and David Austin, "CETA and Aging," *Aging and Work* (Summer 1978): 163–74.

DOUGLAS DOBSON

6

The Elderly as a Political Force

At the turn of the century, only 4 percent of this nation's citizens were sixty-five years of age or older. In the eight decades that have since passed, there have been rather sharp changes in the conditions that influence the age structure of the population. Rapid advances in health-related technologies, for instance, have greatly extended life expectancy. Fertility rates, with the exception of the postwar "baby boom," have continued to decline. Immigration rates dropped sharply after the first two decades of this century and have remained relatively low. As a result, about one out of every ten persons in the United States is presently over the age of sixty-five.[1]

Projecting the age composition of the population into the future is risky, for estimates depend, among other things, on crucial assumptions about rates of fertility and mortality. Present indications suggest, however, that growth in the size of the elderly population is likely to continue unabated until well into the next century. Indeed, if current projections are accurate, we can anticipate rather sharp increases in both the absolute and relative size of the elderly population. By 2035, the U.S. population will have increased by about 40 percent relative to 1980. During the same period, the population sixty-five and older will have grown by more than 130 percent. Thus, at the end of the first third of the next century, over 18 percent of the population (some fifty-six million persons) will be aged sixty-five or older.[2]

Rapid changes in the age structure of the American population potentially could have significant economic, social, and political implications. Indeed, there is little doubt, given present federal policies, current inflation rates, and an increasing number of elderly beneficiaries, that economic effects will be significant. As Hudson has observed,

Total outlays for the aging, survivors, and retirees under OASI, civilian and retirement insurance plans, railroad retirement, SSI, Medicare, and Medicaid were $122 billion in 1977. . . . The corresponding figure for the FY1979 budget- . . . [was] $148 billion, or 29.6 percent of the total [federal] budget. HEW Secretary Califano estimates that, if present trends continue, "real" spending on behalf of the elderly will triple by 2010.[3]

Reasoned speculation about the social and political implications of an aging population is somewhat more difficult. On the basis of sheer numbers, there is little doubt that the elderly have the *potential* to play a significant political role, just as laborers and blacks have done in this century. Moreover, recent years have seen the formulation and rapid growth of a number of interest groups concerned with aging policy.[4] Estimating the likelihood that these potentials will be realized as effective "senior power" in the political process is highly problematic, however, given our present state of knowledge. Neither our theories of social and political change nor our existing data bases have sufficient power to permit precise projections of current values, attitudes, and behaviors—to say nothing of contextual factors—into the distant future.

To say that we cannot provide definitive answers to long-range questions about the political implications of an aging population should not be cause for despair. The question is complex, and research that has been explicitly concerned with the relationships between age and political behavior is of rather recent vintage. Rigorous, empirically based research is even more recent. Thus we are just beginning to sort out some of the dynamic relationships between age and politics. As our understanding grows, so too will our ability to make informed judgments about the future.

In this chapter, we will explore the major lines of research relating age to political behavior. In addition, we will also consider some recent data that provide insight into the contemporary political implications of age consciousness. We will also briefly consider some of the political implications of aging as seen through the eyes of elected representatives. Our principal concern will focus on the question of whether elderly citizens constitute a distinctive political force in American politics.

AGE AND POLITICAL BEHAVIOR

Attempts to understand the relationship between age and political behavior must confront at least two major issues, both of which relate to the influence of age as an explanatory variable. The first issue revolves around the question of how observed differences between younger and older individuals should be interpreted. As a person ages, several processes are at work. There are physiological and psychological processes, which we would generally refer to as "maturation" or "aging." Those processes include changes in both individual body chemistry over time and the cumulative effects of life experiences such as familial socialization and formal education. There are also social, political, and economic circumstances that may be relatively unique to persons born within a particular span of time. For such a "cohort" or "generation," shared experiences *may* lead to shared responses to new social, political, or economic conditions. To the extent that different cohorts have radically different life experiences, such experiences may serve as a basis for explaining observed age-related differences in political attitudes and behavior. We must therefore consider what have been termed "period" effects or "history." Some cohorts may experience wars, depressions, technological developments, or other events that differ from those experienced by both younger and older cohorts. These experiences, no doubt, influence the responses of each succeeding cohort to new social, economic, and political developments.[5]

Perhaps the most straightforward approach to understanding the ways in which these effects serve as competing explanations of age-based differences is to consider a hypothetical example.[6] Suppose that we sampled two groups of individuals; those aged eighteen to twenty-five, and those aged sixty-five and older. Suppose further that we asked each respondent to tell us whether they generally thought of themselves as a Democrat, an Independent, or a Republican, and assume that we found, after tabulating the results, that in the younger group 75 percent were Democrats, 15 percent were Independents, and 10 percent were Republicans. For the older group, assume that results were a mirror image, that is, 10 percent were Democrats, 15 percent were Independents, and 75 percent were Republicans. The question is, do these results support the argument that aging "causes" people to become more Republican in their outlook? Although one can find instances in which such interpretations have been made, [7] it appears that the answer is no.

To see why observed differences between age groups do not necessarily lead to the conclusion that those differences are due to age, we need only change the name of the variable under consideration. Suppose that instead of collecting data on partisan affliliation we had instead asked the same respondents to report their education as more than high school, high school graduate, or less than high school and that we obtained the same percentage distributions as above for the two groups. It is easy to see that interpreting such results to mean that an individual's age "causes" a decline in educational level is fallacious. Indeed, we would expect almost no variation in an individual's educational level after about the third decade of the life cycle. In no case would we expect that an individual's educational attainment would decline with increasing age.

Results such as these are more appropriately understood as cohort differences. With the expansion of the public school system, the enactment of compulsory attendance legislation, and the development of college loan programs, each succeeding generation has experienced higher levels of educational attainment. Thus, in any cross-sectional sample, older individuals are likely to report having completed fewer years of formal education than younger individuals. But such results are obviously independent of the aging process itself.

More recent research has confronted these difficulties by relying upon a series of data collected over the years rather than a single, cross-sectional sample. In this way, researchers have sought to observe changes in the behavior of the same-age cohort over time, thus permitting at least a rough estimate of the relative effects of maturation and generation. Although such an approach has not completely solved the problem of intrepretation of age differences, it represents a significant advance over single-year, cross-sectional approaches. Ultimately, however, resolution will very likely require panel studies that observe the same individuals over relatively long periods of time.

A second major issue in the study of age and political behavior relates to the distinction between chronological and "subjective" age.[8] Chronologically, individuals age at the same rate. But it is unlikely that everyone of the same chronological age perceives themselves to be of the same age subjectively. Indeed, in a youth-oriented society such as that found in contemporary America, there are probably substantial inducements to resist psychologically the notion of "being old." Whether such considerations have significant implications for understanding the relationship between age and political behavior is presently unclear. It is clear, however, that substantially more research on the issue is needed.

With these interpretative problems as background, let us turn to an overview of current findings relating to age and political behavior. In so doing, we shall consider the effects of aging on political involvement, political interest, and political attitudes.

AGE AND POLITICAL INVOLVEMENT

Although the politics of aging often has not been of primary concern, a number of scholars have considered the relationship between age and selected aspects of political involvement. Cross-sectional studies that have examined the relationship between age and political participation generally come to the same conclusion. Participation rates are lowest among citizens in their late teens and early twenties. From that point, the data typically suggest a pattern of increasing participation rates up through middle age with a decline beginning in the fifty- to sixty-year age range.[9] Norman Nie and his associates report that this general pattern holds not only in the United States but in Austria, India, Japan, and Nigeria as well:

Patterns...are remarkably similar.... It would be difficult to imagine a more heterogeneous set of nations in terms of culture, location, or level of development. Each has its own historical sequence, exposing its citizens to different political experiences at different times...this heterogeneity...makes this similarity of pattern more convincing.[10]

While there is a general agreement about the overall pattern of political involvement as shown from cross-sectional studies, explaining why participation rates decline in later years appears to be more difficult. One potential explanation revolves around differences in the sociodemographic characteristics of various age cohorts. Previous research consistently has shown that political participation is related to a number of individual characteristics.[11] Males, persons with more education, higher income, and higher occupational status, tend to participate at relatively high rates. To the extent that cohorts differ with regard to these characteristics, such differences serve as one potential explanation of age-related variation in participation rates. This argument, of course, rejects the notion that the aging process itself leads to lower levels of involvement, suggesting, rather, that observed differences may be due to the fact that contemporary older cohorts are not likely to have characteristics associated with high levels of political involvement.

Nie and his associates addressed this question in their cross-national study by controlling for sex and level of educational attainment. They found that, the "downturn in activity apparent in the uncorrected data was either substantially reduced ... or completely eliminated."[12] Thus, there is some evidence for the argument that the lower participation rates observed in contemporary elderly cohorts are probably due, at least in part, to the unique sociodemographic composition of that group. Nie and his associates went on to suggest that there may be an additional factor related to the aging process itself that accounts for *residual* variation in elderly participation rates. They described the process as one of "slow down," when "old age brings sociological withdrawal as individuals retire from active employment ... [as well as] physical infirmities and fatigue that lower the rate of political activity."[13] To examine this hypothesis, the authors used retirement from the active work force as an indicator of "slow down." Results were not fully consistent across all of the countries examined. In India, Japan, and the United States, working older citizens participated at higher rates than their retired counterparts. In Austria, the results were reversed. Nonetheless, Nie and his associates concluded that "the data are consistent with the 'slow down' explanation of the decline in citizen activity in later years."[14]

A "slow down" interpretation has not been supported by cohort analyses focusing on other aspects of political involvement. Norval Glenn and Michael Grimes, for instance, analyzing some twenty-eight national surveys, examined the relationships among aging, voting, and political interest. With regard to voting, their cohort analysis yielded "no convincing evidence of a decline in voting as people age into their sixties and seventies."[15] Similarly, when they examined levels of political interest, they concluded that the "data [were] ... generally consistent with ... [the] hypothesis that political interest typically increases from young adulthood to old age."[16] They found no support for the idea that aging brings on an inevitale withdrawal.

From yet another perspective, Glenn tested the related hypothesis, suggested by Kenneth Gergen and Kurt Back,[17] that as people age they are less likely to hold or to express opinions.[18] Controlling for both sex and education, Glenn found no support for the hypothesis. In fact, he suggested that, although the data may be subject to differing interpretations, "they suggest that people slowly but steadily become more attuned to current events as they mature from young adulthood to old age."[19]

The ultimate resolution of the meaning of observed age–participation relationships has clear implications for our prognostications about the political roles of future elderly cohorts. If the existing downturn in participation in later life is, as most recent research suggests, primarily due to the unique characteristics of the contemporary elderly, then the gradual replacement of the present cohort with more highly educated individuals should work to increase rates of political participation by future elderly citizens.

AGE AND POLITICAL ATTITUDES

What political values do the elderly hold? Does the aging process inexorably lead to changes in political attitudes? If the elderly had more political power, would they seek to enact public policies that are more liberal or more conservative? These are some of the questions that have been posed by researchers concerned with the relationship between age and political attitudes. As late as 1974, Glenn characterized the study of age and opinions as a "virgin research area."[20] Thus, many questions remain unanswered.

The issue that has been investigated most intensely relates to the widely held belief that, as people age, they grow more conservative in their political outlook. According to this notion, socialization affects age cohorts as political culture changes in content. Attitudes, values, and ideologies vary from generation to generation as older cohorts reflect

greater rigidity, cautiousness, and increasing resistance to change. Further pressures against the acceptance of social and political change become manifest with increasing integration into the social system, which leads to a greater stake in the status quo. Presumably, therefore, older cohorts are not only the bearers of the more traditional political culture, but their members increasingly adhere to the content of their political socialization as they age.[21]

Riley and Foner, in their monumental review of research findings relating to age, reported on several pre-1968 studies that support the above argument.[22] Campbell and his colleagues, for instance, found that the elderly were more resistant to change.[23] Stouffer found older persons to be less tolerant of political and social nonconformists.[24] Early researchers also found elderly citizens to be less favorable toward racial integration in public schools,[25] more opposed to having either a black[26] or a Catholic[27] as president, and generally less favorable toward governmental intervention in social issues.[28] As Glenn concluded in 1974, "The preponderance of evidence from contemporary Western countries shows that at any point in time older people as a whole are more conservative than young adults."[29]

In recent years, these findings relating age to conservative opinions have been seriously questioned. Cutler and Kaufman, for example, pointed out that "much of the support for the aging-conservatism hypothesis has come from single cross-sectional studies."[30] The interpretation problems related to the relative import of maturational, cohort, and period effects once again come into play. Their research, which employed cohort analysis across two surveys completed in 1954 and 1973, focused on Stouffer's finding that older persons tend to be less tolerant of nonconformity. They found that in 1973 younger cohorts were, once again, more tolerant than older cohorts. All cohorts, however, shifted in the direction of higher tolerance; the younger cohorts appeared to have changed toward higher tolerance levels at a faster rate than older cohorts.[31] Thus, Cutler and Kaufman found no evidence for the simple aging-conservatism hypothesis. Their results suggesting that younger cohorts change more rapidly than older cohorts implies, however, that the elderly may always be conservative in a relative sense due to their slower rate of change.

Subsequent work by Cutler, which examined attitudes toward legalized abortion during the period from 1965 through 1977, casts some doubt on the finding that the elderly change their opinions at slower rates than younger citizens. On abortion issues, Cutler found that "older persons . . . change their attitudes over time in the same direction as younger persons," and, moreover, "older persons can change their attitudes to the same extent as younger persons."[32]

Other researchers have approached the aging-conservatism hypothesis from a partisanship perspective. Early cross-sectional studies by Campbell and his colleagues suggested that older persons were more likely than younger ones to identify themselves as Republicans.[33] Given the usual presumption that the Republican party is more conservative than the Democratic party, this finding was interpreted as additional support for the aging and conservatism hypothesis. Crittenden's analysis echoed these results.[34] Neal Cutler, however, analyzed Crittenden's data further, using a cohort design, and found no evidence for linear increases in Republican identification as cohorts aged.[35] More recently, Glenn and Hefner analyzed data from both Gallup and Roper polls between 1945 and 1969. They also found no support for an absolute increase in Republican identification as cohorts aged. They did note, however, that there was some evidence of an increase in the "relative Republicanism of aging cohorts." They interpreted such a finding to mean that "social definitions of the politics of people in the aging cohorts probably changed a great deal even though party identification changed little. . . . [T]his finding suggests that many young liberals have become old conservatives without experiencing appreciable changes in attitudes and values."[36] Thus, the original finds of Campbell and his associates are probably best understood as "intercohort rather than life stage differences."[37]

A final area in which there has been at least some research focuses on the attitudes of the elderly on issues in which they presumably have some degree of self-interest. Campbell, for instance, noted that the elderly are as likely as young people to support government guarantees of low-cost medical care.[38] More recently, Heilig examined support for increased government spending across several issue areas, some of which were presumed to be of particular interest to the elderly, such as health, welfare, cities, and crime.[39] The results were mixed and did not support consistently the hypothesis that the elderly were more "liberal" on issues involving self-interest. Similarly, Epstein and Browne found that older persons were less likely than the young to (1) agree that Social Security should be paid from general income taxes; (2) favor decreasing both Social Security taxes and benefits; and (3) indicate a desire to work beyond the age of sixty-five.[40] On the other three issues they examined, all of which pertained to mandatory retirement, differences between younger and older groups were quite small. Finally, Dobson and St. Angelo examined the relationship between age and a generalized measure of support for government intervention on behalf of the elderly. They found no essential differences between the responses of younger and older citizens.[41]

What, then, is the relationship between age and political attitudes? Earlier findings notwithstanding, recent work appears to lead to the conclusion that aging per se probably has no systematic impact on an individual's political outlook. Or, as Epstein and Browne have suggested, results seem to adhere to the "sometimes it's this way, sometimes it's that way principle," yielding no consistent patterns.[42] To be sure, cohort differences do exist, but there is little support for the hypothesis that those differences are due to maturational factors.

TOWARD A POLITICAL MOVEMENT?

A final set of issues that have concerned observers and scholars is whether, and under what conditions, we might expect to see the elderly coalesce into a unified political force. As Ragan and Dowd have posed the issue,

Whether the notion is couched in the politico's language of a "voting bloc" or in the sociologist's vocabulary of political age group consciousness, the underlying assumption remains the same: The aged, because of prevailing demographic trends in society, will increasingly become aware of their common political and economic plight and will consequently attempt to parlay this awareness into a broad-based social movement.[43]

Some scholars view the development of age-based cleavages, pitting the young against the old, as quite likely. Leonard Cain, for instance, suggests at least two factors that may lead to age-based conflict.[44] First, the increased geographic mobility of both children and their elderly parents will continue to contribute to a weakening of kinship ties. Second, and perhaps more important, the increasing size of the elderly population is likely to create significant pressure on the economic system. According to Cain, as these pressures grow more intense, the tacit intergenerational commitment to provide support for those in a dependent status will be weakened. Indeed, he argues that both the young and the old will have to "struggl[e] for economic support from an intervening middle-aged group."[45] That struggle, in his view, probably will lead to political and social conflict.

In a similar vein, Arnold Rose has noted that there are a number of demographic and social forces that are likely to lead to the development of a "subculture of the aging."[46] Included among those forces are (1) increasing numbers of older persons; (2) the fact that the elderly are physically vigorous due to improved health care; (3) commonality of interest among the elderly in the provision of health-care services at reasonable cost; (4) development of "age-segregated" housing in retirement communities; (5) decreasing integration of the elderly into general society due to increases in early retirement; (6) older people's rising educational and income levels; (7) development of social service programs providing vehicles for interaction among the elderly; and (8) the breakdown of the multigenerational family unit.[47] As a result of these developments, Rose concludes that "The elderly seem to be on their way to becoming a voting bloc with a leadership that acts like a political pressure group."[48]

Other scholars have come to more negative conclusions about the likelihood of an age-based political movement. Binstock, for one, argues that the case for an elderly voting bloc "is impressive only in the most superficial sense."[49] Binstock is drawn to this conclusion, in part, because of what he views as "cricital limitations" on electoral politics as a vehicle for addressing the problems associated with aging. The first of these limitations revolves around a distinction between electoral outcomes and policy adoption. Certainly, the elderly have the potential to influence the outcomes of elections, given their share of the voting population. It is quite another matter, however, to translate electoral victory into concrete policy decisions. Second, Binstock points to the diversity of the elderly. Their partisan attachments, voting behavior, and political values are as diverse as their social, economic, and geographic backgrounds. Such diversity is clearly not conducive to the development of unified political action. Third, Binstock argues that the issues of American politics typically have not been "framed in terms of the special interests of the aged."[50] Thus, even if the elderly wished to vote on the basis of age-related interests, it would be quite difficult to do so.

Anne Foner also has assessed the possibility of age-based political conflict.[51] In large part, Foner views age as operating to structure social and political relations in much the same way that social class does. Such "age stratification" does not, however, necessarily suggest the emergence of age-based conflicts. Age is but one of the many possible bases of stratification. Individuals in a given age stratum may identify with political and social groups on the basis of sex, social class, occupation, race, or religion rather than age per se. Such cross-pressures probably work to reduce the potential for age conflicts. Moreover, age is not static; it changes with the passage of time since there is a "continuous movement of individuals in and out of an age stratum."[52] The fact that membership in any given age group is transient has at least two implications. First, the perpetual influx of new members requires a continuous "rebuilding of solidarity." Second, the inevitable movement of individuals out of a particular age stratum weakens their sense of identification with it.

At the same time, however, there are cross-cutting pressures that may work to heighten age solidarity and thereby increase the potential for age conflict. In Foner's words,

Individuals of like age move together through a particular historical environment. Unlike members of a given social class or ethnic group who have lived varying periods of time and have been exposed to diverse historical experiences, age peers share a common past and face a common future, and this commonality cuts across other lines of stratification.[53]

This statement suggests that it is not age per se that provides a basis for group solidarity but rather a commonality of political orientation presumably derived from shared social and political experiences. Indeed, as Ragan and Dowd have argued, this distinction differentiates between a simple age cohort and a "political generation."[54] They note that only the latter will affect the possibility of age becoming a major factor in political conflict.

In sum, it appears that reasonable arguments can be marshaled on both sides of the question. The changing age structure of the population suggests a potential for the elderly to become a considerable force, a potential that may be reinforced by a number of social and economic developments. On the other hand, there is a large number of other cleavages that can foster political conflict. The transiency of age-stratum membership, along with competing group identifications, are continuing forces that undoubtedly will weaken the potential for age-based political conflict.

AGE AND POLITICAL BEHAVIOR: THE CONTEMPORARY COHORT

In the final section of this chapter, we shall turn our attention to the current cohort of elderly citizens. Our central concern is whether there is any evidence suggesting the existence of age-based political mobilization among the contemporary elderly. Specifically, we will consider the political implication of "age consciousness," and, in addition, we shall provide some evidence on the political impact of the contemporary elderly from the perspective of political leaders.

A common assumption underlying much of the discussion about the political potential of the elderly is that the development of "age consciousness" or "aged-based identification" is necessary for the creation of an age-based political movement. Moreover, age consciousness must have political meaning. That is, age must become "a major referrent in fixing sociopolitical beliefs," and in addition, the political system must "frame relevant policy issues in age-related terms."[55] What about the current generation of older Americans? Do they identify with each other on the basis of age? What social processes lead to the development of age consciousness? Does such an identification have implications for the politics of aging?

To provide at least some tentative answers to these questions, we shall rely upon data from a 1976 election survey completed by the University of Michigan's Center for Political Studies.[56] Since the primary concern here is with elderly citizens, we have included only persons age sixty or older in our analysis. These individuals were born between the turn of the century and the onset of World War I. In their youth, this cohort experienced a catastrophic economic depression, a major realignment of electoral politics from Republican to Democratic dominance, and the beginning of World War II. At the onset of the Great Depression, the bulk of this generation would have ranged in age from their mid-teens to perhaps their early thirties. In many respects, then, the elderly respondents to be discussed below may be characterized as the Depression era generation.

Our measure of group identification derives from a series of questions included in the 1976 survey. Respondents were provided a list of sixteen groups and asked to identify "those groups you feel particularly close to—people who are most like you in their ideas and interests and feelings about things." Having completed this task, the respondents were asked to review the list of groups they felt "close to" and to identify the one to which they felt "closest." The distribution of responses is shown in table 6.1.

Foner's observation with respect to the existence of multiple lines of stratification among the elderly is borne out by these data.[57] Indeed, almost two-thirds of the respondents (63.4 percent) reported a primary identification with some group other than "older people," and an additional 11.3 percent reported feeling close to no group at all. Thus, one respondent in four felt a strong sense of group identification with the elderly. Class ("middle-class people" and "poor people") and occupation ("workingmen," "farmers," and "businessmen") accounted for 21.6 percent and 16.9 percent of reported identifications, respectively. The remaining 24.9 percent of the elderly in this sample reported primary identification with a rather wide variety of groups.

Clearly, the present generation of elderly citizens is characterized by considerable heterogeneity. But the fact that about one-fourth of the respondents report a primary sense of identification with older persons should not be discounted as insignificant. Given a population base of

Table 6.1
Distribution of Group Identifications of Persons Aged Sixty or Over, 1976

Group to Which Respondent Felt Closest	Percent
Businessmen	2.6
Liberals	0.6
Southerners	1.1
Poor people	6.4
Catholics	2.4
Protestants	3.7
Jews	0.9
Young people	2.5
Whites	4.2
Blacks	2.4
Conservatives	3.2
Women	3.9
Middle-class people	15.2
Workingmen	8.7
Farmers	5.6
Older people	25.3
No group	11.3
Total	100.0
Total number	(724)

SOURCE: Compiled by author from 1976 election data. Center for Political Studies, University of Michigan.

roughly thirty-four million persons aged sixty or older,[58] the figures reported in table 6.1 suggest that perhaps as many as eight million elderly have some sense of age consciousness. If such identifications were linked directly to political behavior, the political impact would be quite significant.

As a first step toward understanding the political implications of age-based identification, we analyzed the types of elderly citizens who identified with other older persons. As the data in table 6.2 indicate, respondents who reported feeling closest to other elderly people tended to have the following characteristics: (1) female (29.8 percent); (2) low levels of educational attainment (51.1 percent reported eighth grade or less); and (3) retired (54.8 percent) from the active work force. Elderly respondents reporting primary identification with groups other than older persons were significantly different with respect to these characteristics. Specifically, they were (1) less likely to be females; (2) less likely to report low levels of educational attainment, and more likely to have educational experiences beyond high school; and (3) less likely to be retired.

Table 6.2
Selected Background Characteristics of Persons Aged Sixty and Older, by Identification with Older Persons, 1976

Characteristic	Respondent Feels Closest to:	
	Older Persons (percent)	Other Groups (percent)
Sex*		
Male	29.8	42.4
Female	70.2	57.6
Total	100.0 (153)	100.0 (451)
Education*		
Eighth grade or less	51.1	37.2
Ninth through eleventh grade	16.4	16.6
High school graduate	20.4	24.5
Some college	3.6	12.4
College graduate	8.5	9.3
Total	100.0 (153)	100.0 (447)
Employment status*		
In labor force	9.5	25.2
Retired	54.8	43.1
Permanently disabled	3.9	4.4
Housewife	31.8	27.3
Total	100.0 (153)	100.0 (451)

SOURCE: Compiled by author, from 1976 election data. Center for Political Studies, University of Michigan.

Note: Asterisk indicates significant at .05 or less. Parentheses indicate number.

If the "age-conscious" have background characteristics that are significantly different from other elderly, do those differences have political
significance? That is, do the age-conscious elderly approach politics with
orientations differing from the elderly who are not age-conscious? The
results shown in table 6.3 suggest that they do not, at least in terms of
partisanship and self-perceived ideology. Both groups tend to be Democratic (43.7 percent for the age-conscious, and 45.4 percent for other
elderly). The age-conscious group was slightly less likely than other
elderly to report Republican affiliation and slightly more likely to identify
themselves as Independents. The differences, however, were not statistically significant.

The same pattern emerged when self-perceived political ideology was
considered. About 16 percent of both groups viewed themselves as
having a liberal ideology. The age-conscious were slightly more likely to
view themselves as conservatives. But, once again, those differences
were not statistically significant.

Thus far, then, we have seen that the elderly who identified with older
persons differ from other elderly with regard to selected personal characteristics, but the two groups approached politics with essentially the
same political orientations. If age consciousness had political meaning
among the contemporary elderly, we probably would not have found

Table 6.3

Partisan Affiliation and Ideology of Persons Aged Sixty and Older, by
Identification with Older Persons, 1976

	Respondent Feels Closest to:	
Characteristic	Older Persons (percent)	Other Groups (percent)
Partisan affiliation		
Strong Democrat	25.0	20.0
Weak Democrat	18.7	25.3
Independent	28.9	20.2
Weak Republican	13.3	19.7
Strong Republican	11.8	13.8
Other	2.3	0.9
Total	100.0 (150)	100.0 (449)
Ideology		
Liberal	16.8	16.2
Moderate	28.8	38.4
Conservative	54.4	45.4
Total	100.0 (63)	100.0 (266)

SOURCE: Compiled by author from 1976 election data. Center for Political Studies, University of Michigan.
Note: Parentheses indicate number.

such similarities among our two groups. Rather we would have expected respondents identifying with the elderly to be different from and more homogeneous than other elderly citizens, irrespective of party affiliation or ideology. The data shown in table 6.3 lead us to wonder whether subjective identification with the elderly has political meaning.

Data provided in table 6.4, which shows the relationship between elderly identification and seven indicators of political involvement, are even more compelling. If age consciousness were to serve as a basis for mobilization, we would expect to find that age-conscious older persons would be involved in the political process to a greater extent than other elderly. However, the results shown in table 6.4 suggest just the opposite. Across all seven indicators of political involvement, those who reported primary identification with other elderly were *less* likely to be politically involved.[59]

Table 6.4
Political Involvement of Respondents Aged Sixty and Older, by Identification with Older Persons, 1976

	Respondent Feels Closest to:			
	Older Persons		*Other Groups*	
Respondent Reported Having:	*Percent*	*Number*	*Percent*	*Number*
Voted in 1976 presidential election*	66.6	(153)	76.8	(451)
Tried to influence the votes of others*	22.0	(153)	31.4	(451)
Given money to a party or candidate*	3.0	(150)	9.7	(450)
Written to a public official	18.7	(153)	24.4	(450)
Attended political rallies/meetings	3.0	(153)	6.3	(451)
Worked for a party or candidate	3.0	(153)	5.1	(451)
Worn a campaign button or sticker	2.0	(151)	5.9	(450)

SOURCE: Compiled by author from 1976 election data. Center for Political Studies, University of Michigan.
*Significant at .05 or less.

These findings raise serious questions about the political relevance of age consciousness among the contemporary generation of older Americans. The lack of partisan or ideological homogeneity implies that even if those who identified with the elderly as a group were highly involved in politics, their "participation input," as Verba and Nie have called it, would probably be quite diverse. Certainly, it would be no less diverse than the input of elderly citizens who are less age-conscious. Some older individuals would be inclined to support Democratic candidates, while others would be more likely to support Republican ones. Similarly, the elderly would be as likely to support "conservative" as they would more "liberal" solutions to policy problems. In short, the findings on partisanship and ideology suggest that age has not supplanted more traditional lines of political cleavage among the contemporary elderly.

Such a conclusion is strongly reinforced by the findings on political involvement. A group's political success depends, at least in part, on the ability to maintain high levels of commitment and involvement among participants. Our findings that age-based identification is not associated with high levels of political involvement can be interpreted to mean that increasing levels of age consciousness would not necessarily foster a strong old-age political movement.[60] Indeed, if age consciousness is to serve as a basis for the development of an aging movement, the structure of these relationships will have to undergo a radical transformation.

THE POLITICS OF AGE: A LEGISLATIVE PERSPECTIVE

Given that we find little evidence for the existence of an age-based political movement among the contemporary generation of elderly, one may reasonably wonder at the relative success of aging advocates in the policy process. Indeed, programs for the elderly have served as legislative landmarks at both national and state levels. There are at least two explanations for these developments. First, it may be that legislators view the elderly as a unified and effective political force that they cannot afford to alienate. Undoubtedly, this is the picture that advocates have promoted to legislators. An alternative explanation is provided by Hudson's observation that "the political legitimacy of the aging has rested in the widespread belief that, as a class of persons, they are singularly disadvantaged by low incomes, poor health, and a particular vulnerability brought on by their place in the life cycle."[61] Thus, in his view, legislative successes in aging policy development have not necessarily been due to political power. Rather they have been due to the belief among elites that the elderly are worse off than most other population segments.

In a 1979 survey, Dobson and Karns asked state legislators to report on their perceptions of political involvement and the relative status of older persons.[62] They also measured legislators' support for an expanded state role in the provision of benefits to the elderly[63] and the relative importance which legislators attached to aging issues, in contrast to other types of state policies.[64] They found that state legislators do, in fact, view the elderly as being highly involved in politics. About 75 percent of the state legislators perceived the elderly as voting more regularly than other citizens. Just under one-third (29.3 percent) believed that many elderly were involved in political organizations, and another 60 percent believed that at least some were. Similarly, only 26 percent viewed elderly organization leaders as ineffective, while 74 percent saw them as effective in the policy process.

Legislators were less unanimous about the relative status of the elderly. Only a small fraction of the respondents (2.2 percent) viewed the elderly as "better off" than most other age groups. Just under half (45.1 percent), however, stated that the elderly were "about as well off" as most other citizens. Finally, a slight majority (52.6 percent) believed the elderly to be "worse off" than other citizens.

Tables 6.5 and 6.6 suggest some political consequences of legislators' beliefs about the political involvement and relative status of the elderly. Table 6.5 relates legislators' perceptions to levels of support for state intervention. Table 6.6 does the same for the level of importance that legislators attached to aging issues. In both instances, the results are quite clear. Beliefs about the well-being of older citizens tend to have strong effects on legislators' support for state intervention and the importance they attach to aging issues. Legislators who responded that the elderly were at least as well off as other age groups were considerably less likely to support a positive state role for, or to attach much importance to, aging policy issues.

Table 6.5
Support for an Expanding State Role in the Provision of Benefits to the Elderly and Perception of Elderly Status and Political Involvement among State Legislators, 1979

	Legislator's Level of Support			
Variable	Low (percent)	Moderate (percent)	High (percent)	Total Number
Elderly are:*				
Better off than most	43.4	44.2	12.4	23
As well off as most	54.2	30.4	15.4	458
Worse off than most	36.1	29.2	34.7	543
Elderly vote:				
More regularly than others	43.3	31.3	25.4	758
About as regularly as others	45.8	29.8	24.4	214
Less regularly than others	56.0	12.5	31.5	36
Elderly leaders are:				
Ineffective	42.9	30.2	26.9	271
Effective	44.2	30.5	25.3	741
How many elderly are politically involved?				
Few	46.1	27.1	26.8	109
Some	41.6	31.8	26.6	606
Many	47.7	28.8	23.5	297

SOURCE: Compiled by the author.

*Significant at .05 or less.

Table 6.6

Importance of Aging Issues and Perceptions of Elderly Status and Political Involvement among State Legislators, 1979

	Importance of Aging Issues to Legislators			
Variable	Low	Moderate	High	Number
Elderly are:*				
Better off than most	51.8	35.1	13.1	23
As well off as most	48.6	31.5	19.9	458
Worse off than most	23.6	35.1	41.3	534
Elderly vote:				
More regularly than others	35.6	34.2	30.2	758
About as regularly as others	34.5	33.5	32.0	214
Less regularly than others	31.2	32.4	36.4	36
Elderly leaders are:				
Ineffective	31.6	36.4	32.0	271
Effective	36.0	33.3	30.7	741
How many elderly are politically involved?				
Few	37.1	31.5	31.4	109
Some	34.6	36.9	28.5	606
Many	34.7	29.4	36.0	297

SOURCE: Compiled by the author.

*Significant at .05 or less.

In sharp contrast, legislators' perceptions about the political roles of the elderly had no impact upon either support for state intervention or the perceived importance of aging issues. Although legislators perceive the elderly as being involved in the political process and as having effective political leadership, such views do not appear to translate into policy support. Apparently, as Hudson's remarks suggest, legislators respond to the elderly on the basis of welfare concerns rather than on political considerations.

CONCLUSIONS

The findings presented here as well as those emerging from other research suggest that, although the elderly are an important and perhaps especially regarded group in contemporary American politics, there is little support for the notion that they are a distinctive, unified political force. To be sure, the current generation of elderly differ from the young. They are, for instance, more likely to be conservative in political orientation. Similarly, they are more likely to have partisan inclinations that favor the Republican party. But such findings do not imply that the elderly are a homogeneous political group. Their attitudes and political orientations are about as diverse as the population at large. Such diversity serves to inhibit a realization of the political potential of the elderly, for success in the halls of Congress and the state legislatures depends, at least partially, on uniformity of articulated policy preferences.

Further, among the current generation of elderly it does not appear that "age consciousness" serves as a basis for political mobilization. In fact, it is doubtful that age consciousness has political meaning for *most* elderly citizens. The age-conscious elderly are not more homogeneous than other elderly in either political affiliation or ideological orientation. Perhaps more importantly, the age-conscious elderly are substantially less likely than other elderly to be involved in the political process. If the elderly are a distinctive political force in America, their impact probably derives from an ideology among many political elites supporting the notion that the elderly are uniquely disadvantaged.

It is difficult to say what lies beyond the horizon. There are indications that the elderly may be losing their especially favored political status in the face of staggering inflation and efforts to contain or reduce the size of government programs. This suggests that major political issues will include questions of old age in the coming decades, possibly with fewer benefits accruing to older people. It is unclear, however, whether such changes will foster political mobilization among the elderly. It is obvious, however, that the elderly of the early twenty-first century, will be more highly educated, in better health, and perhaps more politically experienced than contemporary older Americans. As the present cohort is replaced by the politically active 1960s generation, it is certainly possible to visualize scenarios in which age could be a major source of cleavage in the American political system.

NOTES

1. See Matilda White Riley and Anne Foner, eds., *Aging and Society*, vol. 1 (New York: Russell Sage, 1972), pp. 15–38.

2. Donald G. Fowles, *Statistical Reports on Older Americans: Some Prospects for the Future Aging Population* (Washington, D.C.: Department of Health, Education, and Welfare, 1978).

3. Robert B. Hudson, "The 'Graying' of the Federal Budget and Its Consequences for Old-Age Policy," in *The Aging in Politics: Process and Policy*, ed. Robert B. Hudson (Springfield, Ill.: Charles C. Thomas, 1981), p. 274.

4. Since aging interest groups are treated elsewhere in this volume, they will not be considered here. Rather we will focus upon the political behavior of the "mass" of elderly citizens, and our findings will reflect this restricted focus. As Professor Pratt notes in chapter 7, the development of stable aging interest groups is an important phenomenon. It is not really possible to comprehend the politics of aging without paying careful attention to the roles played by aging interest groups.

5. One of the best discussions of these issues may be found in Matilda White Riley, "Aging and Cohort Succession: Interpretations and Misinterpretations," *Public Opinion Quarterly* 37 (1973): 35–49.

6. This example is drawn from Neal E. Cutler and John R. Schmidhauser, "Age and Political Behavior," in *Aging: Scientific Perspectives and Social Issues*, ed. Diana S. Woodruff and James E. Birren (New York: D. Van Nostrand, 1975), pp. 374–406.

7. See, for instance, Angus Campbell, et al., *The American Voter* (New York: Wiley, 1960).

8. See Cutler and Schmidhauser, "Age and Political Behavior," pp. 387–90.

9. See Sidney Verba and Norman H. Nie, *Participation in America* (New York: Harper & Row, 1972), ch. 9; and Riley and Foner, *Aging and Society*, pp. 464–68.

10. Norman H. Nie, Sidney Verba, and Jae-on Kim, "Participation and the Life Cycle," *Comparative Politics* (1974): 326.

11. Verba and Nie, *Participation*, chs. 8–14. See also Lester Milbrath, *Political Participation* (Chicago: Rand McNally, 1965).

12. Nie, Verba, and Kim, "Participation and the Life Cycle," p. 329.

13. Ibid., p. 333.

14. Ibid., p. 335. Note also that the work by Verba and Nie, *Participation*, suggests that their "slow down" interpretation may vary across "modes" of participation. Specifically, while their measure of overall participation showed a residual downturn in elderly involvement after the socio-economic status (SES) effects were removed, the same was not true for their measure of voting involvement. In addition, they found no age-related variation in rates of contacting public officials. Thus, while they do not fully acknowledge it, evidence for a "slow down" interpretation is probably limited to more costly political acts such as campaign involvement or communal activity.

15. Norval Glenn and Michael Grimes, "Aging, Voting and Political Interest," *American Sociological Review* 33 (August 1968): 567.

16. Ibid., p. 572.

17. Kenneth Gergen and Kurt Bach, "Communication in the Interview and the Disengaged Respondent," *Public Opinion Quarterly* 30 (1966): 385–98.

18. Norval Glenn, "Aging, Disengagement and Opinionation," *Public Opinion Quarterly* 33 (1969): 17–33.

19. Ibid., p. 27.

20. Norval D. Glenn, "Aging and Conservatism," *Annals* 415 (1974): 176–86.

21. Stephen J. Cutler and Robert L. Kaufman, "Cohort Changes in Political Attitudes: Tolerance of Ideological Nonconformity," *Public Opinion Quarterly* 39 (1975): 69–70.

22. Riley and Foner, *Aging and Society*, 473–75.

23. Campbell, et al., *American Voter*.

24. Sammuel A. Stouffer, *Communism, Conformity and Civil Liberties* (New York: Doubleday, 1955).

25. Herbert H. Hyman and Paul B. Sheatsley, "Attitudes Toward Desegregation," *Scientific American* 211 (1964): 16–23.

26. Hazel Gaudet Erskine, "The Polls," *Public Opinion Quarterly* 26 (1962): 142–48.

27. Hazel Gaudet Erskine, "The Polls," *Public Opinion Quarterly* 29 (1965): 332–95.

28. H. J. Eysenck, *The Psychology of Politics* (London: Routledge, 1954).

29. Glenn, "Aging and Conservatism," p. 181.

30. Cutler and Kaufman, "Cohort Changes," 70.

31. Ibid., pp. 77ff.

32. Stephen J. Cutler et al., "Aging and Conservatism: Cohort Changes in Attitudes About Legalized Abortion," *Journal of Gerontology* 35 (1980): 115–23.

33. Campbell, et al., *American Voter*.

34. John Crittenden, "Aging and Party Affiliation," *Public Opinion Quarterly* 26 (1962): 648–57.

35. Neal E. Cutler, "Generation, Maturation, and Party Affiliation: A Cohort Analysis," *Public Opinion Quarterly* 33 (1969–70): 583–88.

36. Norval D. Glenn and Ted Hefner, "Further Evidence on Aging and Party Identification," *Public Opinion Quarterly* 36 (1972): 38.

37. Ibid., p. 44.

38. Angus Campbell, "Social and Psychological Determinants of Voting Behavior," in *Politics of Age*, ed. Wilma Donahue and Clark Tibbitts (Ann Arbor: University of Michigan Press, 1962) pp. 87–101.

39. Peggy Heilig, "Self Interest and Attitude Patterns Among the Elderly" (Paper presented at the Annual Meeting of the Midwest Political Science Association, Chicago, 1979).

40. Laurily Keir Epstein and William P. Browne, "Public Opinion and the Elderly: An Explanation of the 'Sometimes It's This Way and Sometimes It's That Way Principle'" (Paper delivered at the Annual Meeting of the Midwest Political Science Association, Chicago, 1979).

41. Douglas Dobson and Douglas St. Angelo, *Politics and Senior Citizens: Advocacy and Policy Formation in a Local Context* (Washington, D.C.: Administration on Aging, 1980).

42. Epstein and Browne, "Public Opinion."

43. Pauline K. Ragan and James J. Dowd, "The Emerging Political Consciousness of the Aged: A Generational Interpretation," *Journal of Social Issues* 39 (1974): 137.

44. Leonard Cain, "The Young and the Old: Coalition or Conflict Ahead?" *American Behavioral Scientist* 19 (1975): 166–75.

45. Ibid., p. 172.

46. Arnold Rose, "The Subculture of Aging: A Framework for Research in Social Gerontology," in *Older People and Their Social World*, ed. Arnold M. Rose and Warren A. Peterson (Philadelphia: F. A. Davis, 1965), pp. 3–16.

47. Ibid., pp 4–5.

48. Ibid., p. 14.

49. Robert H. Binstock, "Interest-Group Liberalism and the Politics of Aging," *Gerontologist* 12 (Autumn 1972): 265–280. See also Robert H. Binstock, "Aging and the Future of American Politics," *Annals* 415 (1974): 199–212.

50. Binstock, "Interest Group Liberalism," p. 118.

51. Anne Foner, "Age Stratification and Age Conflict in Political Life," *American Sociological Review* 39 (1974): 187–96; and Anne Foner, "Age and Society: Structure and Change," *American Behavioral Scientist* 19 (1975): 144–65.

52. Foner, "Age and Society," p. 152.

53. Ibid., p. 153.

54. Ragan and Dowd, "Emerging Political Consciousness."

55. Ibid., p. 143.

56. The data utilized in this section were made available by the Inter-University Consortium for Political and Social Research. The data for the 1976 American National Election Study were collected by the Center for Political Studies of the Institute for Social Research, University of Michigan. Neither the original collectors nor the consortium bear any responsibility for the analyses or interpretation presented here.

57. This conclusion was also supported by inspection of responses to each of the sixteen items, taken independently. The percentage distribution of "feel close" responses for each group was as follows: businessmen, 19.6; liberals, 8.1; Southerners, 18.3; poor people, 38.8; Catholics, 20.3; Protestants, 40.1; Jews, 9.2; young people, 32.9; whites, 44.5; blacks, 12.7; conservatives, 20.0; women, 41.7; middle-class people, 59.9; workingmen, 52.1; farmers, 42.4; and older people, 72.1.

58. U.S., Department of Health and Human Services, Administration on Aging, *Statistical Notes* (Washington, D.C.: National Clearinghouse on Aging, April 1980).

59. The relationships reported in table 6.4 were controlled for both sex and education. Results did not differ substantially from those shown here.

60. See E. Cumming and W. E. Henry, *Growing Old: The Process of Disengagement* (New York: Basic Books, 1961).

61. Robert B. Hudson, " 'Graying,' " p. 274. For a related discussion, see Binstock, "Aging and the Future," pp. 212ff.

62. The state legislature data resulted from a mail survey of legislators in twenty-seven states. For a detailed description of the research, see Douglas Dobson and David A. Karns, *Public Policy and Senior Citizens: Policy Formation in the American States* (Washington, D.C.: Administration on Aging, 1979).

63. The measure of "support" utilized here resulted from a factor analysis of items asking state legislators whether they believed that the state should do much more, should do some more, has done about enough, should do some less, or should do much less across twelve contemporary aging policy issues: lowering cost of prescription drugs; elimination of age discrimination; funding senior centers; reducing crime against the elderly; enabling individuals to work past normal retirement age; providing transportation; reducing utility costs; relieving property taxes; providing alternatives to institutionalization; providing good housing; regulation of nursing homes; and providing adequate health care.

64. The importance of aging policy issues was determined by asking legislators to judge each of the policy issues as "important" or "not important" in contrast to other state issues. Responses were, once again, factor analyzed.

HENRY J. PRATT

7

National Interest Groups Among the Elderly: Consolidation and Constraint

It has been almost exactly half a century since the first tentative steps toward mobilizing senior citizens were taken. In 1933, Dr. Francis E. Townsend, a sixty-six-year-old physician practicing in Long Beach, California, observed three shabbily dressed, elderly women, evidently rendered destitute by the Great Depression, scrounging for food in a garbage dump. As legend has it, this pitiful sight so moved Townsend that he initiated the so-called Townsend Plan, which called for a pension of two hundred dollars per month—a huge sum for those times—for all persons sixty years of age or older on the condition that the two hundred dollars be spent in the United States within a month after its receipt. In a Depression-weary land, the "Plan" appealed to many older people as a means of both giving immediate aid to themselves and reinvigorating the nation's economy through infusion of new purchasing power. By 1934, the first "Townsend Club" had been organized, and the Townsend Movement soon emerged into what Arthur Schlesinger, Jr., would later term "the most striking political phenomenon of 1935."[1] Born out of the agony of hard times, the Townsend Movement began to fade in the late 1930s and early 1940s as defense industries began hiring workers in large numbers and the United States gradually emerged from the Depression trauma. Nevertheless, Townsend's initial success at creating a sentiment among the elderly served as a beacon to later social activists and organizers, and every subsequent decade has brought its own crop of new senior citizen organizations.

Some of these groups, including the Townsend organization itself, have fallen by the wayside, but enough of them endure to justify the claim that their number and variety is nothing short of astonishing. In addition to general-purpose, mass-membership groups, of which the Gray Panthers, the National Council of Senior Citizens (NCSC), and the American Association of Retired Persons (AARP) are by far the largest and most visible, there are several membership bodies composed of retirees in certain occupations, including the National Retired Teachers Association (NRTA)—the sister institution of AARP—and the National Association of Retired Federal Employees (NARFE). In addition, there are a number of small, caucus-type bodies whose leaders seek to address the particular needs of various categories within the elderly population. These include the National Council on the Black Aged, the National Association for Spanish-Speaking Elderly, and the National Indian Council on the Aging. And a number of interest groups have sprung up that are focused on the needs and aspirations of old people although not primarily composed *of* them—the National Council on the Aging (NCOA) and the Gerontological Society of America (GSA). It is difficult to arrive at an overall total for the number of organizations composed primarily of the aged, in view of the obscurity of many groups and their ephemeral character. Yet estimates at least are possible, and one estimate arrived at recently by the Research Department of the American Association of Retired Persons is of considerable interest. Combining those groups with memberships restricted to senior citizens with others that focus on the elderly but with membership not confined to that age group (for instance, the Gray Panthers and National Council on the Aging), AARP concluded that there are currently around one thousand separately organized senior citizens' groups in the United States at the local, state, and national levels. Excluded from this number are the local chapters of national organizations, the total of which for AARP and NCSC alone is in excess of five thousand.

It has become customary in referring to interest groups in the United States to quote de Tocqueville on the point that Americans have a natural propensity to establish and join organized groups. It seemed to him that one of the most significant manifestations of the American democratic spirit was the proclivity of Americans to organize into special groups to advance their own specific interests. At first glance, the great profusion of organizations in the field of aging—some of them composed of senior citizens, others created to meet the "needs" of the elderly, variously defined—seems fulsome testimony to the validity of de Tocqueville's assessment.

Yet, the history of old-age organization on closer scrutiny suggests a need to modify de Tocqueville's thinking in significant ways. Writing about American interest groups generally, E. E. Schattschneider remarked a generation ago that most organized groups have a marked middle-class to upper-class bias.[2] Where de Tocqueville would lead one to expect that interest groups would be most likely to form wherever the objective "need" is greatest, presumably including the poor and near poor, the fact is that the most mobilizable segment of the elderly population has proved to be retirees from higher-status occupations. The most in-depth study thus far conducted into the kinds of people who join politically active old-age organizations provides graphic evidence on this point.[3] Even state-level pension movements whose goals directly relate to the elderly's money-income needs, have difficulty in extending their membership base much below the lower middle class and upper working class of the retiree population. Senior citizen groups resemble most other interest groups in their general inability to involve large numbers of poor and near-poor individuals. Roughly 30 percent of American elderly people fall into this income bracket. Up to a point, of course, the mass-membership groups can endeavor to plead the cause of the truly disadvantaged elderly—in a kind of virtual representation. Yet, senior group leaders remain constrained by their middle-class and higher-income working-class constituencies. They have not, for example, been deeply involved in programs like Medicaid and Supplementary Security Income (SSI) that are targeted at elderly persons toward the bottom of the income scale.

There is also a second respect in which the experience of trying to organize senior citizens calls for modification of de Tocqueville's point about the propensity of Americans to establish interest groups. Many attempts have been made to mold seniors into stable and viable organizations, but these efforts often have proved abortive, and the overall success rate has not been high. At the national level, for instance, there is a fairly lengthy list of groups that existed at some point in the 1960s or 1970s but now are defunct. It includes Senior Advocates International, the Senior Citizens League, Senior Citizens of America, and the National Association for the Advancement of Older People. There is no way of knowing how many similar "bankruptcies" may have occurred during these same years in state government among the many "action groups," "coordinating councils," and "senior lobbies" that tend to arise there. Presumably, such a list would be fairly lengthy. One does not have to probe deeply to understand why it has proved difficult to forge seniors into durable association. The danger of bankruptcy exists for all types of voluntary organizations, not merely ones composed of the elderly. Maintaining an organization on the basis of dues from members is a difficult task under the best of circumstances, and the tangible rewards for the typical entrepreneur/leader are likely to be fairly modest. Absent any marked degree of initial success, a leader can get discouraged and give up the effort. Additional problems are presented when the membership base consists of seniors. Advanced age carries with it an added risk of mental and physical impairment. A majority of senior citizens are no doubt vigorous and hearty, but a substantial number are less fortunate. Impairment also can creep up on a person, diminishing the contribution of someone who, because of earlier vigor and commitment, may occupy an important office in the organization. In addition, the age range from which senior group members are mainly recruited is decidedly narrow, about a dozen years, sixty-two to seventy-five. Older adults who have not yet reached the age range of sixty-two to sixty-five are unlikely in large numbers to identify as "seniors" or be responsive to "senior group" appeals. The "old-old"—those beyond age seventy-five—may experience impaired physical and mental vigor and also, given their much greater tendency to be widowed, tend to be less organizationally involved. Research has shown that single people of all ages tend to be less politically active than those who are married.[4] These are, of course, generalities and do not apply to all individuals. Every senior citizen group can point to individual members, both single and married, who are committed and active well into their eighties, or beyond. But such people are not typical. Even in what might be termed the prime age group for active members— sixty-two to seventy-five—voluntary associations of the elderly must confront the risk of greater member disability or death than other types of groups. For the organization to remain viable, the places of those who die or are disabled must be filled by new recruits. This tends to produce a constant preoccupation with recruitment that can be a drain on resources that otherwise might be used for more goal-directed activity.

It is not surprising, then, that throughout the first third of the present century little thought was given to organizing the elderly into an effective force. (The pension movement of the 1920s, which consisted of organizations like the American Association for Labor Legislation, the American Association for Old Age Security, and the Fraternal Order of Eagles, mainly involved younger adults working on behalf of the elderly.) The period 1900 to 1920 was one of unparalleled organizing effort among other categories of the population. A significant number of national interest groups, representing blacks, farmers, women, consumers, and others, were formed or expanded in these years, and many of these are still in existence today. However, no such effort was made to form groups composed of elderly people.[5]

Nevertheless, even after allowance is made for the needed qualifications in de Tocqueville's assessment, there remains a sense of wonder over the extent to which interest groups in the field of aging have emerged on the scene since the 1930s and a lingering feeling that he was fundamentally correct. Senior citizen mass-membership groups espousing public policy goals would be of interest to political science even if none of their goals were realized, since large organizations are politically important for the effect they have on their members' political attitudes and behavior, quite apart from any direct influence they may exert on public policy. In the case of the elderly, however, the leading senior groups are important both for their effects on rank-and-file members and for their impact on public policy.

The rest of this chapter will be organized into three sections. First, the discussion will probe for factors that have permitted the leading senior citizen interest groups in the past twenty-five years to emerge on the scene and to consolidate. Second, the analysis will consider various ways in which these groups are constrained in their behavior by forces of an internal character. The third part will shift to an external vantage point. Senior citizen groups will be assessed in terms of their capacity to influence public policy, focusing on the political influence of the "gray lobby" in Washington relative to certain other leading lobby groups outside the aging field.

FACTORS IN SENIOR GROUP STABILITY

The founding of the Townsend Movement in 1934 marked the beginning of efforts to organize senior citizens on a mass scale. The movement's leadership, whatever its failings, did succeed in demonstrating that retired Americans can be forged into a major lobbying force capable of exerting pressure on governments and generating vast publicity. Even though its founder and long-time leader, Dr. Francis E. Townsend, never came close to getting his "Townsend Plan" adopted by the Congress, the large number of dues-paying members who were drawn to his banner— six hundred thousand at the peak—and the great interest he aroused served to inspire other "entrepreneurs" to launch their own senior groups with a similar style and membership base. Some of these achieved a fair degree of success in their various state-level pension crusades, extending in some cases through the early 1950s. Nevertheless, by the late 1940s the Townsend Movement and its state-level imitators were mostly in a state of decline, and by the mid-1950s they had ceased to be a significant political force at any level of government. The middle and late 1950s, therefore, represented a hiatus for politically self-conscious senior citizen organizations in the United States.

In the aftermath of the 1961 White House Conference on Aging, however, there occurred a reemergence of senior citizen organizational effort. Over a ten-year period, new groups like the National Council of Senior Citizens (1961) and the Gray Panthers (1970) were organized, and existing ones, such as the American Association of Retired Persons (1958) and the National Council on Aging (1950), gained a much-expanded membership base and an enlarged sense of public policy awareness and concern. In hindsight, one can see that the organizations comprising this senior citizens group "reemergence" are remarkable in terms of their stability and capacity for long-term survival. Whereas the groups of the 1930s and 1940s within a decade of their founding were already in a state of decline, or in some cases actually defunct, the more fortunate of the groups formed in the late 1950s and 1960s, including all of those just mentioned, are still vigorously active in the 1980s, twenty years or more after their inception. What exactly has made for this greater capacity to consolidate? A comparison between the groups of the

Townsend and post-Townsend eras on the one hand and those of the more recent "reemergence" on the other should prove useful in gaining insight into this matter.

One point of contrast has to do with structure. The basis of the Townsend Movement was essentially the personality and charisma of its founder and leader, Francis E. Townsend. Though not by any means a genius at organization—the brains of the movement was Townsend's right-hand man, Robert Clements—Townsend dominated his organization, which was officially known at the outset as Old Age and Revolving Pensions, Ltd. The Townsend style of leadership was followed by other entrepreneurs who emerged in the post-Townsend era of the 1940s. Chief among these latter-day pension crusaders were Robert Noble, the founder of the "Ham and Eggs" Movement, George McLain of the California Institute of Social Welfare, and O. Otto Moore of the Colorado-based National Annuity League. Since in all of these cases the organization tended to be essentially the extension of one man's personality, his idiosyncracies had a marked bearing on organizational behavior. In the early months of popular enthusiasm for the new movement, this generally caused little difficulty and may even have represented a source of strength. Yet, as emotions cooled and the organization endeavored to regroup itself for a more protracted effort, the founding leader's idiosyncracies often became a source of weakness. Right or wrong, his will had to prevail; he and his coterie were "wise," and those voicing opposition were branded as unenlightened and even venal.

The early groups also were beset by a tendency to emphasize political and legislative accomplishment to the exclusion of anything else that might serve to encourage membership. Essentially built on "purposive" incentives, such groups might flourish as long as legislative victories were forthcoming. However, when favored legislation was blocked decisively in the legislature, or even long delayed in coming, there was a marked tendency for rank-and-file disillusionment to set in and for the organization—whose very survival depended on member commitment to the stated political goals—to begin deteriorating. Other possible bases for recruiting members existed at the time, but these could not be developed as long as this political fixation prevailed. A network of local affiliated clubs, for example, wherein inducements of a nonpolitical character might develop, could have served as a basis for sustaining the movement during the inevitable legislative "dry" periods. Such clubs never developed beyond the embryonic stage. The Townsend organization did have a local club structure of sorts, as did the McLain organization and the National Annuity League. But these local clubs were typically poorly attuned to the "headquarters faction" in the organization, and the top leaders tended to regard them with a wary eye. McLain, for example, consciously limited the size of his movement's clubs and kept each one independent from all others. The Townsend Clubs were a constant annoyance to Francis E. Townsend and Robert Clements, the movement's leaders. When at one point restiveness against headquarters policy among Townsend Club leaders reached the point where some of them broke away to form their own organization, the top leaders were compelled to create a machinery through which member organizations could have a voice in policymaking. But this concession was made grudgingly and only to forestall further defections. In practice, it never proved a very effective check on the national group's continued dominance.

Another facet of this abiding preoccupation with political goals was the leaders' inattention during their organizations' critical early years to developing a range of "selective benefits" that might have served as an inducement for potential members to affiliate with them. Only late in its history, and after an irreversible decline had set in, did the Townsend Movement begin to offer a range of goods for sale to its members— Townsend Old-Fashioned Horehound Drops, Townsend Club Toilet Soaps, Dr. Townsend's Vitamins and Minerals—the revenues from which could more closely bind members to the movement while also providing a steady, if modest, source of revenue.

In contrast, the marked stability of the senior movement groups of the contemporary era can be understood in terms of their managing to avoid these debilitating organizational flaws. Although the major legislative breakthroughs on Capitol Hill in the field of aging policy were largely confined to the years prior to 1975, the leading senior citizen groups have continued in subsequent years to attract members in significant numbers. It appears that even though all of them have set forth specific public goals, they do not fundamentally depend on rank-and-file backing for such political objectives as the essential "glue" of the organization. Instead, AARP, NCSC, and the Gray Panthers all have stressed, in differing ways, that support based on political agreement must be matched by a sense of solidarity that transcends narrow political self-interest if the organization is to survive and flourish.

The solidarity element, the main locus of which is the local affiliate chapters in each organization, has been extremely important. AARP has over 3,000 local chapters, NCSC claims over 4,000 local affiliated clubs, and the Gray Panthers, with a much smaller membership base—50,000 as against 12.5 million and 3 million, respectively, for the other two—has 110 local chapters. The national officers and staff make elaborate efforts to ensure that the voice of the local chapters is heard and that national policy is reflective of chapter sentiment. AARP has a provision in its bylaws specifying that not less than half of the delegates to the biennial convention must be from local chapters, even though such members number only around 700,000, or roughly 5.5 percent of the total. The national headquarters provides a training program for local officers at no charge to the chapters, and it otherwise endeavors to enhance their strength. The Gray Panthers carries this a step further, requiring that *all* delegates to the biennial convention be members in good standing in their local affiliate. (The Panthers have roughly 10,000 local chapter members.) The leaders of NCSC prefer not even to talk about the organization's total membership, lest this put the emphasis in the wrong place; hence NCSC stresses that it is "an organization consisting of 4,000 local clubs." Not a great deal is known about the quality of relations between chapter representatives and national officials in any of the three organizations; indeed, research on this point could be extremely useful. But from what little information is available, it appears that the relationship has been fairly harmonious. Certainly, there has been nothing approaching the atmosphere of open revolt that occurred in the case of the early Townsend Clubs with respect to the leaders of that movement. It is highly plausible, moreover, that the existence of clubs in all three cases has served as a major stabilizing element, helping to increase rank-and-file commitment and to avoid what otherwise might be a fairly anonymous relationship between rank-and-file members and the organization.

In addition to incentives such as shared political purpose and solidarity, the three leading mass-membership groups also have recruited members on the basis of direct member services. The case of AARP is legendary in this respect. Indeed, the services bulk so large as to cause some observers to wonder whether the term "voluntary association" is really applicable, or whether instead the association might better be considered a business enterprise for which the membership element serves as a kind of veneer. The list of benefits offered through AARP—or else in close conjunction with it—is extensive. Its mail-order pharmaceutical operation, which offers discount prices on major drug items, is a major enterprise, and its profits add significantly to the organization's revenues. It is not by accident that the U.S. Postal Service has designated a special Zip code for AARP and its sister organization, the National Retired Teachers Association! AARP has entered into an arrangement with Prudential Insurance Company for the sale of life insurance to AARP dues-paying members, with a percentage of the profits being used to help subsidize the association. Prudential is guaranteed the exclusive right to advertise in official AARP publications. (The arrangement with Prudential replaces an earlier longstanding one with the Colonial Penn Insurance Company, whose relationship with AARP was severed recently by court order.) And the list of enterprises goes on—travel services, a preretirement planning program, and so forth.

In the case of the National Council of Senior Citizens, a significant direct service to members consists of certain responsibilities that the leadership undertakes in behalf of the large industrial unions that are affiliated with it. The service consists of the oversight and leadership given to its several unions' local retiree chapters. While the chapters are to some degree underwritten directly out of subventions from the union treasuries, they are also aided indirectly through annual contributions to the NCSC budget. In the latest year for which data are available, 1971, NCSC had its own range of direct member services—a travel tour program, a prescription drug operation, a job retraining program, and so forth. These return some surpluses each year to the national treasury, although none of them even begins to approach the vast scale of its AARP counterpart.

The preceding remarks provide insight into how the leading senior citizen groups have managed to consolidate and sustain themselves. The discussion now can turn to the purposes for which the groups employ their resources, especially regarding the more political aspects of their role.

INTERNAL DYNAMICS AND POLITICAL GOALS

With the exception of the National Council of Senior Citizens and the Gray Panther movement, the leading present-day groups involved in aging issues were founded for essentially nonpolitical purposes and with the objective of governmental representation as, at most, a subordinate element in their organizational mandate. And with NCSC as the only exception, none of the leading groups originally had its national headquarters in Washington, D.C. The pattern among those groups that focus on elderly persons as their primary concern is quite marked in this respect. The National Council on the Aging, founded in 1950 as the National Committee on the Aging, set up its headquarters in New York City. Its original founders, Ollie Randall, Albert J. Abrams, and Geneva Mathiasen, among others, all resided in the New York area. The Gerontological Society of America, an organization of scholars, researchers, and planners in the aging field, established its first headquarters in Saint Louis. Vincent Cowdry, an early GSA president, arranged for the organization to have free office space at Washington University in Saint Louis, where Cowdry was dean of the Medical School. The core of the organization's early leadership—Robert Kleemeier, Herman Blumenthal, and James Kirk (one of the first editors of the society's official journal)—had faculty appointments in various departments at the same university. Likewise, the American Association of Retired Persons, founded by Ethel P. Andrus in 1958, was administered from offices in Long Beach, California, the community where Andrus had her home. AARP did, early on, establish a parallel "headquarters" in Washington, D.C. However, during Andrus's lifetime the Washington office was subordinate; the bulk of the professional staff and the center of decision making in the organization remained at Long Beach. Finally, Philadelphia became the site of the Gray Panthers' national offices when that organization was founded in 1970, Philadelphia being the home of GP founder Margaret Kuhn.

It is remarkable the extent to which these various groups have since opted to relocate their national offices to the nation's capital. NCOA made its move to Washington in 1960, when it also changed its name from "committee" to "council" and substantially enlarged its mandate. AARP did the same in 1968 as part of a reorganizational effort after the death of Ethel Andrus the previous year; the existing AARP Washington office became "headquarters" in fact not just in name, and Long Beach was downgraded to the status of "Western regional office." The Gerontological Society of America relocated to Washington in 1970. Moreover, no leading senior organization, having once elected to locate its headquarters in the national capital, has ever moved away.

The Gray Panthers is presently the only leading senior group organized nationally whose headquarters is not situated in Washington, and conversations with its national staff in 1981 indicated that there is no sentiment among members of the National Steering Committee to shift the headquarters site. To some degree this satisfaction with existing arrangements may reflect the fact that Philadelphia is only a two-hour direct train ride to Capitol Hill. More fundamentally, however, it probably reflects certain attributes of the Panthers' goals, ones that make the need for intimate, day-to-day contact between top staff personnel and Washington officials and lawmakers appear less crucial than is true of the other senior groups. Nevertheless, the Gray Panthers is not insulated from the external forces that impinge on all interest groups in the area of aging. The GP National Steering Committee in mid-1981 was considering a proposal to open a permanent Washington "field" office, a move that probably will be approved. Until now, Gray Panther lobbying in Washington has been conducted by members of the National Steering Committee residing in the Washington area. This has its advantages but has not afforded the intimate day-to-day contact with events on Capitol Hill and in the federal bureaucracy that many leaders deem desirable. In addition, in 1980 the Panthers voted to shift the site of its biennial national convention from Asilomar, California, where it was originally planned, to Washington, D.C., so as to facilitate efforts aimed at the 1981 White House Conference on Aging.

This pattern of shifting office locations and convention sites is a clue to a very important facet of the larger environment that groups concerned with the welfare and advancement of senior citizens must function in. Even though at their beginnings most of them manifested a pronounced nonpolitical stance, all have since become conscious to one degree or another of a strong gravitational pull toward national politics. The initial selection of a headquarters site had been typically a matter of convenience, but time brought with it appreciation of the need for close proximity to the center of political authority, the vortex of national policy-making. The leadership of the National Council on the Aging proved to be unusually farsighted in this regard, since NCOA shifted its headquarters to Washington well before the Congress enacted the remarkable series of legislative breakthroughs on the aging front—Medicare, the Older Americans Act, the nutrition program, Foster Grandparents and Retired Senior Volunteers, the Age Discrimination in Employment Act, the indexing of Social Security to the cost of living, and so on—that marked the period 1965 to 1974. By the 1970s all senior group leaders had come to appreciate the importance of the national government for meeting their own group goals and aspirations.

Indicative of such change is the altered image of the National Council of Senior Citizens. This group, which alone among recent senior citizen organizations was founded out of a perceived need for a vehicle to achieve public policy objectives and has had a marked political coloration ever since, is no longer regarded, as once was the case, as unique by virtue of its strong public policy focus. If there is a difference between NCSC and other senior groups, it now is more a matter of degree than of kind. The difference also consists in certain elements of style—a willingness among NCSC leaders on occasion to employ mass marches, rallies, and other direct-action methods as a means of influencing federal officials and lawmakers, as well as in certain uniqueness of priorities and goals, the nature of which will be discussed below. But all of the leading senior groups, not just NCSC, regularly lobby political officials as an essential part of their mandates.

The public policy objectives of the leading senior citizen groups are convergent in some respects and divergent in others. There is sufficient agreement on fundamentals to serve as a basis for loose, ongoing association. In the early 1970s the top officials of six voluntary associations joined together in a Conference of Interested Agencies in Aging. This eventually fell by the wayside but was replaced later on by a much larger, twenty-six-group, Ad Hoc Coalition of Aging Organizations, which continues to be quite active. Participants in these various coalitions have not as yet seen fit to undertake lobbying activity on a collective basis, but the coalition's behind-the-scenes efforts have helped firm up areas of consensus and have minimized the danger of working at cross-purposes. Loose though they may be, these coalitions are one of the sinews of the "gray lobby."

Pronounced areas of agreement on public policy matters do exist among the national senior citizen groups. All of them can be counted on, for example, to speak with one voice in behalf of sustaining a high-priority status for federal aging programs. Among those groups which at the time were maintaining Washington offices, there was unanimity in support of the 1973 proposal that the House of Representatives should create a Select Committee on Aging. A decade earlier, in what was probably their first collaborative intervention, senior groups had gotten together to denounce HEW Secretary Anthony Celebreeze's decision to downgrade what was then the Special Staff on Aging from its place in the secretary's office and to relocate it under a newly designated commissioner on welfare under a new title, the Office on Aging. The action was doubly offensive to old-age activists, both as threatening to remove aging from the center of focus in HEW and as linking aging with the negative connotations of the term *welfare*. When Secretary Celebreeze refused to back down and restore the special staff to its former location in HEW's center, aging groups turned to the House of Representatives, where their concerns gained a more sympathetic hearing. In 1965, as part of the newly enacted Older Americans Act, they managed to secure legislatively what they had not been in a position to win through administrative channels, namely having *their* agency, now designated the Administration on Aging, restored to a high level of access and visibility within HEW. This was not the end of the struggle, however. Later on in the same decade, the aging groups again coalesced when HEW Secretary John Gardner, successor to Celebreeze, and Undersecretary Wilbur Cohen transferred the Administration on Aging out of the Office of the Secretary and into the newly created Division on Social and Rehabilitation Services. Again, as before, the action aroused a solid wall of opposition from the senior citizen groups headquartered in Washington, and the secretary's move was later modified to some degree under congressional pressure.[6]

Aging groups also can be counted on to unite when there are proposals to eliminate or sharply cut back old-age benefits as provided for in existing legislation. Early in 1981, for example, they joined together in opposing President Reagan's proposed cutbacks in benefits under Social Security. The Reagan administration's retreat on the idea of scaling back early retirement benefits was at least partially a response to the storm of criticism by aging organizations.

One must be cautious, however, not to exaggerate the degree of mutual agreement. There are differences in priorities, some of them so marked as to border on direct clash. A public airing of such points of divergence thus far has been avoided, but not without difficulty. The differences are grounded partly in contrasting philosophies and definitions of basic needs, partly in varying temperaments among the several group leaders, and partly in differing policy preferences that arise out of the contrast in social class composition among rank-and-file members. The latter point is especially worthy of emphasis. Although hard data on social class composition are lacking, it is reasonably clear that AARP and NCSC—by far the largest senior groups presently active—differ fundamentally in this respect. AARP membership is predominantly middle- and upper middle-class; NCSC contains a sprinkling of middle-class members, but its center of gravity is among working-class retirees, especially people who were employed in unionized blue-collar jobs or who represent various ethnic groups such as the Jewish population. The Gray Panthers membership does not appear to fall into any such clear social class pattern.

There is an apparent connection between AARP's middle-class membership base, including many people in the established professions, and its vigorous support over the years for bringing an end to mandatory retirement in all sectors of the American economy. From the very outset, Ethel P. Andrus made opposition to forced retirement a top-priority AARP concern. In a 1959 speech, she declared, "It would be difficult to conceive of a more vast waste of manpower and/or production than that caused by mandatory retirement."[7] Andrus's death in 1967 in no way diminished the organization's strong commitment in this area. In 1971, with the White House conference approaching, AARP, in conjunction with its sister organization the National Retired Teachers Association, published a book of essays, *Options for Older Americans*. Appeals for legislation outlawing mandatory retirement was a persistent theme of the various prominent people who contributed articles. At the White House conference itself, AARP and NRTA representatives fought hard to get a resolution adopted stating that mandatory retirement is unconstitutional. The Conference's Employment and Retirement Section, which had jurisdiction in this field, refused to go all the way with AARP, but its affirmation that "chronological age should not be the sole criterion for retirement" was at least a gesture in that direction.[8] As the decade of the 1970s progressed, the association stepped up pressure. It filed an *amicus curiae* brief in the case of *Weiss* v. *Walsh* supporting a philosophy professor at Catholic University who alleged that Fordham University, having offered him a prestigious humanities chair, withdrew its offer when it learned that he had passed his sixty-fifth birthday. The *Weiss* case was ultimately decided against the plaintiff and against the position favored by AARP.

The mid-1970s brought certain leadership changes on Capitol Hill that were to pave the way for AARP's most significant legislative victory to date. Numerous bills proposing to bring an end to mandatory retirement throughout all sectors of American society had been placed in the congressional hopper over the years, but they had failed to get very far for lack of a strong champion among the lawmakers. For example, an early chairman of the House Select Committee on Aging, Congressman William Randall (D–N.J.) passed up numerous opportunities to recommend action on this front. All this was to change at the beginning of the ninety-fifth Congress in January 1977, when Congressman Claude

Pepper (D-Fla.) replaced Randall as chair of the House aging committee. Pepper's vigor and colorful style, combined wth AARP's vast membership base and firm commitment (augmented by active support from the Gray Panthers after 1976), proved to be a potent legislative combination. As political analyst Laura C. Ford was later to observe in describing this period, "There was no question that the needed spark was provided by the political activism of the American Association of Retired Persons, the National Retired Teachers Association, the Gray Panthers, etc."[9] The final legislative outcome, the 1978 Amendments to the Age Discrimination in Employment Act, raised the allowable age of forced retirement from sixty-five to seventy. Moreover, by implication the measure called into question the whole rationale behind mandatory retirement itself and gave impetus to a drive at the state level to abolish forced retirement outright. The measure was not a total victory for the AARP position, whose subsequent Annual Legislative Guidelines have continued to "recommend that forced retirement based solely on age should be completely prohibited under ADEA." Nevertheless, it represented a major step toward realization of a long-held goal.

In contrast to AARP's singleness of purpose, NCSC's behavior with respect to mandatory retirement has revealed a certain ambivalence. As a matter of principle, NCSC shares the AARP view that mandatory retirement is wrong, since it substitutes the "irrelevant criterion" of chronological age for the more "appropriate" ones of worker capacity and ability to perform. On the other hand, NCSC has taken the position that excessive emphasis ought not to be placed on this particular issue. Moreover, in 1977 the Washington office of the AFL-CIO, which is closely allied with NCSC, voiced opposition to the Pepper bill on the grounds that it would tend to undermine certain contractually arranged retirement benefits for unionized workers, the receipt of which was predicated on worker acceptance of a mandatory retirement age. Moreover, on the related matter of Social Security's so-called retirement test, under which employees who continue to work past age sixty-five must give up one dollar in Social Security benefits for every dollar earned above $6,000 (1982), the NCSC view has been that such a test should be maintained. NCSC argues that payouts to people who continue working well past the normal retirement age would drain the Social Security trust fund unnecessarily. NCSC leaders frankly admit that the group's position is influenced by a pragmatic consideration. Composed predominantly of a blue-collar membership, the organization does not have a large number of people who desire to work full time past age sixty-five. Indeed, a major thrust of the labor movement in recent decades has been to enable workers to retire early. The character of many blue-collar jobs, which are physically draining, monotonous, and unpleasant, has contributed to worker demands for retirement as early as one's fifties—"Thirty and Out" is a slogan popular among autoworkers, for example—rather than for the privilege of continuing on past age sixty-five.

The two groups tend to reverse positions entirely when it comes to issues having to do with income maintenance, especially Social Security benefits. In this area, one finds that NCSC has a deep and abiding commitment, whereas AARP's stance reflects a certain ambivalence. NCSC's sense of resolve was manifested in its original organizational name National Council of Senior Citizens for Health Care Through Social Security. Although the final phrase has been dropped from its name, there endures a fundamental and strong commitment to Social Security and a desire that the program, in terms of both scope of coverage and benefits, be expanded. During the campaign in behalf of Medicare, NCSC was still a fledgling organization with severely limited resources. "When I came down here," NCSC Executive Director William Hutton remarked to an inerviewer in 1965, "the office was a dilapidated flat, the one secretary worked at the kitchen table and kept the press releases in the bathtub, and there was precious little in the way of funds."[10] Yet, despite this, NCSC did manage to play a significant, if secondary, role in the final legislative outcome on Medicare.

In what was probably its most singular political success to date, comparable in key respects to AARP's achievement in helping to secure legislation outlawing forced retirement at age sixty-five, NSCS was a central participant in the campaign leading up to adoption of the 1972 Social Security Amendments. According to a widely held view among informed observers, the 1972 amendments were the most significant enlargement of the Social Security Act of 1935. The final outcome was in large degree a consequence of NCSC representatives managing to find a major congressional ally who was prepared to collaborate with them and who had the political sagacity and clout needed to push the measure along. The ally was the chairman of the House Ways and Means Committee, Wilbur Mills (D–Ark.), whose own presidential ambitions at the time were important in his willingness to break with a customary conservative stance and to champion legislation that, however popular among the elderly, would necessarily entail an enlargement in the federal role.

The behavior of AARP on most income-maintenance programs is generally one of support, but support that falls well short of the all-out commitment it can generate on other kinds of issues. AARP representatives did testify in favor of the 1972 Social Security Amendments, for example, but that was about the extent of the group's involvement. And with regard to the earlier struggle over Medicare, the divergence between AARP and NCSC was very marked. NCSC's all-out commitment to financing Medicare through the Social Security system, a principle that underlay the legislation finally adopted by Congress in 1965, already has been mentioned. AARP, however, never endorsed this view. Throughout the Medicare struggle, which commenced with the introduction of the Forand Bill in 1957, AARP for the most part remained noncommittal. What little the organization did have to say on the issue tended to lean toward the view espoused by the American Medical Association.[11] In testimony on the Forand Bill in 1959, Dr. Andrus advanced a proposal that, although not identical to the "Eldercare" proposal offered by the American Medical Association, was not inconsistent with it. While carefully avoiding the suggestion that Medicare be linked to Social Security, Dr. Andrus proposed the creation of a health insurance plan for the elderly, initiated and administered by a "trusteeship." The dominant partners in this trusteeship would be representatives of the health-care industry, business, and the aged.[12] Labor representatives also would be included, but apparently not as dominant partners.

Conclusive proof is lacking, but it seems quite plausible that AARP's assigning of income maintenance to a slightly less than top priority among the various public policy concerns of elderly Americans is related to the fact that middle- to upper middle-class retirees are less preoccupied with money income concerns than with other potentially disturbing aspects of retirement status. For them, concerns such as the need for a continuing usefulness to society and a sense of belonging may well take precedence over economic issues narrowly conceived.

Despite their points of difference, however, AARP and NCSC seem more akin to one another than either is to the nation's third leading mass-membership organization, the Gray Panthers. In 1970, on the occasion of the Gray Panthers' founding and for some years subsequent, the organization seems to have occupied itself with the politics of culture to the virtual exclusion of the politics of government, at least at the national level. In its formative years the GPs experienced a remarkable enlargement in their membership, from a bare handful of activists at the outset to more than ten thousand members in its various local networks by 1975. This expansion occurred without the movement's national leaders becoming significantly involved in efforts to influence national public policy. This was not a case of simple oversight, since by the early 1970s the national government had become quite important in shaping social policy in the aging field. Rather, the GPs' seeming indifference to national government reflected certain unique features of its leadership, goals, and structure.

More than any other present-day senior group, the Gray Panthers has been the outgrowth of one person, its founding leader Margaret Kuhn. In her appearances at lecture halls and mass rallies, Kuhn has demonstrated a unique ability to arouse warmth and support among her listeners. She is also skilled in the use of the rather different medium of television, over which she succeeds in getting her message out to vast audiences. Active in earlier years as a professional staff member of the United Presbyterian church, Kuhn's thinking had been shaped by traditions of liberal Protestantism and Christian socialism. These philosophies are manifest in Kuhn's present-day anger over exploitive social institutions and in her passion for social justice.

However, at the time of its founding, the Gray Panther organization was not simply a manifestation of Maggie Kuhn's vision and social creed. It also incorporated much of the spirit and organizational thinking earlier embraced by certain social movements that were highly visible at the time—anti-Vietnam War protests, Black Liberation, women's rights, consumer-oriented activities. Influenced by these groups, Gray Panther leaders were determined to avoid a hierarchical governing structure and to develop instead a shared leadership. The idea of having formal membership, dues, specific qualifications for joining (including age), or credentials was rejected. Emphasis was placed on the movement's grass-roots character and on the need to foster "networks" of autonomous local affiliates. There was a corresponding stress on the alleged evils of bureaucracy, which GP activists were convinced would force the organization to develop a large, overstaffed national headquarters at the expense of spontaneity and grass-roots activities. As late as 1981, the national staff in Philadelphia consisted of only six persons. The organization thus came to embrace a philosophy that political scientist Jo Freeman, in analyzing the women's movement, referred to as the "myth of structurelessness."[13]

Radical in organizational structure, the Gray Panther movement was equally so in terms of its professed goals. The celebrated "Goal Five," adopted at the first Gray Panther National Convention and reaffirmed in 1979 by the National Steering Committee after some controversy, has been the clearest expression of its basic stance vis-à-vis the existing social order. The goal commits the group

to act independently and in coalition with other movements to build a new power base to achieve short-term social change and ultimately a new and just economic system which will transcend the profit motive, eliminate the concentration of corporate power, and serve human needs through democratic means.[14]

By emphasizing social change rather than incrementalist politics, and by talking of "transcending" existing societal values and structures, the Panthers purposely placed themselves outside the moderately reformist orientation that typified more mainstream senior citizen groups. As is true of radical organizations generally, this stance initially precluded conventional lobbying activity at the national level of government. Such lobbying would not have been congruent with the strong GP emphasis on grass-roots action, and presumably, too, it might have appeared in conflict with its larger goals.

The organization's main energies during its first decade involved programs related to the politics of culture. Through its National Gray Panther Media Task Force, Panther activists monitored television broadcasts in an effort to isolate and eliminate negative portrayals of old people. Through its Long Term Care Action Project, Gray Panther networks across the country organized to transform the nursing home industry. In 1974 the Gray Panthers staged guerrilla theater skits outside the American Medical Association convention in Chicago in an attempt to draw public attention to the heartlessness of the American health-care industry. In collaboration with Ralph Nader's Retired Professional Action Group, the Panthers helped in the investigation of hearing aid dealers, drawing attention to fraudulent advertising. The group also proposed model state laws for regulating such firms.[15] At the same time, Maggie Kuhn and other Panther leaders worked tirelessly to combat all forms of ageism and sexism, problems they viewed as interconnected. Tish Sommers, a leader of the Older Womens League (OWL), became a regular columnist in the Panthers' official publication, *Gray Panther Network*, while Maggie Kuhn, in her numerous public appearances, spoke out against "gerontophobia" and "ageism," describing herself as a "wrinkled radical."

In a perceptive analysis,[16] sociologists Ruth Jacobs and Beth Hess have identified three fundamental problems that have served to constrain the Gray Panthers. The first is the problem of leadership. Although Maggie Kuhn's energy and personality have been a decided asset, the fact that the organization leans so heavily on her charisma—indeed, may even be said to be based on it—makes it difficult to move new people into leadership positions and to arrange for an orderly succession of authority within the organization. Second, there is the problem of structure. An organization thoroughly imbued with an antihierarchical ethos finds it difficult to pursue any national goals with tenacity and consistency. This is not intended to negate the point made previously that the GPs' network of local affiliates throughout the country represents a stabilizing element within the organization. Yet it does suggest that, in fostering a strongly localistic ethos, the Panthers find it difficult to recruit and maintain a thoroughly professional staff at the national level and that this difficulty has implications for goal attainment. As Jacobs and Hess remark, "Lack of a central organization, however ideologically satisfying, has probably reduced the effectiveness of the Panther movement."[17] Maggie Kuhn is the movement's energizing center, but her presence in no way undercuts the antihierarchical tendency among the GPs, since her leadership derives from personal charisma and not from any office held or formal authority wielded. Until 1977 the GPs had no regular dues structure, and income was uncertain. The group relied mainly on Kuhn's speaking fees and various incidental sources. By the late 1970s, the leaders were beginning to solicit outside sources of revenue—from foundations, industry, and the U.S. government. However, heavy reliance on such outside sources entails a danger of weakening the desired structural integration between the national leadership, which directly solicits the outside aid, and local-level GP activists.

Finally, there is the issue of political orientation. The need to have formal Gray Panther membership was accepted in the early 1970s, and over a decade's time the organization expanded from a mere handful of activists at the outset to over fifty thousand members by 1981. However, the new recruits have consisted in large numbers of persons concerned with enhancing the status and power of old people generally, and only incidentally with enhancing the well-being of economically needy and politically disadvantaged persons regardless of age, which was a cardinal principle of Maggie Kuhn and the other GP founders. As a consequence, certain GP goals, such as nationalization of transportation and the oil industry, enjoy less than wholehearted support among the rank-and-file members. According to Jacobs and Hess, there is a lack of consensus within the organization on many of the more radical Panther goals.[18]

Although the Gray Panther's impact on national policy is not a topic treated in the Jacobs–Hess account, there is little doubt that the constraints mentioned in their analysis have affected negatively the group's lobbying efforts. The initial Gray Panther inattention to official Washington was superseded, beginning in the late 1970s, by a growing public policy awareness. With time, the group became committed to broad national legislative issues, including abolition of mandatory retirement, which would necessitate further modification of the Age Discrimination in Employment Act, an end to sex discrimination under Social Security, enactment of Congressman Ronald Dellums's national health insurance bill (H.R. 2969), and the lifting of federally mandated ceilings on savings account interest rates. Articles appearing in the *Gray Panther Network* tend to show that Gray Panther leaders have come to appreciate the importance of collaboration with other interest groups and with sympathetic politicians. It also appears that, for the present at least, its role in such coalitions is typically a subordinate, not a leading one. Such subordinate status is not, of course, unique to the Gray Panthers. It applies in some degree to all senior citizen groups, none of which can go it alone politically and all of which must on occasion join coalitions in which they may not be one of the leading forces. Nevertheless, whereas NCSC and AARP have succeeded in proving their ability on occasion to exert substantial political clout, the GPs have yet to demonstrate such capacity. NCSC and AARP representatives are accustomed to the corridors of power, whereas Gray Panther representatives are in a sense strangers to power. Panther leaders are obviously attempting to overcome these limitations, but it is not easy when their organization does not even have a Washington field office. Moreover, the internal constraints, leadership, and political orientation render it difficult for the group to have an impact on national policy. In short, the Panthers are beginning to understand that a group's ability to play a significant role in government requires more than merely shifting goals toward legislative issues. The Panthers are discovering that it is not a simple matter for a group deeply imbued at its outset with a radical spirit to transform itself into an effective lobbying body, which must operate within the accepted rules of the political process.

THE GRAY LOBBY'S MODEST REPUTATION FOR POLITICAL POWER

Thus far the leading senior citizen organizations have been examined from the standpoint of internal dynamics—their resources and constraints, political goals, and strategies. An important dimension missing from the discussion is an overall assessment of these groups' political role from an external vantage point. How do they stack up against other lobbies and political interest groups outside the aging field in terms of their capacity to influence and mold public policy? How do informed observers rate them as a political force? It is useful to address these questions since an assessment of senior citizen organizations from an internal perspective exclusively may convey quite a misleading impression and may serve to obscure certain vital truths about the actual role they play?

The preceding analysis has suggested that the larger mass-membership groups among the aged have not been wholly without influence on certain broad policy matters affecting the elderly. Already mentioned were the role played by NCSC in recent amendments to the Social Security Act and the activities of AARP culminating in the enactment of the 1978 Age Discrimination in Employment Act. Also discussed was the growing involvement and acceptance of the Gray Panthers as a partner in various drives to secure legislative reforms in behalf of the elderly.

An important component of senior group power that is significant, although not always easy to assess, is a capacity to keep certain proposed policy changes off the political agenda. As a result of the statutory breakthroughs during the 1960s and early 1970s, numerous protections and benefits for elderly Americans now are available. While these do not by any means provide a guarantee of economic security, dignity, or fulfillment for all elderly persons, they are at least an impressive legislative and programmatic edifice. Few, if any, other disadvantaged groups in the American population have been so favored. In such a setting, the greatest power of senior groups may be in their potential for making trouble when cost-conscious lawmakers or officials propose to cut old-age benefits or trim such expenditures. When it comes to defending the sanctity of existing public programs, the leverage of aging groups is at a maximum; it tends to be easier to veto change than to initiate it successfully.

But it is one thing to mobilize in defense of the status quo and quite something different to initiate new policy successfully or modify existing policies in ways congruent with group demands. Here the consensus among informed observers seems to be that the senior citizen groups have been only modestly influential and certainly not as powerful as certain other groups in American government that enjoy a reputation for first-rank political stature. Robert Binstock remarks,

The aging organizations have sufficient power to maintain themselves and their interests, but the goals articulated and sought by these organizations are not suitable to ... change the general societal status of the aged. While they probably would not have sufficient power to achieve such goals even if they sought them, the very incentive systems that create and sustain their organizational viability— interests of their members and pursuit of their trades and professions—preclude them from testing the extent of their power to achieve fundamental changes for the aging.[19]

In a similar vein Dale Vinyard has argued,

While these modern groups seem to have acquired some skill and sophistica- tion in dealing with national policy, their impact on broad issues affecting the elderly, like that of their predecessors of the 1930s, appears limited ... [they] have sufficiently established their credentials so they are welcome in the coalition, but in such a coalition they play a supporting rather than a leading role.[20]

Slightly more pessimistic than either Binstock or Vinyard, but not out of line with their thinking, is the assessment offered by Robert A. Har- tooyan: "Their [age-based advocacy groups'] record remains unimpres- sive when compared to the influence and political activity of non-age- based interest groups."[21] A survey of federal activity in the field of aging over the past twenty years reveals that, with a few singular exceptions, the major legislative breakthroughs have been engineered by presidents and various members of Congress, with the primary source of interest group support, if any, coming from non-age-based organizations. For example, the enactment of Medicare in 1965, as brought out in Theodore Marmor's study,[22] was pushed through Congress by President Johnson (after being introduced during the Kennedy years). Support from organ- ized labor and from various professional groups in the social welfare field was also a critical element. Similarly, the Age Discrimination in Employment Act of 1967 was an outgrowth of presidential initiative with strong backing from labor. The leading senior citizen groups did testify favorably on the bill when it was pending in Congress, but there is no evidence that their support was in any sense critical to its enactment. The protections in the bill were limited to workers under age sixty-five, and therefore did not directly affect the senior groups, most of whose members are above this age; this may explain why they did not give it higher priority. In the case of the Older Americans Act enacted in 1965, the principal initiative came from members of Congress, not the president. Senior citizen groups manifested considerable interest but were not a major factor in the legislative outcome.[23] One can make the case, and indeed the author has argued this elsewhere,[24] that the failure of senior citizen groups to affect decisively the legislative breakthroughs of the middle and late 1960s stemmed from their not having achieved the "critical mass" of resources and expertise needed to become politically effective and that by the early 1970s—especially in the wake of the 1971 White House Conference on Aging—they did achieve this, in the process realizing an increased level of influence and political stature. Yet, even in the 1970s, Congress enacted some significant age-related legislation in which the aging groups were only tangentially involved—the 1972 nutrition program added to the Older Americans Act, for example, or the Supplementary Security Income program (SSI). While there is evidence that the American Association of Retired Persons played a role in adoption of the 1973 Older Americans Comprehensive Services Amendments, it was a facilitative, and by no means a determinative, role.[25]

It is important to understand some of the reasons why the larger mass-membership groups of the aged have not succeeded in achieving a reputation in Washington for top-ranked power and influence. Given the usual measures of interest group potential, including both tangible and intangible factors, these organizations should be easily capable of realizing such a status. Such apparent potential accrues from at least five elements of their structure and societal position. First, in terms of sheer numbers, their combined membership is enormous. AARP, with close to thirteen million directly contributing, dues-paying members, may possibly be the largest mass-membership group in the nation's capital, save perhaps for some of the larger church organizations such as the United States Catholic Conference. Certain interest groups with very large nominal memberships, like the AFL-CIO with fifteen million people, are in fact federations. The rank-and-file members are actually only indirectly affiliated with the federation officers. The combined total of the three largest senior citizen groups in the nation is approximately seventeen million people. This figure probably exaggerates their numerical strength, since an undetermined number of elderly Americans hold multiple senior group memberships and, in addition, AARP counts both wife and husband in cases when only one is an actual dues-paying member. Yet, even after an adjustment is made for these factors, total membership of all senior groups is quite large and, indeed, represents a major fraction of all aged persons in the country.

A second determinant of group political potential is wealth, and here again the leading senior groups enjoy an advantage. No precise accounting of AARP wealth has ever been rendered, but its assets are generally estimated to be in the hundreds of millions of dollars. K Street in Washington is known as the "K Street Corridor," by virtue of its distinction as the headquarters locale for many interest groups of all varieties. And since real estate holdings are a rough measure of wealth, it is revealing that among all these headquarters offices none is more impressive than the multistoried, modernistic edifice owned and occupied by NRTA/AARP. The headquarters of the NCSC, again a K Street address, is much more modest than that of AARP, a four-story renovated older structure. But even it is more impressive than that of most other headquarters in the same vicinity. Only the Gray Panthers seem decidedly low on such a wealth index.

Another determinant of interest group potential is quality of leadership. Capable leaders can enable a group to compensate for deficiencies in other areas, just as mediocre ones can diminish the influence of an otherwise advantaged group. Judgments regarding leadership quality are to some extent subjective, but the evidence suggests that the present-day senior groups in Washington have been reasonably well served in this area. The abilities of long-time executives like Cyril Brickfield of AARP and William P. Hutton of NCSC appear to be at least equal to their counterparts in other large associations in Washington and may even rank above the average. Unlike the performance of Francis P. Townsend in the 1930s and 1940s—a performance not marked by any great distinction according to a leading study[26]—the leaders of today's Washington-based aging groups have exhibited a fair measure of drive, sophistication, and political savvy.

Finally, the senior groups appear to rate rather high on two other measures of interest group potential, namely the degree of legitimacy in the eyes of the wider society and the absence of internal factional strife which can sap a group's energies and undercut its political interventions. Older people tend to be viewed by the general public as having legitimate needs that deserve public attention. Dale Vinyard argues that such support has prompted many senators to serve on the Senate Special Committee on Aging since they want to be identified with this politically popular constituency.[27] So strong has been the sense of legitimacy attributed to the elderly that they comprise what amounts to an unrivaled minority, a grouping that has no institutionalized or self-proclaimed political opponents such as the constant opposition of militant conservationists to lumbering interests in the western United States.[28] One must be cautious, however, not to overstate the elderly's legitimacy or the utility of a proelderly stance for politicians. The desire of lawmakers to be identified publicly on the side of the elderly may not in all cases, or even in most, necessarily represent a deep personal commitment. It may be simply a matter of political prudence, for as Robert Binstock aptly remarks, "[Old age] interest groups, with their access to politicians and their platforms for framing issues, are in a key position to interpret the interests of millions of aging voters *whom politicians do not wish to offend.*"[29] As will be brought out later in this chapter, lawmakers on Capitol Hill who sit on broadly based committees such as Ways and Means in the House, frequently betray a less than total commitment to the senior citizen cause when supporting that cause would involve offending other politically potent constituencies.

Harmony with outside organizations tends to be mirrored by harmony within the organizations themselves. From what little evidence is available regarding the internal lives of these groups, it appears that serious strife has been held to a minimum. Although the members of each aging group do not have monolithic views, none of the organizations has faced the threat of an internal faction splitting off and forming a separate entity, such as occurred with the Townsend Movement in its early years. Factional stife has not appeared to be a serious problem, and this probably has made it easier for senior group leaders to appear before the public as spokespersons for a seemingly unified view on policy options.

By each of the five criteria mentioned, then—size, wealth, leadership, legitimacy, and freedom from debilitating factionalism—the leading senior groups measure up quite well, very high indeed on some indexes and at least moderately high on others. Given the fact that senior groups enjoy such a ranking on measures of political potential, why, then, have they wielded only moderate amounts of power and influence in Washington? Insight into this question can be gleaned by comparing NCSC and AARP with three other groups, all of which enjoy undisputed reputations for first-class power status. The Gray Panthers will be dropped from the following analysis because of its lack of any long-term involvement in national lobbying activity.

The groups chosen for comparison are the American Legion and the National Rifle Association (NRA). The American Legion for many years has been the most visible element in that awesome force on Capitol Hill known as the veterans lobby. Equally effective whether the party in power be the Democrats or the Republicans, the legion's legislative prowess has been manifest repeatedly throughout its more than sixty years of existence, including some issues in which the stakes were very high. A recent example of its power was the legion's success in getting the

Democratically controlled House and Senate to override President Carter's veto of the Veterans Administration physicians pay bill in August 1980; this was only the second time in thirty years that a Democratic president had been overridden by a Democratic Congress. Likewise, the National Rifle Association has earned a legendary reputation for political prowess. Few knowledgeable observors would dispute the fact that Harlan Carter, NRA's executive vice-president, is among the most effective lobbyists in Washington, D.C. The American Legion and NRA have been able to capitalize on their political assets and potential. In contrast, senior groups have suffered incapacity in this area because of certain inhibitors. These inhibitors can be observed at two levels: at the mass level (attitudes and behavior of rank-and-file senior group members); and at the elite level (expectations that constrain senior group representatives at the point of direct governmental intervention).

At the mass level, the leaders of any interest group face problems when the rank-and-file members do not fully embrace the political objectives set forth by its leaders and ratified at the organization's national convention. The views espoused by the active minority may not always reflect adquately the thinking of its full membership. Data on the level of rank-and-file support for stands adopted in the name of senior groups is lacking, but there is indirect evidence to support the view that such support is not intense or widespread, save for a few exceptional issues on which internal consensus may be high. This is not to suggest that the rank-and-file members necessarily oppose the stands adopted by the groups; obviously, if this were the case, the groups would become immobilized by internal squabbling and factional strife. The problem, it would seem, is more one of apathy than overt opposition, apathy that arises out of the weakness of group members' attachment to the symbols of agedness. The literature on political socialization indicates that, while socialization is not strictly confined to any age span, and while a certain amount of resocialization can occur in middle or old age, the strongest group attachments and political affects are formed during one's adolescent and early adult years. Most people reach old age with their primary affiliations—to family, ethnic group, neighborhood, church, political party—already firmly fixed. Occasionally, events do occur that intensify older people's attachment to old-age organizations, and when this occurs there may be a dramatic surge of self-consciousness and awareness among senior group rank-and-file members. The mobilization of elderly people in California generated by the Townsend Plan during 1934 and 1935 is a vivid example of such a surge in sentiment. But since primary attachments are formed early in life and affiliation with issues and groups related to old age are mostly overlaid upon these, the surge in senior group sentiment typically is followed by a fading of support, such as occurred in the Townsend Movement beginning as early as 1937. In no way is this meant to suggest that senior citizen groups are wholly lacking in mass-membership support for their stands on public policy. It is, rather, to suggest that support for such stands tends to vary widely, with only occasional positions having intense and widespread internal support. Others tend to be weakly supported, along with low-level attachments to the group itself.

Senior citizens can join an organization of the elderly without necessarily subscribing to its public policy goals or even being aware that the organization takes stands on public issues. It is logical to suppose that many persons—not all—join AARP essentially to avail themselves of the direct private benefits to members and remain relatively indifferent to its stands on public matters. Likewise, it seems plausible that among the three to four million members affiliated with NCSC, many joined for a sense of solidarity and emotional support gained through participating in one of NCSC's local clubs and chapters. Such individuals do not necessarily subscribe to the national officers' highly politicized outlook. In sum, membership in an organization may not signify active support for its national policy objectives. While the same could be said of all voluntary organizations, not merely those composed of seniors, it seems to be more marked among old-age groups. Research by Neal E. Cutler reveals that large numbers of persons who are chronologically in the older age group do not define themselves in this manner, preferring instead such alternative descriptions as "middle-aged," "youthful," or "no age-group identification." Furthermore, according to the national survey data analyzed by Cutler, support for senior group goals tends to increase markedly among the 38 percent of sixty-and-older people who do accept the "old" or "elderly" label. This suggests that subjective acceptance of elderly status is associated with an increase in acceptance of senior group demands and aspirations. If the proportion of such persons were higher among the chronologically old, it is likely that the level of support for senior group political goals also would be greater.[30]

The experience of interest groups with first-rank reputation for political influence reveals a lesser tendency toward abrupt surges in support followed by waning enthusiasm. In part, this is related to the fact that their rank-and-file members became identified with the organization during their period of primary political socialization, in their teens and twenties. The relationship of sports enthusiasts and gun lovers to the NRA and of exservice personnel to the American Legion contains a common element: early socialization into the general ethos of the group and stability of support for the group's general societal objectives, including public policy goals. Again, one should be cautious about overgeneralizing on this point; some members of these groups are probably indifferent to its larger social goals and maintain membership only for the direct benefits involved or the sense of solidarity arising out of face-to-face contacts. But it appears that the rank-and-file members of these organizations feel a greater visceral commitment to the organization than is true of senior groups; for some members of the former it borders on a kind of passion. The intensity with which group goals are embraced is probably related to the tendency in these groups toward internal factional strife. The internal affairs of the National Rifle Association have been particularly subject to such acrimony, involving at one point a revolt resulting in the ouster of some long-time leaders who were believed insufficiently dedicated in their opposition to gun control legislation. Obviously, if such factionalism were to go on uncontrolled over any period of time it could seriously weaken, if not undermine, the NRA's capacity to exert political power. However, up to now at least, factionalism has been sporadic and held within limits.

A tendency toward abrupt surges of support followed by a waning of enthusiasm has been a recurrent theme among old-age movements since the earliest days, this being a trait common to the Townsend Movement of the 1930s, the "Ham and Eggs" movement of the early 1940s, the Colorado-based National Annuity League of the 1940s and early 1950s, and the Medicare crusade of the late 1950s and early 1960s. Admittedly, there is some tendency among public interest groups of all kinds for mass enthusiasm to ebb and flow. For example, surges are apparent in the experience of several movements of the present-day and recent-past feminists, environmentalists, peace advocates, and so forth. And, although there is no hard evidence, it appears that this tendency has been less pronounced among such groups than with senior citizens. The fact that one cannot pick up a book or article on old-age political activism without having a surge and decline dimension brought to the fore suggests that, while not different in kind, there is at least a difference in degree in this area between senior citizen movements and ones composed of nonseniors.

Shifting from the mass level to the elite level, the next section will discuss other possible factors contributing to power differentials between the two senior groups and the American Legion and NRA. Data on membership size and wealth show that the four groups all have certain commonalities. As seen in table 7.1, all have large memberships, with even the smallest having no less than 1.8 million people. If anything, the membership advantage goes to the senior groups. There is no direct measure of group wealth—interest group executives are wary of providing this information—but the size of the professional staff is a reasonably sound indirect measure. Here considerable variation emerges, with NRTA/AARP exceeding all other groups by a wide margin. However, this disparity seems less significant in political terms when one notes that the resources devoted by each group to national-level lobbying are of roughly equal magnitude. The comparatively low figures reported for the American Legion and NCSC probably underestimate the actual strength of their lobbying capacity; both are highly politicized organizations that can draw on almost any executive in the national headquarters, even those who are not viewed as lobbyists. The data on congressional appearances can serve as a rough measure of the intensity of the group's interest in national government and public policy. The underlying premise is that groups that are intensely concerned with public policy will appear more frequently before congressional committees and subcommittees. As revealed by the table, there is no great variation among the five groups on this measure; all range between twenty and forty appearances before various congressional bodies during a typical session, a figure reflective of fairly intense legislative involvement in all cases.

Table 7.1
Group Membership, Lobbying Resources, and Lobby Activity

Group	Total Membership (millions)	Washington Staff[a]	National Lobbying Staff[b]	Congressional Appearances[c]
American Legion	2.7	32	3[d]	35
National Rifle Association	1.8	52	5	40
American Association of Retired Persons/ National Retired Teachers Association	12.5	380–400	9	35–40
National Council of Senior Citizens	3–4[e]	18	4	20–30

SOURCE: Compiled by the author.

[a]Includes managerial and professional staff employed in Washington office.

[b]Includes staff employed full time in national lobbying only.

[c]Number of times testifying before congressional committees in a typical session (average of recent years).

[d]Includes full-time registered lobbyists; excludes several support personnel.

[e]4,000 local clubs.

The groups do diverge markedly in the scope of their legislative concern. Interviews were conducted in the fall of 1980 with the chief lobbyist for each of the five groups considered here. Interviewees were all asked to go through the *Congressional Staff Directory* of regular House and Senate committees and subcommittees and identify those which their group is "fairly consistently interested in." The results, summarized in table 7.2, reveal that the five groups fall roughly into two categories. The American Legion and National Rifle Association both had quite short lists—an indication that their range of normal legislative concerns is narrow and sharply focused. A lobbyist for a group such as this concentrates his or her energies on the few committees and subcommittees involved in its specific interests and pays little attention to the great bulk of lawmakers in Congress. The two other groups are not so fortunate. NRTA/AARP and NCSC both cover a wide sweep of the congressional landscape, amounting in the extreme case of AARP to essentially all of the Capitol Hill committees except for those involved in foreign affairs and national defense. Concentration of lobbying energies under such circumstances is normally not possible for old-age groups, except occasionally when an overriding issue presents itself to which all other lobbying activity can be subordinated.

An even more clear-cut line of demarcation emerged when the lobbyists were questioned about the degree to which their friends on Capitol Hill dominate committees and subcommittees of key concern to the group. Informants were asked to designate one or more committees or subcommittees in either house of Congress which the respondent regarded as crucial to his or her group and to select members of each regarded as "friends" or "nonfriends." The term *nonfriends* was used in preference to *enemies* or *foes* so as to avoid the possible confusion presented by lawmakers who could be designated as "neutrals." For the purposes at hand, such a twofold designation seemed preferable to using three or more categories. Table 7.3 reveals the marked disparity existing between the two senior groups on the one hand and the two comparison groups on the other. The American Legion and NRA appear to face an overwhelmingly "friendly" atmosphere in the committees that those groups have identified as organizationally crucial. This signifies not only support on the committee itself but also support on the floor of the House or Senate when a key bill reaches that stage. In contrast, senior citizen lobbyists report that they can count on only about half of the members, at best, on their key committees. This is true, furthermore, even though those lawmakers in the "nonfriends" category in all cases, probably, would verbalize a deep commitment to the needs and well-being of senior citizens.

This raises the obvious question of whether the balance of committee forces favoring the legion and NRA results from their screening out, or perhaps even defeating at the polls, potential "nonfriends" and at the same time rewarding "friendly" members through electoral support. Although our data here do not permit an answer to this question, it can be presumed that the high levels of committee support for these groups is more than mere happenstance.

The spokespersons for senior citizens groups are attempting to represent both their own dues-paying members and a particular group in the U.S. population, many of whom may not be members. In both senses it is

Table 7.2
Congressional Committees of High Interest

Group	House	Senate	Total Number of Committees (Subcommittees)
American Legion	Veterans Affairs Appropriations (2)* Small Business	Veterans Affairs Armed Services	5 (2)
National Rifle Association	Appropriations (2)* Armed Services Governmental Operations (1) Interior and Insular Affairs (2) Judiciary (3) Merchant Marine and Fisheries (2) Rules	Appropriations (3) Armed Services Energy and Natural Resources (1) Governmental Affairs Judiciary (2)	12 (16)
National Council of Senior Citizens	Agriculture (2)* Appropriations (6) Banking, Finance and Urban Affairs (6) Budget Education and Labor (3) Interstate and Foreign Commerce (2) Judiciary (6) Post Office and Civil Service (2) Public Works and Transportation (1) Rules Ways and Means (5) Select Committee on Aging (4)	Appropriations (3)* Banking, Housing and Urban Affairs (4) Budget Energy and Natural Resources (1) Finance (4) Governmental Affairs (2) Judiciary (3) Labor and Human Resources (5) Special Committee on Aging Veterans Affairs	22 (59)

American Association of Retired Persons/ National Retired Teachers Association		31 (36)
	Agriculture Appropriations (4)*	Agriculture (2)
	Appropriations (4)*	Appropriations
	Banking, Finance and Urban Affairs (1)	Banking, Housing and Urban Affairs
	Budget	Budget
	Economic Stabilization (1)	Commerce, Science and Transportation
	Education and Labor (3)	Energy and Natural Resources (1)
	Consumer Protection (3)	Finance (2)
	Government Operations (2)	Governmental Affairs
	Interior (1)	Judiciary
	Interstate and Foreign Commerce (1)	Labor and Human Resources (3)
	Judiciary (1)	Small Business
	Post Office and Civil Service (4)	Veterans Affairs
	Public Works and Transportation (1)	Special Committee on Aging
	Rules	
	Small Business	
	Ways and Means (2)	
	Veterans Affairs	
	Select Committee on Aging (4)	

SOURCE: Compiled by the author.

Note: Asterisks indicate "high interest" subcommittees.

Table 7.3
Lobbyists' Perception of Balance of Forces—"Friendly" and "Nonfriendly"—on Senate and House Committees Considered of Key Importance to Group Members

Group	Key Committees	Balance of Forces on the Committee
American Legion	Veterans Affairs (House and Senate)	All members "friendly."
	Armed Services (House and Senate)	All members "friendly."
National Rifle Association	House Judiciary (full committee)	Solid majority "friendly" to the "gun" position.
	House Judiciary, Subcommittee on Crime	Except for subcommittee chair (Rep. John Conyers) all nine members "friendly."
National Council of Senior Citizens	House Ways and Means	"Not a lot of residual strength there for us and it's gotten worse over time." At most 18 "friends" out of 36 total.
American Association of Retired Persons/ National Retired Teachers Association	House Ways and Means House Education and Labor	"In both cases it's about the the same. On any given issue you can generally count on about half being with you."

SOURCE: Compiled by the author.

a difficult task considering that the structure of national government tends more to frustrate than to facilitate political interventions on behalf of elderly people, or indeed any aggregate of the U.S. population. With only a few exceptions, the federal government is not set up on a categorical group basis. Instead, it tends to be structured on the basis of major purpose or function. This was not always the case, of course. From the middle nineteenth to the early twentieth centuries, several cabinet departments were set up on an essentially categorical group or clientele basis. The Interior Department represented a concession to cattlemen and ranchers in the West; Agriculture was designed to cater to the interests of farmers. Commerce was set up at the behest of business, and the Labor Department involved an accommodation to organized labor. Beginning in the middle part of the present century, however, there was a marked trend away from this pattern, both in theory and in practice. The 1949 Report of the Commission on Organization of the Executive Branch of Government (First Hoover Commission)—since accepted as the bible of government reorganization—affirmed the urgency of "Placing related functions cheek by jowl." In part, this proposal was justified on the basis of eliminating overlaps between agencies and of reducing costs. But the commission insisted that more than this was involved: "of even greater importance *coordinated policies can be developed*"[31] (emphasis added). In the words of a perceptive student of governmental reorganizations, Lester M. Saloman, the view that government should be organized on the basis of major purpose came to be accepted as an article of faith. It had a political, not merely an administrative, logic to command it:

Organizing for effectiveness [by grouping programs by major purpose] means arranging the operating units of government in such a way as to achieve enough balance and diversity in the political forces surrounding the major points of decision to permit broad national interests to hold their own against the more narrow, parochial interests embodied in particular programs.[32]

Those officials involved in arranging reorganizations found the logic of this compelling, so much so that in the three and a half decades since the First Hoover Commission was appointed (1947) almost all restructuring of the federal bureaucracy has been on the basis of major purpose. For example, of the six new cabinets created during the period 1947–80— namely, Defense; Health, Education, and Welfare (recast as Health and Human Services in 1980); Housing and Urban Development; Transportation; Energy; and Education—all were of this type. Very frequently, moreover, the bureaus and agencies that were merged so as to create these large, new bureaucracies, and thus suffered a loss in status, were of the clientele variety. For example, when HEW was created in 1953, its component parts included, among others, the old Office of Education, whose clients consisted of organized educators and classroom teachers, the Federal Security Agency, Social Security and public welfare recipients, and the Childrens Bureau, children. While the major-purpose form did not wholly sever the preexisting ties between agency and clientele group, it did force the various clienteles represented in the merger to compete directly against one another and thereby prevented any one of them from gaining ascendency over the agency officials.

Only the strongest and most powerfully organized clientele groups in the country have been in a position to resist this bias against clientele-based organization and in favor of organization by major purpose. It is one of the supreme achievements of the veterans lobby, for example, that the Veterans Administration remains an independent agency not submerged within any larger cabinet department. However, this is singularly unusual.

Senior citizen groups, unable to mobilize power sufficient to force presidents and other officials responsible for reorganizations to accept a separate, clientele-based agency to administer federal old-age programs (for example, a Department of Elderly Affairs paralleling the VA), are obliged to confront an executive branch in which such programs are scattered about among more than a score of major purpose departments and agencies. There is no target for them to focus on. Although logical from the standpoint of agency officials, promoting as it does program coordination and freedom from excessive clientele group pressures, from the standpoint of the "gray lobby" the arrangement represents an enduring source of frustration.

The lobbyists for the elderly in Washington did not create the legislative and administrative environment that they are obliged to operate in, and it is a tribute to their skill and tenacity that they have been able to engineer, occasionally, breakthroughs on the age-policy front. As mentioned previously, NCSC appears to have accomplished this on some issues related to income security, and AARP on ones related to the status concerns of its predominantly middle-class constituency. In order to achieve legislative success, old-age groups must transform their memberships' customary apathy toward public policy goals into active commitment. At the elite level the senior groups' usual diffuse interests need to become more sharply focused. In combination, these changes may be sufficient to offset competing priorities that normally occupy the attention of general purpose committees, such as House Ways and Means or Senate Finance, that senior group leaders must deal with on issues of concern to them. There may be a similar effect when the senior groups can succeed in focusing their strength on a single administrative agency in the executive branch. In general, however, the inhibitors at both the mass and elite levels tend to prevent senior groups from fully capitalizing on the political potential inherent in their large memberships and unusual reputations for political legitimacy.

NOTES

1. Arthur Schlesinger, Jr., *The Politics of Upheaval* (Boston: Houghton Mifflin, 1958) p. 40. For Townsend Movement background, see ibid., ch. 3.

2. E. E. Schattschneider, *The Semi-Sovereign People* (New York: Holt, Rinehart and Winston, 1960), pp. 30–36.

3. Frank A. Pinner, Paul Jacobs, and Philip Selznick, *Old Age and Political Behavior: Case Study* (Berkeley: University of California Press, 1959), p. 285, table 4.

4. Raymond Wolfinger and Steven J. Rosenstone, *Who Votes* (New Haven: Yale University Press, 1980), pp. 44–46.

5. Wilbert Andrew Achenbaum, *Old Age in the New Land* (Baltimore: Johns Hopkins University Press, 1978), ch. 6.

6. For full treatment of these events, see Henry J. Pratt, *The Gray Lobby: Politics of Old Age* (Chicago: University of Chicago Press, 1976), ch. 8.

7. Quoted in *AAUP Bulletin* (June 1978): 6.

8. 1971 White House Conference on Aging, *Section Recommendations on Employment and Retirement* (Washington, D.C.: Government Clearing House), pp. 3–4.

9. Laura C. Ford, "The Implications of the Age Discrimination in Employment Act Amendments of 1978 for Colleges and Universities," *Journal of College and University Law* 5 (1978–79): 178.

10. Quoted in Richard Harris, "Annals of Legislation," *New Yorker*, July 16, 1966, p. 51.

11. Pratt, *Gray Lobby*, ch. 11.

12. U.S., Congress, House, Committee on Ways and Means, *Hearings on Hospital, Nursing Home and Surgical Benefits for OASI Beneficiaries, H.R. 4700*, 86th Cong., 1st Sess., July 13–17, 1959, pp. 510–11.

13. "Gray Panthers First Decade," *Gray Panther Network* (July–August 1980): 5; Jo Freeman, *The Politics of the Women's Liberation Movement* (New York: Norton, 1975).

14. Quoted in *Gray Panther Network* (July–August 1979): 4.

15. "Gray Panthers First Decade," pp. 4–5.

16. Ruth H. Jacobs and Beth Hess, "Panther Power: Symbols and Substance," *Long Term Care and Health Services Administration Quarterly* (Fall 1978).

17. Ibid., p. 240.

18. Ibid., pp. 239–40.

19. Ibid. pp. 208–9.

20. Dale Vinyard," Rediscovery of the Aged: Senior Power and Public Policy," *Society* (July–August 1978): 28.

21. Robert A. Hartooyan, "Interest Groups and Aging Policy," in *The Aging in Politics: Process and Policy*, ed. Robert Hudson (Springfield, Ill.: Charles C. Thomas, 1981), p. 80.

22. Theodore R. Marmor, *The Politics of Medicare* (Chicago: Aldine, 1973).

23. Pratt, *Gray Lobby* p. 129.

24. Ibid., chs. 9, 10.

25. For discussion of AARP's involvement, see Pratt, *Gray Lobby*, pp. 148–49.

26. Abraham Holtzman, *The Townsend Movement* (New York: Bookman Associates, 1963), ch. 3.

27. Dale Vinyard, "The Senate Special Committee on the Aging," *Gerontologist* 12, part 1 (Autumn 1972): 300.

28. Pratt, *Gray Lobby*, p. 83.

29. Robert Binstock, "Aging and the Future of American Politics," *Annals of the American Academy of Political and Social Science* 415 (September 1974): 206. Emphasis added.

30. Neal E. Cutler, "Age and Political Behavior," in *Aging: Scientific Perspectives and Social Issues*, ed. Diana S. Woodruff (New York: D. Van Nostrand, 1975), p. 389.

31. U.S. Commission on the Organization of the Executive Branch of Government, *Report on General Management of the Executive Branch* (Washington, D.C.: Government Printing Office, 1949), p. 34.

32. Lester M. Saloman, "The Goals of Reorganization," *Administration and Society* 12 (February 1981): 487.

DALE VINYARD

8

Public Policy and Institutional Politics

In recent decades, as was related in detail in earlier chapters, the national government has made a substantial policy commitment to the elderly. Indeed, one commentator has suggested that "a revolution has occurred" in this area of public policy.[1] One measure of this commitment is that financial outlays for the elderly dwarf social expenditures for other constituents. For example, Michael Harrington has estimated that two-thirds of welfare state expenditures are for the income and medical needs of the elderly.[2]

With the development of new or expanded programs for the elderly, governmental bodies and agencies to implement them have proliferated. Among the earliest was the agency created to administer old-age insurance and other programs under the Social Security Act—originally the Social Security Board, which was eventually reorganized and renamed the Social Security Administration. This unit, which today is part of the Department of Health and Human Services (HHS), is the largest source of public funds for elderly programs, primarily those for income maintenance. The Administration on Aging (AOA), an agency in what is now HHS, was created as part of the Older Americans Act of 1965. AOA has worked to create state and local offices or commissions on the elderly to funnel federal grants. The Older Americans Act also established the Federal Council on Aging, whose members are appointed by the president, to review and evaluate federal policies and to advise the president on matters affecting the elderly. Many federal departments and agencies created offices or advisor positions on policy issues related to the elderly.

The development of special units on the elderly has not been confined to the executive branch. Congress on three occasions has passed laws providing for White House conferences on the elderly. These conferences were convened in 1961, 1971, and 1981. While such conferences are venerable institutions of American government—one of the earliest was on conservation, called by Theodore Roosevelt in 1908—the elderly have been their focus more often than any group except children.[3] Indeed, it appears that a tradition has been established since a White House confer-

ence has been set approximately every ten years to make recommendations and review elderly policies. Although such conferences obviously
perform a number of different functions, which will be discussed in more
detail later in this chapter, one of them is to keep issues affecting the
elderly on the public agenda and to support the enactment and expansion
of age-related policies. Both houses of Congress also have created special
or select committees on the problems of the elderly; the Senate acted first
in 1961, the House followed somewhat later in 1974. These committees
are not legislative and thus lack the authority to report bills to the floor.
Rather they are viewed primarily as study and investigating bodies. In
practice, however, they also act as lobbies for the recommendations they
develop from their deliberations.[4]

Numerous commentators see the existence of such bodies as crucial to
the development and implementation of policy for the elderly. The late
Fred Cottrell distinguished the politics of the elderly before and after the
passage of the Social Security Act of 1935.[5] He regarded that act as a
landmark in the politics of the elderly because prior to that time older
people lacked a bureaucracy both to perform services for them and, more
importantly, to be advocates for their interests. The 1935 act not only set
up a program of old-age and survivors benefits but eventually became the
basis of federal financial support for state and local social services. Cottrell did not view the primary importance of such agencies as the Social
Security Administration in terms of their mandate to carry out prescribed programs but rather in their role as de facto proponents for
program renewal and expansion. Whether seen from a somewhat cynical
perspective as bureaucratic "empire building" or, alternatively, as encouraging greater awareness and knowledge of the needs of a particular
clientele, agency advocacy efforts are almost inevitable. However, in the
case of the elderly, the argument is often made that they are in particular
need of such advocates because older people tend to be powerless and
unaware of their interests and how to defend them. This rationale for
bureaucratic advocacy on behalf of the elderly is, of course, debatable.

There is, however, a strong advocacy theme in the pronouncements of
many of the governmental bodies for the aging. For example, a recent
congressional evaluation of AOA concluded that the latter should not be
just another government bureau. The report argued that AOA should
have broad authority to inspire and promote new and meaningful programs for the benefit of the elderly as well as to coordinate existing
programs aimed at providing the elderly with a better life.[6] Similarly, the
charge to the Federal Council on the Aging, initially enacted under the
1973 amendments to the Older Americans Act, has been to serve as a
spokesperson on behalf of older Americans and to inform the public
about their problems.

Social welfare and professional organizations also have been instru-
mental in encouraging the maintenance and expansion of special govern-

mental agencies and programs for the elderly. Such groups often function as allies for relevant agencies in a kind of symbiotic relationship. As one commentator has noted, the definition of client needs and the establishment and location of services tend to be determined by the relative power of competing professional groups or established agencies.[7] This phenomenon has been described by Daniel P. Moynihan as the "professionalization of reform."[8] He argues that the chief pressures for new or revised social policies now come predominantly from organized professional interests (governmental and nongovernmental) that are affected by them. In emphasizing the importance of professionals in promoting legislative and administrative reform, Moynihan contends that social change today lacks the mass political support or intellectual leadership prevalent during the 1930s.

A trend toward "professionalism" is evident in the aging field. A growing elderly population, along with expanding programs, services, and administrative structures created to meet their needs, has fostered a new field of professionals—the gerontologists. Based in universities, foundations, research institutes, and social welfare agencies, gerontologists are drawn from a variety of backgrounds. They include social scientists, social workers, physicians, nurses, psychologists, and others who are bound together by an interest in the elderly. In recent years, such individuals have played a prominent role in supplying technical information to policymakers as well as in generating new ideas and proposals. They also have attempted to heighten the visibility and public awareness of the elderly and to mobilize popular and political support for them. For example, a substantial number of witnesses before the House and Senate special committees on the aging tend to be gerontologists. They have been prominent on the staffs of and as delegates to the White House Conferences on the Aging. Many are affiliated with the Gerontological Society of America or other professional associations such as the National Council on the Aging (NCOA). The latter, which includes health, social work, and community action agencies as well as individuals, has served as a technical consultant to organizations and governmental bodies with concerns in the aging field.

Scholarly studies tend to emphasize the dominating role professional gerontologists have played over public policy decisions affecting the elderly. In her award-winning book on Social Security, Martha Derthick shows how policymaking in this area has been dominated, until recently, by a small group of specialists. Policy was set by a relatively constricted group, the program executives, who had a strong proprietary concern for the program and a high level of consensus on guiding principles. As Derthick puts it, "Initiatives and choices generally followed paths well defined by programmatic doctrines and were treated as if they were technical matters. Major alternatives were hardly considered. The dominant mode was maintenance and enlargement of the program."[9]

Robert Hudson notes that the campaign for social services for the segment of the population aged sixty-five and older, which began in the 1950s, was led by professionals in the field of aging.[10] Moreover, Carroll L. Estes argues that the act reflected "the growing visibility of interest groups for the elderly and the awakening of academic, recreational, and social work professionals to a new field of work."[11]

The influence of professionals over policy decisions, however, can be a mixed blessing; there is an ever-present danger that their prescriptions will advance their own needs and interests rather than those of the elderly. One of the most biting indictments of professionals in the aging field comes from Maggie E. Kuhn, national convenor of the Gray Panthers. She contends that:

The government-funded service delivery system to old people has been designed in such a way as to foster ... a self-perpetuating service delivery network. ... Since the service system exists at the behest of the providers of the services, rather than the consumer, it is not surprising that it serves primarily the needs of practicing gerontologists and only secondarily those of older people.[12]

Several studies that have found sharp differences between professionals and their clientele as to the types of services preferred corroborate Kuhn's observation. For example, Mark Riesenfeld and his associates found that, while agency personnel choose site-based facilities for meeting older people's needs, the elderly themselves would rather have services such as special bus routes or reduced transportation costs.[13] Although the body of literature on this topic is limited, it does suggest divergence of interest between professionals in the field and older people.[14]

Some commentators have suggested that a "policy system," or subgovernment, has emerged in the area of aging policy.[15] That is, public policy is formulated, adopted, and implemented by those groups most immediately concerned with and affected by age-related issues. Largely ignoring institutional boundaries between the legislature and the executive and the distinction between public and private bodies, such a system generally includes key members of relevant congressional committees and their staff, administrative officials, and representatives of interest groups. Among such participants there may well be "almost continuous interchange from the first glimmer of an idea to compromises in conference and to administration of the act."[16]

Examples of "policy systems" in education, aeronautics, and agriculture, respectively, are: the Department of Education, the House and Senate committees dealing with education, and the major educational associations; the National Aeronautics and Space Administration, the space committees of both chambers, and the aerospace contractors; and the Department of Agriculture (especially its various commodity bureaus), the relevant congressional committees, and major commodity groups. Despite the significance of these subsystems, there is a paucity of studies on them. Scholars have preferred to focus on one set of participants, such as administrative agencies, rather than on the full range of actors or the interrelationships among them.

It appears that the aging subsystem plays an influential, often decisive role in policymaking. One component of that system consists of interest groups, including both age-based organizations and professional associations. Age-based interest groups were somewhat late to develop but nevertheless have acquired a degree of public legitimacy and access to public officials that makes them an important part of the aging policy system. Service providers in both the public and private sectors are also influential components, bringing their expertise and self-interest to the policymaking process. Other participants in the aging subsystem are the large number of government agencies and offices that have been created to carry out programs for the elderly. Reflecting the fragmented character of policy in this broad issue area, such units frequently have their own particular interests and goals to pursue and pressures to respond to. Finally, Congress plays a crucial role in the development of aging policies and programs, primarily at the committee and subcommittee levels. Indeed, the special or select congressional committees on aging in both chambers are important parts of the subsystem. Despite the relatively recent origin of the aging policy system, its various elements tend to function successfully in an interrelated fashion.

It is also clear that governmental programs designed to affect the elderly are wide in scope, thus posing some difficulties for the subsystem. One recent inventory suggests that there are more than eighty federal programs that directly or indirectly benefit the elderly.[17] The House select committee on the elderly identified forty-seven major ones.[18] One might distinguish between programs for which the elderly qualify because of their age (Social Security, Medicare) and programs in which eligibility is based on other factors such as income level (food stamps, Medicaid). However classified, there is considerable diversity, fragmentation, and specialization. The programs under the Department of Health and Human Services are the most important because of the amount of money expended and the number of recipients involved. Old-age and Survivors Insurance, Supplementary Security Income, Medicare, Medicaid, and the Administration on Aging's programs are located here. Programs under the purview of other departments range from food stamps and low-income housing to veterans' benefits and energy assistance.

As a result of this diversity and fragmentation, specialization within the aging subsystem has emerged. In fact, Frederick Eisele has suggested that there may be at least three aging subsystems, rather than one.[19] Eisele delineates the three subsystems as income maintenance (the first, and in some ways the most important one to develop), health care, and social services. Other researchers point to additional ones such as housing and employment.[20] Although each functions independently, with its own interest groups, agencies, and congressional committees, the subsystems frequently overlap.

Given the importance of the aging policy system for understanding the politics of old age, the following sections will analyze its major components in depth. Since interest groups in the aging field are analyzed elsewhere in this volume, this chapter will concentrate on the congressional and legislative parts of the aging subsystem.

CONGRESS AND THE ELDERLY

Over the past several decades, Congress has been central to the initiation and improvement of aging programs. In the past, increases in Social Security benefits have been readily and overwhelmingly adopted, with increases in election years and payroll tax increases generally effective the following year.[21] Impetus for the Older Americans Act also came from within Congress rather than from the executive branch. In addition, Congress authorized the calling of three White House conferences on the elderly. Although some of this activity is primarily symbolic—designed to reassure the elderly as to their place and standing in American society without providing tangible benefits—an array of programs that provide concrete benefits to some of the elderly has been enacted.

Congressional activity on behalf of the elderly can be explained in part by what has been referred to as "their singular legitimacy as a policy constituency and their political utility to other actors in the policy process."[22] By and large, the elderly have public approval. In opinion polls, programs of aid to the elderly receive high levels of approval, in some cases, virtually unqualified approval.[23] Indeed, programs aiding the elderly have higher approval rating than programs for any other group.[24] Fay Lomax Cook, in a recent study, found strong support for governmental programs that distribute benefits to the elderly as compared with similar programs for other age groups.[25] Although in recent years there is some evidence of a backlash against the elderly—concern about and negative reactions to the size, cost, and range of aging programs—the elderly still command substantial public support.[26]

Older people's legitimacy as a policy constituency, to use Hudson's phrase, makes them especially useful to elected representatives. In his study of congressional behavior, David Mayhew outlined three types of activities engaged in by congressmen seeking reelection, all of which are relevant to the elderly: advertising, credit claiming, and position taking.[27]

Mayhew defines advertising as any effort to disseminate one's name among voters so as to create a favorable image, even if messages are devoid of issue content. He argues that in the second type of activity, credit claiming, a member of Congress seeks personal recognition for congressional enactments. Such activities may provide particularized benefits to an individual group or geographical area or nonparticularized benefits such as passage of a major piece of legislation. According to Mayhew, when a congressman engages in position taking he or she attempts to declare positions or attitudes publicly. Since the elderly have substantial public legitimacy, programs and activities aimed at this group tend to elicit favorable responses from all sectors of society. As one observer noted, "Once upon a time, politicians kissed babies for votes, but these days they're more prone to jolly up senior citizens at retirement homes and gatherings for the aging."[28] Moreover, the variety and size of governmental programs for the elderly have provided innumerable opportunities for congressmen to take personal credit for services and benefits accruing to older people. Finally, most congressmen want to be viewed as supportive of public programs for the elderly. For example, Social Security appears to be the type of policy that is accepted and valued by large numbers of voters and with which all parties, officeholders, and candidates try to identify themselves. Programs such as the Older Americans Act and Medicare generally attract little opposition because they are viewed as having a high degree of legitimacy.

Furthermore, programs for the aged tend to be distributive rather than redistributive. Robert Binstock has suggested that congressmen prefer to treat aging policy as distributive politics (with no apparent losers) so as to avoid a reallocation of power and resources. Although redistributive programs would be more beneficial for the most needy among the elderly, they also generate controversy, thus increasing the political costs of such actions.[29] Consequently, across the board, Social Security benefit increases are more popular with congressmen than pension improvements focused exclusively on the elderly poor. Distributive policies also are popular among the middle-class age-based interest groups, professionals, and agencies comprising the aging subsystem.

Despite the prevalence of political support for old-age distributive programs, advocates for the elderly face a fragmented, decentralized policy structure in Congress. For example, the House Ways and Means Committee and the Senate Finance Committee are both responsible for program initiatives related to Social Security, whereas Education and Labor in the House, and Labor and Human Resources in the Senate affect the Older Americans Act, pension plans, and age discrimination in employment. Furthermore, priorities and goals set by substantive committees can be altered considerably by the appropriation committees and their subcommittees in both chambers. Consequently, proponents of aging programs are forced to watch over a fairly diverse legislative terrain. Just as important, committees such as Ways and Means have a variety of interests to serve and numerous priorities to meet. None of the legislative committees focuses exclusively on the needs of the elderly. Indeed, old-age policies and programs often are peripheral to the primary concerns of a committee. Although aging groups usually do not have to overcome strong opposition to programs for the elderly, they do have to compete with other, often powerful interest groups seeking attention and benefits from congressional committees on their own behalf.

As noted earlier, only the Special Committee on Aging in the Senate and the Select Committee on Aging in the House are concerned primarily with issues related to the elderly. Although they have a wide mandate and can move beyond narrow, jurisdictional boundaries in exploring overall problems of old age, these committees lack authority to report bills directly to the floor. However, as a result of other roles they play, the special aging committees have been effective vehicles for publicizing the social ills experienced by the elderly and for providing old-age interest groups with direct access to the political process. In particular, their functions include (1) symbolic recognition of older people's needs; (2) public forums for addressing their problems; (3) legislative catalysts; and (4) monitors of executive agencies implementing aging programs.

In a number of interviews with congressional representatives conducted by this author, respondents suggested that the primary role of the aging committee is symbolic: legislative recognition of and concern for the elderly. Some comments are illustrative: "Everybody is for the old folks." "The senior citizens must be accorded recognition just as have the farmers, the veterans, the laboring men." "There are a lot of old folks and they, unlike the young, vote." Moreover, although special or select committees tend to be short-lived, the aging committees have become permanent structures of Congress. According to several respondents, the durability of the committees is due to their symbolic function. As one senator put it: "Who wants to be put in the position of opposing the elderly?" However, support for the existence of these two committees is not necessarily based on any consensus as to what problems the elderly face or what are viable solutions to their problems. Rather the emphasis is on offering verbal assurances and recognition to the aged, and their interest groups, as to their continuing importance in American life.

As study and investigatory bodies, the special aging committees also provide forums for groups and individuals interested in aging issues. They tend to be useful vehicles for age-based groups since committee hearings attract media coverage. They also provide opportunities to introduce material and recommendations before generally sympathetic legislators.

The aging committees have had fairly close relationships with the major age-based interest groups. For example, the Select Committee on

Aging in the House has held hearings in conjunction with conferences sponsored by the National Council of Senior Citizens and the National Council on Aging. In addition, the aging committees have provided numerous opportunities for professional gerontologists to express their views, supply technical information, provide legislative proposals, and evaluate ongoing programs. Both committees have worked closely with such individuals, who have comprised a large percentage of the witnesses at their public hearings.

The aging committees also are vehicles or forums for the committee members themselves. For most, membership alone on such a committee is enough to convey a representative's concern with the elderly. Where membership is for symbolic reasons, legislators usually do not have extensive involvement in committee activities, although they may take advantage of opportunities to receive publicity through field hearings in their state or district. On the other hand, for those who have become deeply immersed, membership can become a vehicle for developing policy expertise and public recognition such as that achieved by the late Patrick McNamara of Michigan and the current House chair, Claude Pepper of Florida. These policy entrepreneurs can command attention and influence as well as help set the legislative agenda on aging issues. Furthermore, the inactivity of most members of the aging committees allows activists considerable autonomy in pursuing their interests in the directions they prefer.

A third function of the special aging committees has been to act as legislative catalysts. Although they were not given authority to report bills directly to the floor, these committees do attempt to influence legislation. This has taken several forms: as initiators of new legislation; as watchdogs over legislative changes that affect the elderly; and as internal lobbyists for older people overall. The aging committees outline dimensions of problems, analyze solutions in depth, and recommend priorities for action. But they still must persuade relevant legislative committees to act favorably on any proposals they suggest.

The Older Americans Act (OAA) of 1965 illustrates how the special aging committees can affect legislation through their role as catalysts. The Senate Special Committee on Aging not only originally proposed OAA but also successfully pushed and prodded it through the congressional maze. Moreover, on several occasions, as during consideration of amendments to the Older Americans Act in 1968, the aging committee did most of the staff work for the Senate Labor and Public Welfare Committee.

Perhaps of greater significance has been the aging committees' efforts to ensure that legislation in a wide variety of areas, regardless of origin, does not neglect the interests of the elderly. Thus, in areas such as poverty, taxation, housing, and employment, the aging committees have supported amendments that specify that the elderly should receive a share of program benefits or that add provisions geared to their specific needs.

Another aspect of the catalyst role, that of internal lobbyists, is illustrated by efforts of the House Select Committee on Aging to eliminate mandatory retirement. Although the idea did not originate with the committee—elimination of mandatory retirement had been in the legislative hopper for years—the aging committee played an important role in maintaining the momentum of the legislative campaign from 1976 to 1978. Claude Pepper introduced a number of the diverse bills on the topic and throughout the campaign he played a prominent role. In addition to holding extensive hearings in Washington and in the field, members of the select committee testified, sometimes as a group, before relevant legislative committees, including Education, Labor, and Post Office and Civil Service committees. During the floor debate on the issue, members of the aging committee took an active part, especially Pepper. When the Senate and the House passed different versions of the bill, Pepper was named as a house conferee, although he was not a member of the relevant legislative committee. Indeed, the supportive role of Pepper and other members of the Select Committee on Aging was specifically recorded in the Congressional Record by the chairman of the Education and Labor Subcommittee.[30]

The role of the Senate Special Committee on Aging as a lobbyist was evident during the struggle over Medicare in the 1960s. Numerous commentators have suggested that the principal reason for the creation of the Senate committee itself was to help secure passage of Medicare. Although the committee's attention was never completely monopolized by the Medicare issue, it was its primary concern. Most members of the aging committee and its staff regarded health care as the most pressing problem of the elderly. Their particular target was the Kerr-Mills Act (state assistance under a federal grant-in-aid for health services for the indigent population), arguing that the Social Security approach would best meet the medical needs of the elderly. In 1963, an opponent of Medicare, George Smathers of Florida, became chairman of the Special Committee on Aging. However, committee members created a subcommittee under their former chairman, which continued to lobby for Medicare with its own funds and staff. The final enactment of Medicare in 1965 (P. L. 89-97) did not end the interest of Senate committee members in the program. On subsequent occasions it successfully recommended corrective amendments such as those related to nursing home standards.

It is evident that the aging committees, despite their lack of formal legislative authority, have attempted in a variety of ways to influence legislation. Assessing the extent of their impact, however, is a difficult task. During the Medicare controversy, for example, the roles of others, such as the president and interest groups (that is, organized labor), were more powerful.[31] For less divisive issues, such as housing and transportation, the aging committees appear to have greater ability to modify and shape programs. The committees also have been most effective when supporting distributive policies ("passing out the goodies") rather than reallocating power and major resources.

In addition to attempting to exert influence over legislation, the aging committees also have paid attention to the way executive departments and agencies administer policy, a role commonly referred to as legislative oversight.[32] But they lack some of the traditional weapons possessed by standing legislative committees to secure compliance with their objectives. Most importantly, the aging committees do not have authority over the statutory and fiscal needs of agencies within their jurisdiction. Moreover, given the number of federal programs affecting the elderly, the magnitude of the legislative oversight function is considerable. Agencies also tend to have diverse priorities and a large number of interests to serve, limiting their responsiveness to the aging committees. Even where special units exist to administer programs for the elderly and where the aging committees have close and continuing relationships with them, such units tend to be peripheral to the larger organization of which they are a part. Consequently, their impact on policymaking may be limited.

On the other hand, given the limited overt opposition to programs for the elderly, the aging committees often can achieve their administrative goals by publicizing ways in which policies and agencies could serve the special needs of the elderly more effectively. Committee members and their staffs, along with representatives of concerned interest groups, also confer informally with agency officials, urging them to pursue particular policies or interpretations of legislative intent. However, where such efforts would adversely affect powerful and entrenched interest groups, the agency is less likely to respond positively to the aging committees.

In sum, although the two aging committees are important cogs in the aging policy system, there are significant limitations on their effectiveness, including those imposed by their own special status. And while the aging committees can make symbolic gestures, such as public hearings, and influence distributive policies, they appear to have insufficient resources for affecting policies that would reallocate power or income to the elderly poor.

THE EXECUTIVE BRANCH AND THE ELDERLY

Proponents of aging programs are confronted by the same fragmentation in the executive branch that they face in Congress. While numerous departments and agencies have programs affecting the elderly, a recent report of the Federal Council on the Aging described them as "a contradictory, overlapping, complex fiefdom of shredded and gapping services, group concerns, and actions."[33] And on another occasion the House aging committee referred to "the chaotic fragmentation in federal programs serving the elderly."[34] Elizabeth Kutza has noted that instead of having an intentional, coherent plan regarding what the federal government should do for older people, national efforts are "a direct and indirect outcome of many different programs.... New programs have developed unsystematically, usually with little regard to programs that already exist."[35]

As was indicated earlier, such programs are carried on by a large number of departments and agencies, and, except for the Department of Health and Human Services, most of them view aging programs as peripheral to their primary missions. In addition, agencies with jurisdiction over programs affecting the elderly tend to have strong ties to more powerful interest groups than age-based ones. The organization of many departments and agencies along functional rather than clientele lines virtually ensures this. Although some aging groups have argued for the establishment of a Department of Elderly Affairs (for example, this was recommended at the 1971 White House Conference on the Aging), such requests have not received a favorable response from political leaders. Furthermore, existing agencies and their cluster of allies tend to protect their respective turfs and thus would be opposed to any new department, which would inevitably entail a loss of programs under their jurisdiction.

The creation of the Administration on Aging (AOA) was one attempt to overcome fragmentation in the area of social services for the elderly. It was also expected to serve a symbolic role, similar to that of the special congressional aging committees. Starting at a relatively modest level—$7.5 million for fiscal 1966—funding for AOA soon reached into the hundreds of millions of dollars. By 1981 it was dispensing over $700 million in grants to state and local agencies on aging, service providers, and professional groups. While the growth of AOA programs is impressive, it is consistent with the overall grants syndrome highly characteristic of federal social policy in the 1960s and 1970s, which Theodore Lowi labeled distributive politics.[36] A variety of actors have worked to increase AOA funding: elected officials seeking constituency support; professionals advancing their own careers; civil servants protecting and strengthening their agencies; and the clients of such programs. Given the retrenchment politics of the 1980s, such growth is unlikely to continue.

To some of the proponents of aging programs, the most important role of AOA was not to distribute grants but rather to oversee, evaluate, and coordinate all federal programs affecting the elderly. However, given the magnitude of the task, compounded by inter- and intradepartmental rivalries, AOA was not in a position to coordinate the large and diverse number of programs. Most importantly, AOA had neither the political power nor the resources to achieve such a goal, and consequently it plays primarily a symbolic role. Some proponents of aging programs argue that AOA's lack of success is due to its organizational position in the overall hierarchy of HHS. It is currently a subunit within the Office of Human Development Services, along with units for children, handicapped, and native Americans. Although age-based groups have lobbied for an independent agency, the evidence suggests that the location of AOA would not enhance considerably its ability to meet the service needs of older people. For one, the assigned task may be impossible; the range of programs for the elderly are not only numerous and diverse but are scattered among various departments and agencies. Furthermore, other groups that benefit from these programs are powerful supporters of the status quo. Indeed, age-based groups tend to devote a disproportionate amount of their energy on AOA, considering its relatively limited impact on the elderly. However, the symbolic benefits for age-based groups and the financial support for professionals in the field have fostered significant interest in and concern over AOA activities by these organizations.

White House conferences represent further attempts to generate programs for the elderly and to encourage their coordination. Although the primary impetus for each of the three official White House conferences on aging came from within Congress, they were convened by the president and organized by the executive branch.

Although White House conferences on various issues are a well-established tradition, their format and objectives may differ. For example, one type is designed primarily as an official sounding board for particular programs or policies. It is characterized by limited advance notices and outside preparation (whatever preparation does take place is largely within the bureaucracy); few, if any, officially sponsored or sanctioned preliminary meetings leading up to the conference; plenary sessions with formal addresses; and little attempt to develop actual recommendations. Examples of this type of conference were those held on health in 1965 and on conservation in 1962. Another format, which might be labeled the grass-roots model and which has predominated in recent years, is characterized by considerable advance preparation involving clientele groups, state and local political leaders, and private citizens; numerous preliminary meetings where issues are developed for the conference; extensive use of subgroups to deal with specialized topics; few plenary sessions; development of concrete conference recommendations; and the establishment of followup or monitoring mechanisms. The three aging conferences held in 1961, 1971, and 1981, as well as those held on the handicapped in 1977 and on children in 1970, have followed this model. Other conferences, such as those held on civil rights in 1966 and on food, nutrition, and health, used this basic model but without a complex pattern of preliminary meetings and initial grass-roots involvement.

The form and frequency of conferences on aging suggest that they perform multiple functions for political leaders, agency personnel, and interest groups. One such function is agenda setting; supporters of aging programs attempt to focus national attention on the problems of old age, mobilize support for placing aging issues on the political agenda, and alter the relative standing of these issues in terms of national priorities. Roger Cobb and Charles Elder note that a distinction can be made between a systemic agenda and an institutional or governmental agenda.[37] The former consists of the full range of problems that are salient to society and that are viewed as legitimate concerns of government. The latter represents particular subjects already scheduled for active consideration by some level or unit of government. White House conferences are only one of the many different routes or combinations of routes that can be utilized to achieve a place on either agenda. Some of the advantages of the White House conferences on aging have been their large size and widespread sponsorship, which attracted national attention and raised the visibility of aging issues. Official conferences also put a stamp of legitimacy on the findings and recommendations of concerned groups. Generally White House conferences also serve as a stimulus to other activities, such as legislative proposals, executive initiatives, interest group mobilization, and litigation in the courts that can solidify the position of the problem on the agenda. The first National Conference on Aging in 1950 was designed primarily to place aging issues on the system agenda by attracting public attention to the elderly. On the other hand, the 1961 and 1971 White House conferences attempted to mobilize support for items already on the government agenda. The one held in 1961 was important in mobilizing support for passage of Medicare, while the 1971 conference helped push expansion of social services for the elderly.

Another function of White House conferences is policy analysis and formulation. Conferences patterned on the grass-roots model are expected to develop recommendations for legislative or administrative action, or both. They attempt to take a "new fresh look" at issues, and to develop "broad innovative" programs. As part of this function, some or all of the following activities may take place: collection and analysis of information; development of alternative courses of action; and endorsement of particular courses of action. In recent years, most conferences have presented a fairly lengthy set of recommendations, a veritable "wish list." According to one compilation, the 1971 White House Conference on the Aging presented 663 recommendations. Even after the elimination of duplicates and those too general or vague to be acted upon, 193 recommendations remained.[38]

Furthermore, conferences increasingly have been concerned with existing governmental programs, primarily due to the vast proliferation of programs during the 1960s requiring review. Thus the concern shifted from an initiation of new programs to the facilitation, expansion, and modification of existing ones. In effect, conferences have become monitors of present policies. Another new development has been the creation of mechanisms to check on whether, or how well, a conference's recommendations are carried out. Implementation of recommendations is a major test of the success of a conference as a policy formulator. A variety and combination of methods have been utilized. The 1971 Conference on the Aging established a postconference board that issued a followup report in 1973. Congressional committees also have been used, including the Senate and House committees on aging.

Another function of White House conferences is pacification; the purpose is to "cool things off" and to "take the heat off" the administration by delaying or avoiding action while appearing to do something. The convening of a conference by the president reassures groups who feel aggrieved or neglected. Rhetorical flourishes and broad nonspecific policy goals at the conference, which are symbolic rather than tangible benefits, tend to predominate at White House conferences. Such an approach may be particularly successful when a conference deals with a broad topic in an area with a weak or nonexistent clientele group. But, as Henry Pratt has pointed out, age-based groups are more powerful in the 1980s than they had been when earlier conferences on aging were held. As a result, this clientele group is no longer content with symbolic rewards and has specific and tangible goals.[39]

Conferences also have latent functions in addition to their manifest or primary ones. Latent functions are those that are either incidental to or unintended consequences of manifest functions. For example, Clark Tibbitts has noted that a number of people who attended White House conferences on the aging as nonspecialists and lay persons later became activists for the elderly. Thus new cadres of workers and leaders were generated.[40] Many delegates also experience a greater awareness of problems such as ageism as a result of the vast outpouring of facts, figures, policy proposals, and alternatives presented at the conferences.

As Elias Cohen has suggested, every White House Conference on Aging "is a different ball game."[41] Although each takes place in its own unique social and political environment, it is possible to offer some general conclusions as to their significance. On the whole, the conferences have not produced new ideas or proposals. Moreover, only modest, incremental gains have been achieved. They have had the most immediate impact when dealing with specific, concrete recommendations such as a fixed amount for increases in funding for social services or higher Social Security payments. They have less impact when they express general philosophical views or recommend solutions for broad problems deeply rooted in the social or economic system. On the other hand, the momentum generated by the conferences has fostered congressional and administrative action on proposals that were already pending; the White House conferences merely provided some modest pressure. Moreover, White House conferences can lead to substantial policy change in the long run. Ideas and policies may be on the agenda for years; conference efforts often are part of a continuing campaign to achieve their realization. Finally, recommendations by a White House Conference on Aging have become a benchmark by which to judge progress in meeting the needs of older people.

To be effective a conference cannot be a one-shot effort. Rather, formal arrangements are needed to follow up on the recommendations. A White House conference also will have a greater chance of success if it is part of an ongoing effort where congressional hearings, presidential commissions, and efforts by interest groups mutually reinforce each other. In addition, any conference operates within the constraints of its particular time. The 1950 aging conference was held when there was little public policy for the aged outside Social Security and when age-based groups were weak or nonexistent; the time was not ripe for political reform. On the other hand, the 1961 conference occurred when an age-related issue, Medicare, was a priority national concern and age-based groups were becoming active. The aged also were increasingly regarded as legitimate and deserving claimants. Many of the same conditions prevailed during the 1971 conference.

The political climate during the 1981 White House Conference on Aging was less supportive of new policies and programs, and a backlash against rising costs for aging programs may prevent actualization of its recommendations. Questions are being raised by political leaders and the general public as to whether a disproportionate share of society's resources is devoted to the elderly. Therefore, the conference participants were forced to defend existing policies and programs rather than to suggest new or expanded initiatives. They also had to establish priorities instead of presenting a long list of demands as well as to focus on specific sectors of the elderly such as the poor, women, minorities, and others who are viewed as "vulnerable."

Finally, the aging conferences have been vehicles for and largely dominated by professionals in the field of gerontology and service providers. Prior to 1981 only a minority of delegates were elderly (age sixty-five and over)—13 percent in 1961 and 35 percent in 1971.[42] On the other hand, the law setting up the 1981 conference required that at least 50 percent of the delegates had to be age fifty-five or over. However, the overall effect of such a change on conference recommendations or their implementation will be difficult to assess.

In addition to AOA and White House conferences, presidential involvement and commitment to the elderly potentially could ameliorate the problem of fragmentation of age-related programs. The president could provide a central focus, as well as considerable clout and resources. But an examination of the record suggests that such involvement and commitment is very intermittent. It also has been confined to a few peak issues such as the drive for passage of Medicare or incremental changes in the Social Security system in order to keep it solvent. Presidential efforts for the elderly tend to be symbolic—speeches or public appearances—and usually do not result in tangible commitments.[43] There is often a gap between presidential rhetoric and performance.[44] Part of the problem is the nature of the modern presidency: the numerous, often conflicting demands he faces and the many departments and agencies reporting to him. The president also is forced to deal with domestic issues that are urgent and compelling or foreign policy. Problems that are viewed by the press or public as "crises," and thus could be politically harmful if not dealt with immediately, are high on a president's priority list.

In conclusion, although the executive branch is not as sympathetic as Congress to the problems of old age, it is an important if not decisive arena. Since Congress provides program administrators with broad grants of discretionary authority and power, implementation of policies is a critical stage in the decision-making process. And here, as in the legislative arena, policies and programs related to aging are highly fragmented. Although AOA, White House conferences, and presidential initiatives potentially could improve the situation, as yet they have had only limited impact.

NOTES

1. James Schulz, "Economics of Old Age," in *Quality of Life*, ed. Leo E. Brown (Acton, Mass.: Publishers Science Group, 1975), p 163.

2. Michael Harrington, "Big Lie About the Sixties," *New Republic*, November 29, 1975, pp. 15–19; see also R. L. Clark and John A. Menefee, "Federal Expenditures for the Elderly," *Gerontologist* 21 (1981): 132–37.

3. Dale Vinyard, "White House Conferences and the Aged," *Social Service Review* 53 (December 1979): 655–71.

4. Dale Vinyard, "The Senate Special Committee on the Aging," *Gerontologist* 12, part 1 (Autumn 1972): 298–303; and "The House Select Committee on the Aging," *Long-Term Care and Health Services Administration Quarterly* 3 (Winter 1979): 317–24.

5. Fred Cottrell, "Government Functions and the Politics of Age," in *Handbook of Social Gerontology*, ed. Clark Tibbetts (Chicago: University of Chicago Press, 1960), pp. 624–65.

6. See U.S., Congress, Senate, Special Committee on the Aging and Subcommittee on Aging of Labor and Public Welfare Committee, "Evaluation of AOA and White House Conferences on the Aging," 92nd Cong., 1st Sess., 1971,. p. 53.

7. Arnold Rose and Warren Peterson, eds., *Older People and Their Social World* (Philadelphia: F. A. Davis, 1965), p. 372.

8. Daniel Moynihan, "Professionalization of Reform," *Public Interest* (Fall 1965): 6-16.

9. Martha Derthick, *Policymaking for Social Security* (Washington, D.C.: Brookings Institution, 1979), p. 7.

10. Carroll L. Estes, *The Aging Enterprise* (San Francisco: Jossey-Bass, 1979), p. 224.

11. Robert Hudson, "Client Politics and Federalism: Case of the Older American Act" (Paper delivered at the Annual Meeting of the American Political Science Association, New Orleans, 1973).

12. Maggie Kuhn, "Open Letter," *Gerontologist* 18 (October 1978):423.

13. Mark J. Riesenfeld, et al., "Perception of Public Service Needs: The Urban Elderly and the Public Agency," *Gerontologist* 12 (Summer 1972): 185-90.

14. Judith Turner, "White House Report: Conference on Elderly Seeks Change in Attitude Toward Elderly," *National Journal*, September 25, 1971, p. 1966; Stephen McConnell, "Income vs. In-Kind Services for Elderly," *Social Service Review* 51 (June 1977): 337-56; also P. L. Kasschau, "The Elderly as Their Planners See Them," *Social Policy* (1976): 13-20.

15. Ralph K. Huitt, "Congress—the Durable Partner," in Elke Frank, ed., *Lawmakers in a Changing World* (Englewood Cliffs, N.J.: Prentice-Hall, 1966), pp. 18-19.

16. Huitt, *"Congress,"* p. 19.

17. Estes, *Aging Enterprise,* p. 116.

18. Estes, *Aging Enterprise,* p. 264; see also Louis Lowy, *Social Policies and Programs on Aging* (Lexington, Mass.: Heath, Lexington Books, 1980); Elizabeth Ann Kutza, *The Benefits of Old Age* (Chicago: University of Chicago Press, 1981).

19. Frederick Eisele, "Policy Strategies for Older Americans," in *Analyzing Poverty Policy*, ed. Dorothy James (Lexington, Mass.: Heath Lexington Books, 1975), pp. 45-51. See Henry J. Pratt, *The Gray Lobby: Politics of Old Age* (Chicago: University of Chicago Press, 1976), ch. 15.

20. Pratt, *Gray Lobby*, pp. 210-11.

21. Edward R. Tufte, *Political Control of the Economy* (Princeton: Princeton University Press, 1978).

22. Robert Hudson, "The 'Graying' of the Federal Budget and Its Consequences for Old-Age Policy," *Gerontologist* 18, part 1 (October 1978): 428.

23. Louis Harris and Associates, Inc., *The Myth and Reality of Aging in America* (Washington, D.C.: National Council on the Aging, 1976).

24. *Fortune*, (October 1977): 214-15.

25. Fay Lamar Cook, *Who Should Be Helped: Public Support for Social Services* (Beverly Hills: Sage, 1979).

26. Pauline Ragan, "Another Look at the Politicizing of Old Age," *Urban and Social Change Review* 10 (1977): 6-13; Robert Samuelson, "Busting the U.S. Budget: The Costs of an Aging America," *National Journal*, February 18, 1978, pp. 256-60.

27. David Mayhew, *Congress: The Electoral Connection* (New Haven: Yale University Press, 1974).

28. Jack Anderson, *Detroit Free Press*, January 26, 1978.

29. Robert Binstock and Martin Levin, "The Political Dilemmas of Intervention Policies," in *Handbook of Aging and the Social Sciences*, ed. Robert H. Binstock and Ethel Shanas (New York: Van Nostrand Reinhold, 1976), pp. 511-35.

30. U.S., Congress, *Congressional Record,* 95th Cong. 2nd Sess., March 21, 1978, H2267.

31. Theodore R. Marmor, *The Politics of Medicare* (Chicago: Aldine, 1973). See also James Sundquist, *Politics and Policy* (Washington, D.C.: Brookings Institution, 1968), ch. 7.

32. Morris S. Ogul, *Congress Oversees the Bureaucracy* (Pittsburgh: University of Pittsburgh Press, 1976).

33. U.S., Department of Health, Education, and Welfare, Federal Council on the Aging, *Public Policy and the Frail Elderly,* December 1978, p. iv.

34. U.S., Congress, House, Select Committee on the Aging, *Hearings, Fragmentation of Services for the Elderly* (Washington, D.C.: Government Printing Office, April 4, 1977), p. 139.

35. Kutza, *Benefits of Old Age*, p. 7.

36. For a critical view of such social policy, see David A. Stockman, "The Social Pork Barrel," *Public Interest* (Spring 1975): 3–30.

37. Roger W. Cobb and Charles D. Elder, *Participation in American Politics: Dynamics of Agenda-Building* (Boston: Allyn and Bacon, 1972).

38. U.S., Congress, House, Select Committee on the Aging, *Impact of 1971 White House Conference on the Aging Recommendations, Hearings,* 94th Cong., 2nd Sess., 1976, p. 18.

39. Henry Pratt, "Symbolic Politics and White House Conferences on the Elderly," *Society* (July–August 1978): 67–72.

40. Personal communication, November 1978. He has been for many years one of the foremost analysts in social gerontology.

41. Elias Cohen, "White House Conference on the Aging: Will It Fail?" *Aging and Human Development* 1 (1970): 51–54.

42. See figures cited in Vinyard, "White House Conferences and the Aged," pp. 633–65.

43. Unpublished paper by the author, "Political Rhetoric and the Elderly," that deals with such gestures, available from him.

44. Pratt, *Gray Lobby*, pp. 180–81. He contrasts the words of Richard Nixon at the 1971 White House conference with his policy action little over a year later that elderly groups saw as undoing some of their programs.

DAVID K. BROWN

9

Administering Aging
Programs in a Federal System

Aging and human services programming in the United States, and the
values implicit within them, predominantly reflect the political administrative characteristics inherent in the federal system. From an administrative perspective, federalism may be defined as a geoadministrative
design featuring decentralization of levels of government, circumscribed
and fixed boundaries and jurisdictions, and political prerogatives of
authoritative decision making that are fragmented among these jurisdictions. Of necessity, the level from which bureaucrats and administrators
view their roles and prerogatives in program development and policy
implementation is colored by their position in the federal system, be it
national, state, or local.

From an administrative point of view, the wide dispersal and fragmentation of power and authority in the federal system bears upon agencies
charged with the implementation of programs and services for older
adults, with the result that they are seldom given sufficient power and
authority to carry out their mandates. As Carroll Estes has stridently
pointed out, such existing power and institutional arrangements prohibit
legislative mandates such as the Older American's Act from solving the
problems of the aged, since they are seldom realistically confronted.[1]
From another perspective, Henry Pratt studied age-based interest
groups that comprise the "senior movement" and attributes their early
ineffectiveness in influencing legislative aspects of the Older American's Act to the lact of coherent and integrated policy and program
goals.[2]

Any discussion of the administration of aging programs in the United
States has to consider at the outset the ordering mechanisms and value
assumptions of the federal system in which administrative units are
imbedded. Decentralization, jurisdictional sprawl, fragmentation of
power, and the purposive avoidance of the concentration of authority—
especially within implementing agencies—are all aspects of the federal
system that have a critical impact upon program administration.

AGING THEORY AND ADMINISTRATIVE PREMISES

The major theories in social gerontology are rooted in the micro assumption that an aging individual or cohort is the basic unit of analysis. Such theories are reductionist in the sense that they purport to explain the aging process in isolation from the impact of social institutions on aging. Incipient in these theories is the further assumption that aging is exclusively a biological, psychological, or sociological phenomenon for which, in the latter case especially, the onus of preserving and maintaining life-satisfying roles and status is upon the individual and not the social system. Little attention is paid to why and how sociopolitical institutions and the administrative structures that sustain them contribute to the displacement and dislocation of individuals from previously held roles of status and prestige as they grow older. Even less attention is given to the steady erosion of elderly status in societies experiencing rapid social change and political and economic modernization.[3]

For example, disengagement theory holds that aging individuals gradually separate themselves from former roles, thus reducing their level of social interaction, and that such rites of passage are necessary and functional for the equilibrium of the social system.[4] By such disengagement, sociopolitical and economic roles are left for younger members who have a longer life-span contribution to make to society.

On the other hand, activity theory holds that successful aging is dependent upon the maintenance of activity patterns established in the younger years. The assumption behind the activity approach is that older individuals choose either to remain active or to decline into inactivity.[5]

To perpetuate the ongoing debate among social gerontologists as to the relative merits of disengagement and activity theory is beyond the scope of this essay. The central issue here is that the maintenance of social equilibrium is a given under these positions. Such "victim-blaming" approaches require that full accommodation and compromise be made by aging individuals and not by the social system that conditions and shapes values, attitudes, and role structures for the entire human group.[6]

Moreover, from an administrative point of view, such theories shape the way in which aging policy is interpreted, managed, and implemented. For example, Estes has pointed out that the pervasive ideology in America toward the aged segments them from the rest of society and legitimates an emphasis on particularistic services.[7] One consequence is that service providers, planners, and suppliers tend to reify the isolation of the elderly in order to justify their own service market or program existence, spawning an aging administrative and service industry—the "aging enterprise." Estes further asserts that the service and administrative strategy of the Older Americans Act itself establishes a network of segmented services and organizational mandates couched in euphemisms such as coordination, pooling, and advocacy. The responsibility for implementing the latter, which falls to the Area Agencies on Aging (AAA), requires considerable political skill across a broad range of complex sociopolitical institutions within the local community. Even if expertise were available to meet this administrative responsibility, AAAs would not have commensurate political authority to do so.[8] The bifurcation of program responsibility and implementing authority, together with age-segmented programming, has been a consistent administrative dilemma throughout all levels of the aging organizational network since its inception.

The roots of the dilemma lie in the nature of the federal system, the prevailing social mythology of aging in the United States, and the administrative ecology and service delivery strategy of aging programs that reflect extant sociopolitical institutional arrangements. The administrative bias inherent in the aging network is keyed to the maintenance and equilibrium of these institutional systems, the acquiescence of the aged to socially determined role assignments, and the bureaucratic solidarity of the existing service system.

THE ADMINISTRATIVE DEVELOPMENT OF THE AGING NETWORK

This section will suggest a number of issue areas and analytical approaches for students concerned with the administrative development of aging programs. Its central focus will be upon the Administration on Aging, state aging commissions, and the area agencies. An ecological approach, which presents environmental–organizational interaction as the major point of attention, will be suggested.

The way in which social welfare programs have evolved in the United States has generated an ongoing administrative dilemma because the United States has never established a nationally integrated administrative system of social service program delivery.[9] The result has been fourfold. First, each new program initiative requires its own unique administrative structure. Second, a premium is put on rapid delivery of services or other tangible and demonstrative projects before a sound management system to accommodate program priorities is established and tested. Third, neophyte social services management systems simultaneously face the dual problems of enhancing rapid service delivery on the one hand and increasing organizational efficiency on the other. At the same time, the efficient exercise of new functions clash with the old traditions of residualism and incrementalism. Fourth, each new program area carries along with it state and local administrative subdivisions that are charged with planning and program implementation responsibilities.

For example, the Federal Appalachian Regional Development Act of 1965 created the local development districts (LDDs) on the multicounty level, which had the responsibility for planning local economic development. In like manner, the National Health Planning and Development Act of 1974 established a network of local health systems agencies, which are to develop plans for health-care systems in their localities and, like the LDDs, coordinate these plans at the state level. LDDs and HSAs perform functions in their respective program areas that are similar to AAA program responsibilities for older people. Such administrative sprawl and overlap have led to a situation where, if one were to impose the boundaries and catchment area of each of these service entities on the map of a given state, it would resemble a plate of spaghetti. The history of the administration development of the Older American's Act manifests a similar tradition.

The term *aging network* is used to connote the totality of agencies, organizations, interest groups, service providers, and mangement and professional staff that is broadly concerned with aging policy, services, and program development. Figure 9.1 depicts the major administrative components of the network, including the Administration on Aging, state aging commissions, and the area agencies. This network includes fifty-seven state units, over six hundred area agencies, and nearly twelve thousand nutrition sites.

The Older American's Act of 1965 created the Administration on Aging (AOA), which is to serve as a national focal point and spotlight for the needs and concerns of the nation's elderly. Among AOA's functions are the distribution of information concerning the nation's elderly, technical assistance, and more effective utilization of available resources on behalf of the elderly. AOA's mandate not only includes the distribution of categorical grants to the states but is to serve as a federal mobilizer of a national effort to address aging problems as well. The act passed with only one negative vote in the entire Congress. A federal commissioner on aging, chosen by the president and serving at his will, provides executive leadership. The Federal Council on Aging serves AOA in an advisory capacity.

All new agencies face the challenge of what Anthony Downs has termed the "initial survival threshold," which can occur even before a new agency emerges as an autonomous entity.[10] To meet this challenge, the neophyte agency has to carve out a clearly defined clientele, maintain clear jurisdiction over a set of functions unqiue to itself, and demonstrate a clear area of competence. By this means, the organization can remove threats to its identity and assert an assured claim to ongoing and sustaining resources. In other words, a new agency must quickly (1) find a market and (2) satisfy its customers. In this way, its "products" come to be valued as socially significant, and the agency's activities are legitimated and socially supported. The extent to which society is willing to bear the costs of keeping that agency functioning is related to how well the agency has successfully surmounted the initial threshold of survival.

Figure 9.1
Major Components of the Aging Network

1. Statutory Mandate
2. Program Priority, Review & Evaluation
3. Statutory Mandate
4. Coordination
5. Planning, Administration and Review
6. Consent-Building
7. Program Review

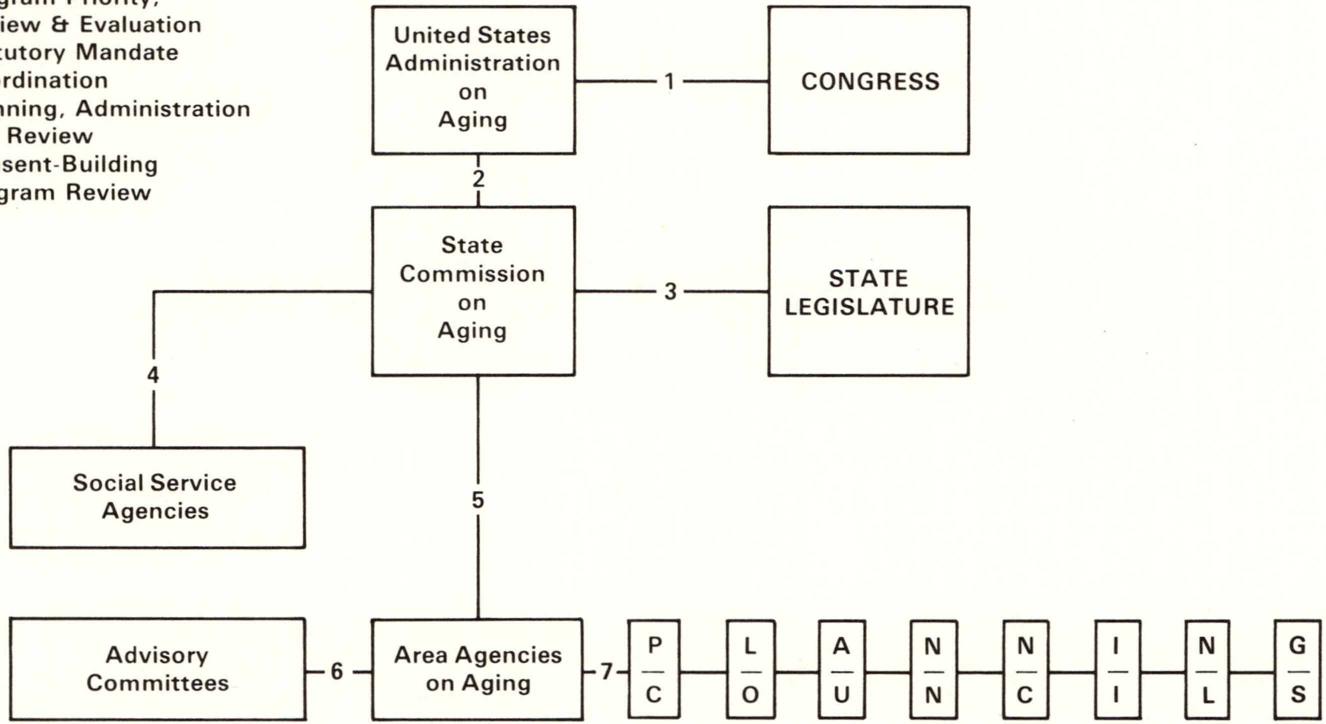

The evidence suggests that the entire administrative development of the aging network, and especially AOA, has involved the struggle to establish sufficient autonomy and legitimacy to confront the initial survival threshold and move beyond. However, it has experienced several interrelated problems. First, wide disparity between AOA's broad legislative responsibility and meager political authority has hampered its effort to arouse and mobilize other federal agencies in a concerted attack on problems facing the elderly. Second, the relative autonomy from AOA of the National Association of State Units on Aging (NASUA), which consists of executive directors of state aging offices, and the National Association of Area Agencies on Aging (N4A), a body composed of AAA directors, has worked against the firm integration of the major administrative units that comprise the aging network. Third, because of its national administrative exposure, AOA is likely to bear the brunt of public and legislative scrutiny and criticism as the larger society increasingly becomes unwilling to support the rising costs of aging and human services programs. Robert Hudson graphically develops the point:

The question now arises as to whether AOA will become the scapegoat for ongoing problems which are not of AOA's making. . . . The agency which serves to recognize a constituency in a benign environment is transformed into a lightning rod attracting problems in a hostile environment. The lofty language expressing concern becomes a legislative mandate demanding results.[11]

In his view, the "honeymoon" phase of social acceptance of aging programs is rapidly coming to an end. Neal Cutler even envisions the onset of an aging backlash and increased political conflict in society between age-supporting and age-dependent groups. Should the analysis of Hudson and Cutler bear out, AOA will face increasingly severe tests of its legitimacy, support, and survival threshold. How AOA meets ongoing challenges of organizational development, maturity, and consumer acceptance is an issue that requires the closest scrutiny by students of the administrative development of aging programs and social policy.

Another factor to be considered in the analysis of the administrative development of AOA is the fiscal and budgetary relationship it has had with successive presidential administrations. Assuming that such a benchmark is an indication of general political support, or the decline thereof, such a comparative analysis is revealing. However, the external factors in the larger political environment weigh upon this assessment. The general political philosophy and ideological leanings of various presidents, party majorities in Congress, and overall economic conditions all have a direct impact on the distribution of resources to social programs. The political-administrative acumen of successive AOA commissioners and their ability to detect and constructively activate levers of power and authority in Congress, the White House, and among age-related interest groups also require careful consideration.

Political observers such as Vinyard have asserted that over the last decade or so society has been willing to pass the costs for elderly care on to government.[12] And these costs for older people have been significant. Former HEW Secretary Califano has pointed out that in FY 1978, more than $94 billion was paid out to persons sixty-five and over for Old Age Assistance, Medicare, Medicaid, Supplementary Security Income, and the Black Lung benefits program.[13] Another $18 billion went to elderly citizens in the form of housing subsidies, food stamps, and military and civil service retirement. Totaling $112 billion, this program cost 5 percent of the GNP, or 24 percent of the federal budget, for that year. Califano further projected that by the years 2010 and 2025, when the "senior boom" peaks, expenditures are likely to reach $635 billion, or more than 10 percent of the GNP, and 40 percent of total federal outlays. While the significance of these outlays can be assumed to be an indicator of positive social commitment, such costs also raise serious questions concerning the tolerable limits of taxpayers' generosity.[14]

These tolerable limits are futher crystalized by the contemporary political mood for across-the-board tax relief and reduction of the nature and size of government involvement in social programs. Successful legislative initiatives by the Reagan administration, both in budgetary and tax reductions, are at present riding the crest of popular opinion. Table 9.1 outlines projected cuts proposed by the administration.

"Pocketbook" issues related to rising inflation, high interest rates, and increased government spending are currently in vogue, receiving an impetus from the administration's emphasis on tax relief incentives to the supply or producing sectors within the economy and its deemphasis on benefits to consumers. The impacts of such an approach most centrally confront the vulnerable elderly—the frail, the old-old, minorities, and widows. In recent testimony to the House Select Committee on Aging Subcommittee on Human Services, the director of New York's SUA (state unit on aging) decried the Reagan administration cuts in Title XX, food stamps, and Medicaid, the move toward block grant programs, and age-irrelevant social programming, as having potentially disastrous effects on the country's elderly population. On the other hand, since substantial numbers of older people pay little or no income tax, they receive little benefit from proposed income tax reductions. In addition, organizational changes have further decentralized AOA's fiscal authority by assigning this responsibility to Human Development Services staff at the regional level.

Administrative and program development follows the vicissitudes of economic growth of the larger society and the collective public policy decisions based thereupon. Who is president and what party controls

Congress do matter—greatly. As Table 9.1 shows, given the fiscal strategy of the Reagan administration, AOA faces a critical period of cutback management. Thus, administrative agencies continually are affected by public decision making in the political environment.

Table 9.1
Program Budget Cuts Proposed by the Reagan Administration

Program	Proposed Nationwide Reduction
Medicaid	Cap imposed $100 million reduction in FY 1981 $1 billion cut in FY 1982
Social services (Title XX)	Included in block grant 25% cut in FY 1982
Food stamps	$15 million cut in FY 1981 $1.8 billion cut in FY 1982 Lower income eligibility levels imposed
Energy assistance	Included in block grant 25% reduction
Weatherization	Transferred to new Community Development Assistance Grant merged with Urban Development Action Grant Program CDAG and UDAG merged, plus loss of $12 million in 1982
Social Security minimum benefit	Elimination of minimum benefit
Comprehensive Employment and Training Act	Elimination of Titles II-D and VI
Subsidized housing	12% cut nationwide in section 8 and public housing 7% cut in section 202, due to inflation

SOURCE: New York State Office for Aging, "Impact of Reagan Budget and Tax Cuts on Elderly in New York State," n.d. See also U.S., Congress, House, Committee on Education and Labor, *Oversight Hearings on the Effects of Cutbacks Proposed by the Reagan Administration*, 97th Cong. 1st sess., April 29, 1981.

Another aspect from which to consider the administrative development of AOA is the management and leadership style of its various commissioners. Management style has been defined as the process of influencing organizational activities in efforts toward goal attainment.[15]

Strategies of managerial leadership and influence building revolve around the roles a manager adopts to get things done. Mintzberg has delineated the role structure of leadership into interpersonal, informational, and decisional aspects.[16] These roles range from symbolic and figurehead types to information, support building, negotiation, and conflict resolution. The weighing, balancing, and judicious use of these roles, given sensitive, ever changing political and economic nuances in the environment, are the central challenges facing leadership.

Henry Pratt has examined this point from an administrative and interest group perspective, dealing with the administrations of early AOA Commissioners Bechill, Martin, and Flemming.[17] The first two commissioners, William Bechill and John Martin, were immediately faced with initial survival threshold problems, such as consolidating unified and coherent support among age-related interest groups, integrating resource allocation roles among the various state units on aging, and negotiating a unique, autonomous function for AOA within the federal bureaucracy. These leadership roles were never fully and firmly established by AOA so that this "managerial phase" of its evolution fell short of fully institutionalizing the legitimacy of the agency on the federal level, within the states, and among aging interest groups and clientele.

The individual who finally brought together the various national aging groups such as NCOA, NCSC, and AARP, and who was to become the architect of the emerging aging coalition, was Arthur Flemming. With skill and deftness, Flemming, almost by force of his personality, drew these and other aging groups together at the occasion of the 1971 White House Conference on Aging. Though debates over issues, priorities, and organizational strategy and tactics abounded at the conference, Flemming was able to forge the coalition and hold it together so that the conference served as a significant springboard for old-age advocates and interest groups to access the political system. Flemming typified Mintzberg's leadership role structure referred to earlier. His prowess at handling negotiation, conflict resolution, and symbolic figurehead roles not only consolidated the aging coalition but brought to it a modicum of political sophistication and maturity that enabled it to influence future legislative and policy development.

Dan Fritz takes the view, however, that none of these commissioners fully institutionalized the advocacy role AOA was mandated to play as an agency of national focus on aging problems.[18] He attributes this benign neglect to presidential constraints related to expansive social welfare programs. He contends that limited staff, lack of bureaucratic authority, and administrative concern with various and sundry routine programmatic components continue to conspire against AOA's assumption of a systematic advocacy role. While supporting Fritz's analysis, Charles Fahey also observes that AOA's advocacy role is seriously constrained by the fact that it both contributes and is subject to Department of Health and Human Services (HHS) policy development.[19]

Other issues in the administrative evolution and development of AOA persist. Not the least of these are the administrative location of AOA and contention over its visibility and prestige within the federal bureaucracy. AOA is housed in the Department of Health and Human Services, but this decision was preceded by considerable political infighting and administrative jousting.[20] In 1973, it was removed from the department's Office of Social and Rehabilitative Services and placed in the Office of Human Development Services. Organizational charts, however, are smokescreens. What really matters is the political commitment to the functions of an office. There is widespread agreement that this commitment has not been made and that AOA's goals remain vague and nebulous and its responsibilities woefully fragmented. As Robert Benedict, who succeeded Flemming as AOA commissioner, put it, "we are not yet at a point where the government fully understands the meaning of the population changes, problems, and needs of an aging society. AOA's efforts—its statutory authority and its discretionary funds—are directed at shaping national policy in ways that reflect those changes."[21]

Another national spokesperson on aging issues, Msgr. Charles J. Fahey, chairman of the Federal Council on Aging (FCA), has echoed these concerns in recent congressional testimony:

The FCA found considerable ambiguity and conflicting goals within the Older American's Act. The act eschews means testing, yet at the same time it calls for directing resources to those in greatest economic or social need. It urges local responsibility in building community support systems, yet directs that substantial proportions of available resources be allocated to programs mandated by Congress.[22]

In summary, ongoing issues in the administrative evolution of AOA are whether it will emerge as an autonomous, legitimate, and effective focus and advocate for aging programs within the federal bureaucracy; the management challenge of programs cutbacks; integration and consolidation of its role and mission throughout the network; and the political effectiveness of current and future commissioners in influencing presidential and congressional allocation decisions.

THE STATE AND AREA AGENCY NETWORK

State units and area agencies also work within the context of the federal system and are susceptible to the constraints and potentials inherent in that system. Their response to nuances in state and local political environments bear crucially upon their ultimate effectiveness.

The functions of a state unit on aging are: (1) to serve as a management linkage between the national and local level (between AOA and the area agencies); (2) to act as a broker for area agencies and to facilitate the flow of fiscal and program resources to them; (3) to prioritize, negotiate, and coordinate the annual state aging plan; and (4) to arouse and mobilize a statewide commitment to the needs and concerns of its elderly population. Under the terms and conditions of the Older American's Act, SUAs were to be the only state agencies responsible for administering and coordinating planning programs for the elderly. Through the use of federal grants-in-aid, they were mandated to facilitate and implement program goal setting and planning and to assist local agencies in this process.

In most states, the governor is given authority to select the members of the state aging commission, the latter serving concurrently with the governor. The commission usually is led by an executive director chosen by the governor and serving at his or her will. The administrative configuration of the office and its location within the bureaucracy vary from state to state, depending on the type of administrative structure a governor prefers and can establish. Administratively, state aging units have characteristics similar to that of AOA. The executive director, like the AOA commissioner, is a political appointee who is vulnerable to changes in administration, executive preference, legislative majorities, and interest group pressures. (For example, in Alabama, the original executive director served for eight years. Since the 1978 gubernatorial election, there have been four different directors.) Similar to AOA, state units are exposed to changing program philosophies and reorganization strategies. The visibility, activity, and effectiveness of SUAs tend to depend on the intensity of the particular state's commitment to older people.

As on the federal level, program goals required to meet the needs of the elderly cannot be neatly compartmentalized within existing state bureaucratic structures. Agencies have boundaries in addition to political jurisdictions; they are established along functional programmatic lines and take on a territoriality of their own. In other words, each agency jealously struggles to confront its own survival threshold.

THE STATE AGING PLAN

A central function that energizes aging activities within the states is the annual aging plan. The plan, at least in theory, is not merely a formal document but a series of commitments, both human and material, that arouse and mobilize the state network for a concerted, integrated response to the needs of older citizens. Nor is the state plan only a grant proposal for federal funds. In spirit, the annual plan delineates a series of goal and task orientations that focus and direct administrative behavior;

fiscal outlays that depict community investment in aging programs; and implementation strategies that involve discrete, tactical interrelationships of political support and influence building. This latter point is the most crucial aspect of the planning process.

Historically, professional bureaucrats and administrators within the social welfare network have been among the most active interest groups advancing causes of social welfare policy.[23] The lesson learned from the history of the evolution of the aging movement is that building political support and influence is indispensable to sound, effective program planning. A politically weak plan is an ineffective plan. A politically weak agency is an ineffective agency. The planning process, therefore, is potentially one of the most effective instruments state and area agency personnel have at their disposal.

The preparation of the area and state plan establishes a spotlight on aging issues and concerns. The plan is a focal point that draws the attention of state and local elected officials, a variety of interest groups, service providers, and suppliers, and especially the elderly themselves. The plan has the potential to become the cutting edge of community arousal, awareness, and support. Strategic use of public hearings, media formats, training events, and related conferences and workshops can generate political education on the aging process. In the world of the aging program administrator, every public contact is a potential springboard to harnessing greater resources. In fact, the establishment of the informal resource procurement process may be the most critical function of a manager or administrator. At the least, it is folly for an administrator to assume that federal and state legislative mandates and fiscal resources obtained through the grant-in-aid process are in and of themselves sufficient levers of political legitimacy that indicate broad public acceptance of aging program goals. Nor does the process of labeling individuals as planning experts ensure more than the aura of legitimacy.[24] To the contrary, the formal authority given to an SUA and AAA to represent older populations is just a starting point. What really matters is the effectiveness of the administrator and program planner when confronting the political system. It is within this arena that paramount decisions are made that determine what actually gets done in behalf of the elderly.

Robert Dahl has distinguished between potential and actual resources.[25] The transformation of the former to the latter is determined by the mix of resources an actor has at his or her disposal, the level of willingness to use these resources for decidedly political ends, and the actor's political skill level. Dahl's analysis suggests that in order to gain actual political power, state and local aging program directors would need to develop and utilize a stategic mix of resources from the community, drawing upon the political skills and capabilities at their disposal. The implication is that program administrators need to broaden and enlarge their resource base beyond that offered through the formal resource allocation system (for example, contracts and grants). Political skills for building support and influence are the major techniques through which this decisive function can be played out. The planning process is the key strategy system at the administrator's disposal. Through such planning, the administrator potentially can arouse, mobilize, and harness community support and resources both necessary and sufficient for getting things done in behalf of elderly citizens. Beyond writing "correct" goals, objectives, action steps, and target dates, the annual plan, in this perspective, is a change process inspiring political legitimacy for aging agencies and community acceptance of the elderly as valuable members of the social system.[26]

From a bureaucratic perspective, however, the annual plan is often viewed as a burden at worst and, at best, statistically mundane. Too often, the plan is looked upon as a static document, the preparation of which involves significant staff overload, organizational stress in meeting completion deadlines, and nebulous and convoluted program guidelines. In addition, major emphasis is placed during the process on routinizing document trails and paper flow and standardizing report formats. Inordinate concern is placed upon prioritizing components of the service system.[27] Much less attention is paid to developing political strategems for effective program implementation.

In most states, area agencies are attached organizationally to regional planning and development councils, or councils of governments (COGs). Within this context, area agencies are geoadministrative, multicounty planning and coordinating bodies. The original mandate of the AAAs in 1965 precluded them from offering direct services. Instead, they were to coordinate and pool untapped resources within the community in behalf of the elderly and detect and fund "gap-filling" services.

The regional approach to both physical and human services planning has been in vogue since the mid-1960s. Regionalism brings together, in a common planning setting, several counties and the corresponding municipalities within their boundaries. The functions of a regional council are to plan for the orderly growth and development of the area. Regionalism is justified by the fact that it transcends and consolidates jurisdictions served by development planning and thereby facilitiates the planning process. It is a relatively new approach for coordinating intergovernmental relations and has, in some areas, aroused significant public opposition.[28]

At the onset, AAAs were organizationally attached to regional groups not of their own choosing and were vulnerable to the general criticism leveled against regional development schemes. Additionally, they were joined to planning regions whose major emphasis was on "bricks and mortar" and planning physical infrastructure. Human services was a decided secondary priority. How area agencies come to be integrated with these planning bodies and how physical and human services planning is coordinated within them is a fertile issue for further study. Another important issue when examining the administrative development and organizational behavior of AAAs lies in an analysis of the intraorganizational relations and role integration of both the area agency director's office and the executive director of the regional development council. There is some evidence to suggest that staff size, urban–rural location, and dispositions of county and municipal officials to human services programming are important variables to consider.[29] AAAs are also responsible to public advisory councils and boards of directors, comprised largely of elected officials with some citizen participation. The relationship of the AAA to these groups is another fertile field for careful study.

It is generally maintained that all organizations strive toward self-maintenance, goal attainment, and environmental adaptation. Administrators and bureaucrats, in seeking these ends, work in three worlds: the behavioral world, the institutional world, and the world of process.[30]

The behavioral world consists of a myriad of complex interpersonal relations in which the administrator is enmeshed. As we have seen, AOA commissioners deal with federal bureaucratic peers, Congress, the White House, and nationally organized interest groups. State commissioners, likewise, interact with governors, state legislatures, other state agencies, and state-based pressure and interest groups. In the same vein, AAA directors interact with locally elected officials, for example, county commissioners and city councils, other local agencies, boards and committees, and citizen groups. Out of the labyrinth of these encircling human exchanges and interactions flow many of the support resources the administrator needs to accomplish the goals of the organization.

The administrator also operates within an institutional world composed of the sociopolitical institutions in which the organization is imbedded. These institutions are shaped by ordering mechanisms such as federalism, regionalism, and state jurisdictions. Each of these institutional configurations have manifold impacts, both positive and negative, upon program development and implementation. The administrator feels constant pulls and pushes from these institutional forces. For example, the impacts of federalism upon the aging network, as discussed earlier, are systemwide and all-pervasive. Likewise, the regional, geographic positions of state units and area agencies constrain and influence their organizational efforts.

The third world of the administrator is that of process. By their nature, administrative functions tend to move toward routinization and inevitably become part of organizational structure. The effects of process are formalism, rationality, careerism, and doing things "by the book." The administrative accouterments related to process emphasize the self-maintenance of the organization, and goals dealing with institutional and social change become largely displaced. How these evolutionary patterns continue to manifest themselves in the future growth and development of the aging network are critical issues and should be studied carefully.

THE AGING NETWORK AS DEVELOPMENT ADMINISTRATION

Convincing arguments have been presented to support the view that the most significant impacts upon a society's older population are the sociopolitical and economic forces of development and modernization.[31] Modernization is defined as a comprehensive sociopolitical process of rapid economic, technological, and social change. The goals of modernization are the rapid modification of social institutions, technological application to the means of production, and the enhancement of centralized political authority. Development necessitates the emergence of new social groups occupying novel socioeconomic roles within the community. Usually, these groups will involve youth, skilled labor, the military, political elites, and bureaucracy. Moreover, these groups must be mobile and adaptable. Alex Inkeles has succinctly summarized this process:

Modern society has been characterized as a participant society. It requires of its citizens a readiness for new experience and an acceptance of innovation, a concern with public issues at the community and national levels, a sense of efficacy that encourages and supports programs of social change, and the ability to move freely from place to place and to integrate one's self with new coworkers and new neighbors in new living arrangements.[32]

This pattern of development suggests that structural changes in the social system undercut the special position of the aged. In other words, as old norms and traditional ways of doing things rapidly erode, the elderly are dislocated from formerly held social roles and status. In fact, these security generators the elderly once held become increasingly superfluous to the ends of modernizing social systems.

Table 9.2 presents a model that is suggestive of the socioecological characteristics of traditional and modernizing societies. Discrete ecological dislocations in the life systems of the elderly due to the modernization process are directed at family and kinship roles, territorial authority and value systems, and economic roles. It is within the complex and comprehensive reconfiguration of these social structures that displacement of the aged occurs. Moreover, it is within this context that the challenge of meaningful program development and administration must occur if the aging network is to respond effectively to our elderly population. Donald Cowgill and Lowell Holmes have further hypothesized that the status of

Table 9.2
Socioecological Characteristics of Traditional and Modernizing Social Systems

Traditional Social Systems (Ideal Type)	Modernizing Social Systems (Ideal Type)
Sedentary range of human interaction.	Mobile, expansive range of human interaction.
Territorially conscripted value systems.	Universal, diffusely oriented values.
Kinship dependence, socialized by family.	Nuclear, transitory, interfamilial independence.
Localized, territorially based, socio-political allegiances.	Sociopolitical allegiances directed to emerging, centralized levels of government.
Determined, fixed, sacred-based value systems.	Secularized, rational, differentiated value systems.
Relatively undifferentiated economic roles.	Highly specific economic roles, techno-logical orientation.
Ascribed, age-based roles of gerontocracy status maintenance.	Achievement, production-based roles of socioeconomic status.
Patriarchal residence over means of social legitimation.	State-centered, mass-oriented means of social legitimation.

SOURCE: Compiled by the author

the aged is inversely proportional to the rate of social change inherent in the modernizing process.[33]

Leo Simons, in illustrating the impacts of modernization on the elderly, writes:

There is a pattern of participation for the aged that becomes relatively fixed in stable societies but suffers disruption with rapid social change. In the long and steady strides of the social order, the aging get themselves fixed and favored in positions, power, and performance. They have what we call seniority rights. But when social conditions become unstable and the rate of change reaches a gallop-ing pace, the aged are riding for an early fall, and the more youthful associates take their seats in the saddles.[34]

If the modernization process has these comprehensive and dislocating impacts on the aged, as we argue they do, then the special needs and conditions concomitant to the aging process are significantly social, eco-nomic, and political in nature. Therefore, the value dispositions, theoreti-cal assumptions, and administrative structures upon which aging pro-grams are built and from which aging policy decisions and implementation strategy flow must take these factors into account. Such an approach suggests that the aging network needs to be transformed from a mainte-nance bureaucracy model to that of development administration.

The model of development administration flows from characteristics inherent in the definition of the modernization process. As such, development administration refers to an administrative structure and organizational behavior necessary to implement policies and programs fostering socioeconomic and political change. Its overall framework encompasses strategies aimed at improving the social system.[35] The focus is on institution building, not singularly upon service delivery schemes.

Institutionally, the model assumes that the organization should undertake a continual and ongoing support-seeking interaction with its surrounding environment in order to introduce and guide significant change in that environment. On the strategic level, the institutional-building process involves an assessment of the extent of environmental hostility to change, acceptance of innovative norms within the organization, and attempts to legitimate program goals and ends throughout the social system.

On a logistics level, Samuel Eldersveld has linked the development process to bureaucratic citizen exchange and has offered the following criteria for this interaction: (1) penetration, or bureaucratic outreach to the most alienated and distrustful potential clients; (2) information, or dissemination; (3) belief, or wide-ranging bureaucratic contact for purposes of developing a consensual support of plans and programs; (4) confidence, or extended client interaction for purposes of developing trust in the agency; and (5) action, or motivation to achieve their own goals.[36]

A change strategy also directs the priorities and objectives of the development plan, which primarily seeks to modify social institutions while simultaneously seeking to develop a service delivery modality that most effectively meets clients needs. The development plan is such a change strategy, rather than an outline of services as in traditional and current plans. The assumption behind the model is that, since sociopolitical dimensions bear crucially upon the aging process, social and political changes are needed to address it.

Within the social system, the model assumes that discrete changes should be targeted toward the stratification system, which entails status-consciousness building among clients. That is, clients are made aware of their position in the social system with respect to others as well as of the advantages and disadvantages of a given status position they may occupy. They also are engaged in role testing (exploring the legitimate limits of their roles and experimenting with them). Clients are encouraged to become future-oriented so that they understand changes in their life chances, and can attempt to alter some aspects of their situation so as to fulfill their expectations more adequately.[37] In the context of the model, administration means providing new institutions, modifying existing ones, and utilizing administrative decision making as a change process.

The elderly are especially vulnerable and victimized by the vicissitudes of social, political, and economical change, largely due to the comprehensive loss continuum experienced in the later years (loss of job, loss of income, loss of status, loss of family, and so forth). Dissatisfaction has been expressed throughout the aging network with program development, planning, delivery, and advocacy efforts. The roots of this dissatisfaction lie partly within the network but also within the social environment. Much has been done for the nation's elderly, but much more remains to be accomplished. The model of development administration discussed above can serve as a point of departure for laying new strategy directions for program goals. Clearly, any approach seeking to improve substantially the well-being of America's elderly population must consider the socioeconomic realities inherent in the aging process and change mechanisms within the federal system of government. Such factors are the foundation for the evolution of meaningful development administration in aging programs.

NOTES

1. Carroll L. Estes, *The Aging Enterprise* (San Francisco: Jossey-Bass, 1979).

2. Henry J. Pratt, *The Gray Lobby: Politics of Old Age* (Chicago: University of Chicago Press, 1976).

3. Donald Cowgill and Lowell Holmes, *Aging and Modernization* (New York: Appleton-Century-Crofts, 1972).

4. Elaine Cumming and William E. Henry, *Growing Old: The Process of Disengagement* (New York: Basic Books, 1961).

5. Robert C. Atchley, *The Social Forces in Later Life*, 2nd ed. (Belmont, Cal.: Wadsworth, 1977).

6. Jack Levin and William C. Levin, *Ageism: Prejudice and Discrimination Against the Elderly* (Belmont, Cal.: Wadsworth, 1980).

7. Carroll L. Estes, "Barriers to Effective Community Planning for the Elderly," *Gerontologist* 13 (1973): 178–83.

8. Robert H. Binstock and Martin A. Levin, "The Political Dilemmas of Intervention Policies," in *Handbook of Aging and the Social Sciences*, ed. Robert H. Binstock and Ethel Shanas (New York: Van Nostrand Reinhold 1976), pp. 511–35.

9. Jane Axinn and Herman Levin, *Social Welfare: A History of the American Response to Need* (New York: Dodd, Mead, 1975).

10. Anthony Downs, *Inside Bureaucracy* (Boston: Little, Brown, 1967).

11. Robert Hudson, "The 'Graying' of the Federal Budget and Its Consequences for Old-Age Policy," *Gerontologist* 18, part 1 (October 1978): 438.

12. Dale Vinyard, "Rediscovery of the Aged: Senior Power and Public Policy," *Society* (July-August 1978): 24-27.

13. Joseph Califano, "Aging of America: Questions for the Four-Generation Society," *Annals* 438 (July 1978): 96–197.

14. Robert Clark and John Menefee, "Federal Expenditures for the Elderly," *Gerontologist* 21 (April 1981): 132–41.

15. Robert Tannenbaum, et al., *Leadership and Organization: A Behavioral Approach* (New York: McGraw-Hill, 1961).

16. Henry Mintzberg, *The Nature of Managerial Work* (New York: Harper & Row, 1973).

17. Pratt, *Gray Lobby*.

18. Dan Fritz, "The Administration on Aging as Advocate: Progress, Problems, and Prospects," *Gerontologist* 19 (April 1979): 141–50.

19. U.S., Congress, House, Committee on Education and Labor, Subcommittee on Human Resources, Testimony of Msgr. Charles J. Fahey, Hearing, 97th Cong., 1st sess, April 29, 1981.

20. Pratt, *Gray Lobby*.

21. Robert Benedict, "TG Interview," *Gerontologist* 20 (April 1980): 132.

22. Fahey, Testimony, p. 14.

23. Vinyard, "Rediscovery of the Aged."

24. Carroll L. Estes, "Community Planning for the Elderly: A Study of Goal Displacement," *Journal of Gerontology* 29 (1974): 684–91.

25. Robert Dahl, *Modern Political Analysis* (Englewood Cliffs, N.J.: Prentice-Hall, 1965).

26. Robert Hudson, "Rational Planning and Organizational Imperatives: Prospects for Area Agencies on Aging," *Annals* 415 (September 1974): 41–54. In this essay, Hudson distinguishes between rational and social system models in the early evolution of the area agencies. The former approach is based upon utilizing formal mandates and planning goals as stated in the Older American's Act as the sole basis for organizational legitimacy. The latter model places stress on factors of environmental support building.

27. Westat, Inc., *Evolution of the Area Planning and Social Service Program*, vol. 1: *Focus on Changes in Service to Older Persons: The Area Agency Role* (Rockville, Md.: Westat, 1978).

28. David Brown, "Public Reception to Regional Development Schemes," *Growth and Change* 1 (January 1977): 16–21.

29. Larry Gamm, "Standards and Regulations in State-Local Administration: Analysis of Views of Directors of Pennsylvania Area Agencies on Aging" (Pennsylvania State University, Gerontology Center), 1977.

30. Robert T. Golembiewski, et al., eds., *Public Administration: Readings in Institutions, Processes, Behavior* (Chicago: Rand McNally, 1966).

31. Cowgill and Holmes, *Aging and Modernization*.

32. Alex Inkeles, "A Model of Modern Man: Theoretical and Methodological Issues," in *Comparative Modernization*, ed. Cyril Black (New York: Free Press, 1976), pp. 322–23.

33. Cowgill and Holmes, *Aging and Modernization*.

34. Leo Simons, "Aging in Modern Society," in *Toward a Better Understanding of the Aging* (New York: Council on Social Work Education, 1972), p. 4.

35. V. A. Panandiker, "Development Administration: An Approach," in *Readings in Comparative Public Administration*, ed. Nimrod Raphaeli (Boston: Allyn and Bacon, 1967), pp. 199–210.

36. Samual Eldersveld, "Bureaucratic Contact with the Public in India," *Indian Journal of Public Administration* 2 (1965): 216–35.

37. David Apter, *Some Conceptual Approaches to the Study of Modernization* (Englewood Cliffs, N.J.: Prentice-Hall, 1968).

DAVID BRODSKY

10

Future Policy Directions

Public programs and expenditures on behalf of older American's have increased dramatically since the passage of the Social Security Act in 1935. These expanded efforts in programs and funding, due in large measure to legislative initiatives, improved benefits, and growth in the elderly population, have contributed to marked advances in the living conditions of many older persons. Critics have, nevertheless, begun to question the effectiveness and costs of such age-related programs as Social Security retirement benefits, Medicare, and social services provided under the Older American's Act and Title XX of the Social Security Act. Consequently, the old-age policy agenda includes a myriad of conflicting proposals. Some call for the expansion of existing governmental efforts on behalf of older citizens and the introduction of new programs to address unmet needs. Others call for a reduction of governmental expenditures on behalf of elderly persons. This chapter assesses the likely outcomes of the current policy debates. To this end, it describes the contemporary policy environment and discusses major policy issues and specific proposals in the area of retirement income security, health care, and social services.

Taken together, the models most often used as explanations of old-age policy outcomes appear to offer a comprehensive picture of the factors influencing the development of policies for older Americans. However, they fail to examine adequately or explain the effects of macroeconomic conditions on the structure of social policies, including those for the aged population.

EXPLAINING OLD-AGE POLICY OUTCOMES: A POLITICAL ECONOMY APPROACH

If one traces the development of current social policies, several constants stand out from the overall mosaic of change in the policy environment. First, despite dramatic transformations in the U.S. economy and despite increased government intervention in the country's economic life, the economy remains basically a private enterprise system. Second, most elected and appointed public officials believe in the virtues of the private enterprise system, accept its superiority to alternative economic systems, and hold a commitment to its preservation and growth.[1] Third, social policies, including those benefiting elderly Americans, represent one set of tools used by political decision makers to ensure the stability and growth of the economic system.[2] Finally, this commitment to the private enterprise system limits the options policymakers consider as they attempt to deal with issues and problems.

The circumstances surrounding the emergence of the Social Security system illustrate the links between the needs of the economic system, as perceived by public decision makers, and the development of social welfare policies.[3] During the 1920s and 1930s, such factors as declining wages, rising unemployment, the loss of savings, and inadequate aggregate demand contributed to the Depression. The political system's response to these economic problems involved an expanded government role in the economy. The Social Security Act of 1935 served as a major element of this response, and although its component programs enhanced the economic security of retired persons and other individuals, the act focused on the twin problems of umemployment and inadequate demand. Accordingly, its retirement and old-age assistance provisions sought to reduce unemployment by removing older workers from the labor force, thereby opening up jobs for younger workers. Its sponsors also sought to stimulate consumption through the distribution of cash benefits as well as through the increased purchasing power available to formerly unemployed younger workers.[4] In sum, policymakers tailored Social Security to the economic circumstances of the 1930s.

THE POLICY ENVIRONMENT

A number of factors "explain" the development of growth of the federal programs benefiting older Americans. These same factors will undoubtedly have an impact on future policy developments. The overall state of the economy and the commitment of political leaders to maintaining the private enterprise system will to some extent constrain the range of available policy choices. Decision makers will have to formulate old-age policies in the midst of an economic crisis marked by a slowdown in economic growth, an increase in inflation, and an increase in unemployment. Their choices will necessarily reflect a consideration of the effects of old-age policy on the economic well-being of the nation, a necessity manifested in the current policy debates surrounding such questions as the impact of Social Security on personal savings and on the formation of investment capital.[5] Policy decisions will also have to take into account the influence of changing economic conditions on the performance of old-age policies, a need illustrated by the effects of continuing inflation and unemployment on the fiscal integrity of the Social Security program.[6]

Existing programs will affect the direction of future policies. American policymakers, including those concerned with older persons, have consistently demonstrated a preference for coping with public problems through incremental modifications to existing policies rather than through new program initiatives.[7] This suggests that future developments in old-age policy will take the form of adjustments to existing programs. However, this prospect may prove problematic.[8] The current array of economic and social policies was rooted in efforts to cope with the major problems of the Depression. To achieve this end, the federal government accepted responsibilities for promoting economic growth and stability through expenditures and other demand management policies. The government also assumed a role in protecting individuals and businesses from the unpredictable turns of the market. For individuals, this protection took the form of alternative sources of income and benefits, including Social Security retirement benefits, old-age assistance, and unemployment compensation. For business, protection took the form of government spending programs, government protection from foreign competition, and a reluctance to allow major corporations to fail.[9]

On the one hand, these policies contributed to the growth of the American economy in the post–World War II period and supported improvements in the economic status of many Americans, including a substantial proportion of the elderly population. On the other hand, by their very success in stablizing the economy and providing a previously unknown measure of economic security, these policies have contributed to current economic problems by reducing restraints on wages and prices and by creating a climate in which many groups, including older Americans, feel entitled to rising economic benefits from the government. Moreover, these groups possess sufficient political resources to protect their interests. Thus, these programs directly stimulate inflation by creating an imbalance between the claims made upon the economy and the economic benefits it can deliver and indirectly contribute to rising unemployment when government attempts to control inflation by using monetary and fiscal policies to slow the economy.[10] Although any debate over old-age policy will surely include at least a partial assessment of the macroeconomic effects of programs for older Americans, the bias toward incrementalism may limit the range of corrective actions considered and the effectiveness of the policies ultimately adopted.

Finally, several other factors may also influence future policy developments by contributing to a decline in public support for government programs that assist older persons. Over the past several years public opposition to government spending, especially for social programs, has increased to the point where the Reagan administration prevailed in its initial efforts to reduce significantly federal expenditures for social welfare purposes. Although Social Security and other programs primarily for elderly persons generally escaped extensive reductions, the overall commitment to curbing social expenditures will almost certainly affect future levels of financial support for these programs. At the same time public opposition to government spending has risen, so has public concern about the future of such programs as Social Security and Medicare. These trends taken in conjunction with the relative improvements in the overall condition of the aged population may reduce support for any expansion of programs for older persons and may, in fact, lead to demands for cutbacks in existing programs.[11]

THE POLICY ISSUES

Three basic issues appear likely to emerge in future debates about specific aging programs—cost, adequacy, and age or need entitlement.

Policymakers will have to contend with the costs inherent in the federal government's present commitments to older Americans and the budgetary impact of any proposed changes in existing policy.[12] At present the federal government expends one-fourth of its annual budget outlays on programs for aging persons. Current trends, including the graying of the baby boom into a senior boom, growth in the older and most vulnerable segments of the aging population, and increases in the number of early retirees, point to future increases in federal expenditures to a level where they will constitute 40 percent of budget outlays shortly after the turn of the century.[13] As a consequence, decision makers will have to decide whether the federal government can afford to continue or increase its efforts on behalf of older persons or whether increasing budgetary costs require a reduction in programs for the aged segments of the population.

Those concerned with old-age policy will also have to address the question of adequacy. Despite consuming one-fourth of the federal budget and a large share of state expenditures, current programs leave millions of elderly Americans to suffer the effects of poverty, ill health, and inadequate social services. Benefit levels in the Old Age and Survivors Insurance program and the Supplementary Security Income program (SSI) fail to provide many recipients with incomes at the federal government's official poverty line.[14] As many as half of the potentially eligible older persons fail to participate in the SSI program.[15] Rising "coinsurance" requirements in the Medicare program and increasing out-of-pocket health expenses place a heavy burden on elderly persons, especially those solely dependent upon Social Security benefits. Social service programs under the Older Americans Act and Title XX of the

Social Security Act serve only a fraction of those with legitimate needs, a shortcoming illustrated by the low rates of participation (2 percent of those eligible to participate do so) in federally supported nutrition programs for older persons.[16] Given the often devastating effects these shortcomings have on the lives of many older persons, any attempts to improve old-age policy will have to balance considerations of cost with a concern about need.

The last major issue facing policymakers involves a choice between alternative approaches for determining eligibility for income support and social service programs. At present, many of the major programs for older adults, including the retirement portion of Social Security, Medicare, and the service programs provided under the Older American's Act, determine eligibility on the basis of age rather than on the basis of need.[17] Although this approach has successfully reached many older persons in need, the past few years have seen a growing concern with the overall effects of age-based eligibility standards, especially on the inability of these programs to serve effectively elderly individuals most in need. Proponents of a shift to a more universal approach based on need entitlement see several advantages. First, such an approach would recognize the heterogeneity of the older population and might prove more effective in directing scarce resources to those with the greatest need. Second, universal eligibility standards based on need will not segregate older persons by singling them out as recipients of preferential treatment.[18] And, finally, shifting to a more universal approach may help avoid a potential backlash if other sectors of society come to see themselves as unfairly bearing the costs of programs serving a relatively well-off elderly population.[19]

The next several years will see a continuing debate over old-age policy. Whatever form this debate takes, the participants will have to balance the often competing goals of providing adequate benefits to those in need and of holding costs to economically and politically feasible levels. The way in which policymakers resolve the issue of choosing between age-based and need-based entitlement may significantly affect their ability to achieve a reasonable balance between the objectives of cost control and benefit adequacy.

THE AGING POLICY AGENDA

Although the aging policy agenda for the 1980s has yet to emerge fully, three policy areas—retirement income security, health, and social services—are already commanding the attention of official decision makers, concerned professionals, and the general public. The early appearance of these concerns on the policy agenda derives from such factors as public uncertainty about the financial solvency of the Social Security retirement program, concern with the rising costs of Social Security and other federal income-support programs, and reaction to the Reagan administration's successful efforts to cut various social service programs.

America's efforts to provide a secure and adequate retirement income for its elderly citizens have resulted in a mix of private pensions, public employee and veteran's pensions, and government programs under the Social Security Act. These programs have made a substantial contribution to improving the economic status of the aged population. They have become, nevertheless, the focal point of an intense policy debate between those who criticize perceived inadequacies in the benefits provided and those who perceive the costs of providing current benefits as excessive.[20]

THE SOCIAL SECURITY TRUST FUNDS

The Social Security trust funds—Old Age and Survivors Insurance (OASI), Disability Insurance (DI), and Hospital Insurance (HI)—will pay more than $175 billion to the retired, the disabled, their survivors, and their dependents in fiscal year 1982.[21] An impending deficit in the OASI trust fund and the sheer magnitude of Social Security expenditures have stimulated numerous suggestions for reform. Supporters of Social Security have focused their recommendations on alleviating the short-run financial crisis, meeting the increased demands likely to occur when the baby boom retires after the turn of the century, and restoring public confidence in and support for the program. Opponents, in contrast, have attacked Social Security on a variety of grounds including what they see as its negative impact on savings and capital formation,[22] its low rate of return to contributors,[23] and its structure of compulsory participation.[24] Those opposed to Social Security have also called for gradually reducing its role in providing future retirees with secure incomes.[25]

The financial difficulties currently facing Social Security stem largely from economic conditions outside of its control. Slow rates of economic growth, high levels of unemployment, and high rates of inflation have interacted to reduce payroll tax revenues and to increase expenditures from the trust funds in accordance with indexing provisions that automatically adjust benefit payments to increases in the Consumer Price Index. Despite these economic circumstances and the balance of political power in Washington, there appears little chance that the government will enact any legislation calling for dramatic changes in the Social Security system. However, in keeping with the incremental pattern historically followed in modifying Social Security, the present difficulties will likely result in the enactment of more modest changes to the program.[26] Significantly, unlike past reforms, which usually sought to expand coverage and to raise benefit levels, these efforts may stress either improving Social Security's revenue base or reducing the program's long-term costs.

The Reagan administration's reform proposals focus on controlling costs through a series of benefit reductions. In contrast, the proposals favored by the National Commission on Social Security, the 1979 Advisory Council on Social Security, many organizations representing older Americans, and, perhaps most importantly, many congressional Democrats seek to improve the program's revenue base and provide slightly more adequate benefits. Differences of this magnitude might normally preclude cooperative action. However, the very real short-term funding problem in the OASI trust fund and the rise in public concern about the future of Social Security may generate pressure sufficient to produce compromise legislation.

Compromise appears most likely on several proposals designed to meet the OASI trust fund's short-range difficulties. First, although Congress has, in the past, relied on payroll tax increases to replenish the Social Security trust funds, a more likely outcome involves a change in the formula allocating payroll tax receipts among the three trust funds. After the allocation formula incorporated into the Social Security Amendments of 1977 contributed to decreasing balances in the OASI trust fund and increasing surpluses in the DI trust fund, the ninety-sixth Congress authorized a reallocation procedure for 1980 and 1981. This congressional action increased the portion of the payroll tax going to the OASI trust fund while decreasing the share allocated to the DI trust fund, in effect boosting OASI revenues without increasing the payroll tax. Congressional approval of legislation extending this reallocation procedure beyond 1981 seems certain. Second, the Social Security trust funds will probably receive authorization to borrow from each other. This action would allow inter–trust-fund borrowing when necessary to ensure the timely payment of cash benefits. At present, this could mean that the OASI trust fund, the fund most likely to experience difficulty in meeting its obligations, could borrow from the DI and HI trust funds, the funds currently thought to have more than adequate reserves. A reallocation of payroll tax revenues for interfund borrowing would probably delay the impending cash shortfall in the OASI trust fund until 1985, thereby allowing additional time to formulate strategies for dealing with long-range trust fund problems.

Another set of proposals seeks to alleviate Social Security's financial problems by adding general revenues to the trust funds. In its 1977 proposal to Congress, the Carter administration proposed introducing general revenues into the trust funds whenever unemployment exceeded 6 percent. The amount of general revenues transferred would have equaled the difference between what payroll tax revenues would have been at 6 percent unemployment and the actual payroll tax receipts.[27] Other proposals, including those offered by the 1979 Advisory Council on Social Security and the National Commission on Social Security, recommend introducing general revenues into the HI trust fund and then transferring to the OASI trust fund some fraction of the payroll tax previously allocated to fund hospital insurance benefits.[28]

Although these and similar proposals have not fared well in the past, the introduction of general revenues to the Social Security system will receive renewed consideration as Congress and the administration grapple over the program's future. Policymakers have, for the most part, resisted introduction of general revenues into the OASI trust fund, on the grounds that such a change would significantly alter the relationship of benefits to contributions based on wages. In contrast, proposals to introduce general revenues into the HI trust fund have received more support because a person's medical expenses after retirement have no direct relationship to his or her work history. Concern over rapidly rising health-care costs may also generate more interest in the use of general revenues in HI funding. Nevertheless, the short-range prospects for the introduction of general revenue funds into Social Security do not seem promising.

The future of other proposals is less clear. Congress has, heretofore, resisted taking action that visibly reduces the benefits provided through the cash benefit trust funds.[29] Nevertheless, several proposed changes which will effectively reduce future benefits seem likely candidates for implementation. Proposals by congressional Republicans, the 1979 Advisory Council on Social Security, and the National Commission on Social Security calling for gradually increasing the normal retirement age—the age at which eligibility for full benefits and Medicare coverage begins—from sixty-five to sixty-eight some time around the turn of the century will receive serious consideration. As the normal retirement age advances toward sixty-eight, the age at which reduced benefits become available will also increase from sixty-two to sixty-five. The proponents of gradually raising the retirement age argue that it will: (1) reduce the burden on the Social Security trust funds (especially OASI) by delaying the onset of benefit payments and by extending the time workers and their employers pay into the funds; (2) increase general federal revenues through the additional income taxes paid by workers remaining in the labor force; (3) contribute to the overall health of the economy by keeping the labor supply high; (4) and allow older persons to maintain their independence and sense of self-worth for a longer period of time, one more in line with current mortality and morbidity rates. Opponents, including Robert M. Ball, former commissioner of Social Security, believe that increasing the retirement age, as a practical matter, reduces the benefits for someone who planned to retire at age sixty-five with full benefits but who would, if the retirement age were changed, retire at the same age with the reduced benefits paid to early retirees.[30] Moreover, Ball believes that proposals to delay retirement fail to take into account the employment problems likely to face older workers, especially those trying to find rather than maintain employment after age sixty.

The 1979 Advisory Council on Social Security and the Reagan Administration recommended eliminating the Social Security minimum benefit. This provision of the Social Security Act allowed persons who worked 40 quarters (10 years) in a job covered by Social Security to qualify for a minimum primary insurance amount of $122 per month, regardless of their earnings history. Congress intended for the minimum benefit, as it evolved, to raise the retirement income of long-term, low-wage workers. In practice, however, the minimum benefit provision frequently supplemented the incomes of relatively affluent retirees with other pensions.[31] Advocates of repeal wanted to eliminate these windfall benefits and to rely on the means tested Supplemental Security Income (SSI) program to provide cash assistance to elderly persons with low incomes.[32] Although the ninety-seventh Congress eliminated the minimum benefit for all present and future retirees, it later took steps to modify its decision by restoring the minimum primary insurance amount for all persons eligible for benefits as of December 31, 1981, and by permitting members of religious orders to become eligible until December 31, 1991. Despite these actions, future initiatives intended to restrict the minimum benefit to long-term, low-wage workers or to replace it with some combination of OASI and SSI benefits appear likely.

The indexing formulas used to adjust automatically benefits for retirees and the earnings records of those still in the work force have increased the costs of the Social Security program at the same time as they have made the benefits paid more adequate. The National Commission on Social Security and the Reagan administration, among others, have proposed controlling costs either by adjusting the indexing formulas or by delaying the effective dates of benefit adjustments, respectively. The changes proposed in the indexing formulas include a cap or limit on the annual cost-of-living adjustments to the benefits received by retired workers,[33] changing the effective date of their adjustments from July to October—the start of the government's fiscal year—and shifting the basis for adjusting earnings records (and the benefits for future retirees) from the current wage-indexed formula to one based on prices.[34] Each of these changes would reduce trust fund expenditures by reducing future benefit increases. Despite their negative impact on benefit levels, Congress will probably enact some adjustment to the indexing provisions in order to reduce the effects of economic conditions on Social Security expenditures.

One current proposal—reduction or elimination of the Social Security earnings test—appears likely to negotiate successfully the legislative shoals even though its enactment will increase Social Security expenditures.[35] In its 1981 reform package, the Reagan administration recommended phasing out, by 1986, the earnings' test for persons age sixty-five and older who continue working after beginning to draw their Social Security benefits. Many groups including the National Council on the Aging (NCOA), the National Retired Teachers Association/American Association of Retired Persons (NRTA/AARP), and the President's Commission on Pension Reform have expressed support either for some modification of the earnings test or for its outright repeal.[36] The proposal's supporters argue that changing or eliminating the earnings test will enhance the independence and financial security of older persons, contribute to the economy, and partially pay its own way through the payroll taxes collected from older workers who continue in the labor force.

In the foreseeable future, concern with avoiding deficits in the trust funds will dominate the Social Security agenda. Consequently, policymakers will direct their attention to strategies intended either to increase revenues (unlikely) or reduce costs (highly likely). More importantly, the emphasis on cost control will mean that proposals to improve the adequacy of benefits, including the 1979 Advisory Council on Social Security recommendation that minimum Social Security retirement benefits for full-time minimum-wage workers provide an income at least equal to the official poverty index, will receive less attention as will efforts to correct aspects of the law that negatively affect working women. The prospects for other improvements in Social Security benefits appear equally dim.

On balance, substantial changes to meet the long-term problems of Social Security seem unlikely at present. Instead, Congress and the Reagan administration will probably continue to opt for policy changes that meet the system's short-term difficulties. Such a strategy will ensure that Social Security continues to occupy a prominent place on the old-age policy agenda.

SUPPLEMENTARY SECURITY INCOME

In 1972 the federal government enacted the SSI program to replace separate welfare programs for the aged, the blind, and the disabled. Several factors indicate that this program will occupy a prominent place on the old-age policy agenda during the next few years. First, the Reagan administration has responded to criticism of its successful efforts to eliminate the Social Security minimum benefit by arguing that SSI will provide cash assistance to retired low-income workers whose minimum benefit payments constituted a major portion of their retirement income. In the words of OMB Director David Stockman:

In fact, the great majority of low-income retirees who are receiving additional assistance through the Social Security system minimum benefit provisions are also receiving cash SSI payments. The irony, however, is that the additional dollars they receive through Social Security . . . are offset, dollar for dollar, by

reduced SSI benefits. Totally eliminating the minimum benefit provision, therefore, would not reduce cash assistance to the truly needy . . . by as much as one
dollar.[37]

Second, SSI plays a prominent role in many proposals for alleviating
financial difficulties facing the social security trust funds. Essentially
these recommendations distinguish between two competing objectives,
individual equity and social adequacy, which determine the distribution
of Social Security benefits.[38] Individual equity refers to the extent to
which the program gives benefits in proportion to tax payments or
contributions. Social adequacy refers to the extent to which benefits are
given on the basis of need. Since its inception, the Social Security system
has pursued both objectives, although the current program emphasizes
social adequacy more than individual equity. Recent critics of Social
Security argue that the most effective route to reform lies through a
separation of the program elements directed toward achieving individual
equity and those intended to achieve social adequacy.[39] Reduced to their
most basic form, these proposals call for using the trust fund elements of
Social Security, especially OASI, to provide an equitable return on tax
contributions and for transferring the social adequacy or welfare function to the means-tested SSI program.

Finally, shifting any of Social Security's welfare functions to SSI will
require many changes in that program. These include adjusting the
minimum age for elderly SSI recipients (sixty-five) to match the early
retirement age for OASI (currently sixty-two), modifying the SSI limits
on financial resources and other assets, revising the SSI earnings test,
and increasing appropriations for the SSI program. Such an intensive
review of SSI would also provide an opportunity to consider inadequacies
in current SSI guarantees with an eye to raising the minimum SSI benefit
to the official poverty line.

PRIVATE PENSIONS

The present controversy surrounding the Social Security system has
led to recommendations for expanding the role played by private pensions in providing adequate retirement income for older workers.[40] The
debate over public policy regarding private retirement programs will
focus on three major issues: the appropriate mix between private pensions and Social Security; the extent and adequacy of private pension
coverage; and the provisions for integrating private pensions with Social
Security retirement benefits.

The Social Security system covers approximately 90 percent of the
work force and provides relatively high benefits to eligible individuals. At
the same time, private pension programs also contribute to the income of
many retired workers. However, the mix between public and private

programs has changed dramatically over the past thirty years. Social security in 1950 paid slightly more than 25 percent of all retirement, disability, and survivors' benefits disbursed in the United States. By 1980, its share of payments had more than doubled, a trend that helped spark a continuing debate over the appropriate mix of public and private programs, a debate reflected in the contrasting recommendations recently reported by federal commissions studying retirement income programs.[41] The President's Commission on Pension Policy, on the one hand, criticized the nation's overreliance on Social Security benefits and proposed encouraging additional private coverage through a combination of universal mandatory private pensions and tax incentives to encourage personal savings.[42] Enactment of the commission's proposals would significantly increase benefit payments from employee pension plans, and, although Social Security benefit payments would remain essentially unchanged, Social Security's share of total benefit payments would decline by approximately 13 percent. The National Commission on Social Security, on the other hand, questioned the feasibility of mandating universal private pension coverage.[43] Instead, it recommended expanding Social Security coverage to the entire work force and continuing to rely on Social Security as the primary program for assuring workers a basic level of retirement income. Although Congress will probably not favor a dramatic decrease in the role played by either Social Security or private pensions, it has already acted to encourage increased private savings for retirement through such actions as authorizing "all saver's certificates" and making individual retirement accounts available to all workers and more attractive financially.

Future discussions of retirement policy will also address the related issues of private pension coverage and benefit adequacy.[44] Testifying before Congress, P. McColough, chairman of the President's Commission on Pension Policy, described the causes and consequences of the uneven distribution of private pensions:

One class of workers fares reasonably well in retirement because it can count on Social Security, as well as employee pensions and some personal savings. Another class of retirees has failed to become eligible for employee pension benefits and therefore must rely primarily on Social Security benefits. Inability to vest is often the result of lengthy pension plan service requirements, job mobility, or lack of a pension plan at a worker's place of employment.[45]

Proposals to improve the extent and adequacy of private pensions range from those compelling employers to provide universal private pensions incorporating provisions that accelerate vesting and facilitate portability to those providing substantial tax incentives to employers implementing private plans for their workers. Action mandating univer-

sal private pensions appears highly unlikely. Growing business opposition to government regulation and the depressed state of the economy
suggest that substantial segments of the business community would
oppose such a plan. Second, President Reagan's commitment to cutting
back the social welfare activities of the federal government indicates that
the administration will not recommend mandatory pension programs.
However, the use of additional tax incentives as devices to encourage
voluntary efforts by employers appears more likely. Such an approach
would fit well with the ideological orientation of the Reagan administration and would also build on the limited steps taken in this direction
during 1981, even though they would offer no help to highly mobile
workers.

OTHER ISSUES

With the enactment of Medicare and Medicaid in 1965, the federal
government assumed responsibility for protecting the retirement incomes of older persons by helping them meet their medical expenses.
However, the exact contours of this commitment remain undefined.
Three issues appear likely to dominate the health policy agenda: the costs
of funding medical care for elderly people; the adequacy of current
programs in protecting retirement incomes; and the effects of existing
policy on the mix of services provided to aged citizens.

The costs of Medicare and Medicaid programs have risen dramatically
since their enactment.[46] Concern with these rapidly increasing expenditures led to a series of reforms intended to reduce the budgetary outlays
associated with each program. In Medicare, the cost containment strategy focused on gradually increasing the share of medical expenses paid
for by elderly citizens through raising the coinsurance and deductible
payments mandated in the Social Security Act. Congress also attempted
to reduce total Medicare expenditures by removing the restrictions that
limited coverage for home health services to those necessary for treatment of conditions for which the claimant received inpatient hospital
care. To control Medicaid expenditures, the state and federal governments have employed a variety of strategies, most of which reduce
services or benefits. At the state level, these include discontinuing coverage for specific services, tightening eligibility requirements, and lowering reimbursements to service providers.[47] At the federal level, the
actions directed at containing costs focus on "capping" or limiting the
federal share of Medicaid outlays, strategies that place additional pressure on already strained state budgets.

While the federal and state governments have assigned a high priority
to limiting their expenditures for medical care on behalf of older persons,
others have given some attention to the issue of adequacy. The National
Commission on Social Security recommended several changes intended

to improve the income protection offered to elderly individuals by Medicare.[48] The commission proposed to reduce the out-of-pocket expenses incurred by individuals for medical care by modifying the cost-sharing (coinsurance and deductibles) requirements in Medicare and by establishing a two-thousand-dollar annual limit on the cost-sharing payments made by individuals.

The recently liberalized Medicare coverage for home health visits, although enacted, in part, as a cost-saving measure, also represents an effort to meet more adequately the long-term health-care needs of older adults by providing an alternative to institutional (hospital or nursing home) care, an action that raises an additional issue—the appropriate mix or balance between institutional care and home or community based care. Certainly, the varying needs of the older population suggest the desirability of providing a continuum of services and facilities. Nevertheless, no consensus exists as to whether public policy should support long-term care arrangements on the basis of their cost effectiveness or on the basis of their ability to meet effectively the diverse needs of elderly persons and their families.

Continuing increases in the cost of medical care do not bode well for those advocating more adequate and flexible Medicare and Medicaid programs. Although future health-care policy may continue to encourage a shift away from institutional care, there appears little chance of any policy enactments that effectively reduce the financial burden medical expenses impose upon older persons. Instead, future initiatives appear likely to embody strategies for further reducing government's share of the medical bills incurred by aged individuals, especially in light of forecasts indicating that the HI trust fund will run out of money in around 1990.

A final issue area—the provision of social services to older adults—will also appear on the policy agenda. The choices confronting policymakers and advocates involve the selection of service delivery strategies most likely to meet the needs of elderly individuals, especially in light of historically inadequate funding, rising need, and resistance to increased government spending. At present, the aged population receives services primarily from categorical programs funded through the Older American's Act and Title XX of the Social Security Act. For the most part, these programs determine eligibility on the basis of age rather than need or a combination of age and need. Consequently, the few dollars (relative to total need) allocated to these programs frequently fail to assist those segments of the elderly population with the greatest need.[49] As appropriations available to these programs suffer because of budgetary reductions or the effects of inflation, policymakers will have to choose between either spreading the appropriated funds across the entire aged population or targeting funds to those most in need. Several factors, including the risks associated with a shift in entitlement formulas, the self-interest of aging network organizations, and a reluctance to change an approach that has worked in the past, indicate that a significant change toward need-based entitlement will not occur. Instead, the existing web of programs will continue with minimal increases in funding and, perhaps, with the adoption of a bloc grant approach not only for Title XX funds but also for some funds provided under the Older American's Act.

CONCLUSION

A forecast of future directions in old-age policy cannot ignore today's reality. The old-age policy environment has changed over the past few decades in several important ways that could limit future policy developments. Inflation and slow economic growth have replaced unemployment and inadequate demand as the macroeconomic problems future economic and social policies will attempt to alleviate, a change reflected in the debates over Social Security's effects on capital formation and the macroeconomic consequences of early retirement. Existing retirement income security, health care, and social service programs have, despite their flaws, improved the living conditions of older Americans to the point where elderly citizens, as a group, appear relatively well off and not the segment of the population most deserving of additional public assistance. Public support for governmental efforts to help those in need has eroded as has the public's willingness to pay the taxes necessary to finance social welfare programs. And, finally, official decision makers, including the president and many members of Congress, now question the desirability and effectiveness of public intervention on behalf of the needy.

Within this policy environment, considerations of cost rather than adequacy appear most likely to influence the policy choices made by decision makers. Consequently, the prospects for either significant improvements in presently inadequate cash benefit and service programs or substantial new policy initiatives look dim. Instead, future policy decisions will emphasize directing scarce resources to older persons with demonstrable needs and trimming, where politically feasible, the benefits provided under existing programs.

Finally, the changes in the policy environment suggest that older people and the groups active on their behalf will have to launch and maintain an intensive lobbying effort first to protect existing programs and appropriations and then, if possible, to secure passage of new programs. As noted in earlier chapters, any such mobilization of the elderly will be neither an easy process nor an inevitable occurrence. This factor further erodes the political prospects for maintaining the gains elderly Americans have won in the past few decades.

NOTES

1. R. Miliband, *The State Capitalist Society* (New York: Basic Books, 1969).

2. J. O'Connor, *The Fiscal Crisis of the State* (New York: St. Martin's, 1973).

3. Miliband, *State Capitalist Society*.

4. W. Graebner, *A History of Retirement* (New Haven: Yale University Press, 1980).

5. Martin S. Feldstein, "Social Security, Induced Retirement, and Aggregate Capital Accumulation," *Journal of Political Economy* 82 (1974): 905–26; Alicia H. Munnell, *The Future of Social Security* (Washington, D.C.: Brookings Institution, 1977).

6. Martha Derthick, *Policymaking for Social Security* (Washington, D.C.: Brookings Institution, 1979).

7. Charles Lindblom, "The Science of Muddling Through," *Public Administration Review* 19 (1959): 79–88; and Carroll L. Estes, *The Aging Enterprise* (San Francisco: Jossey-Bass, 1979).

8. The following analysis draws heavily on Thomas Weisskopf, "The Current Economic Crisis in Historical Perspective," *Socialist Review* 11 (1981): 9–53.

9. Ibid.

10. L. C. Thurow, *The Zero-Sum Society* (New York: Penguin Books, 1981).

11. Robert B. Hudson, "The 'Graying' of the Federal Budget and Its Consequences for Old-Age Policy," *Gerontologist* 18, part 1 (1978): 428–40.

12. The term *cost*, as used here, refers only to budgetary costs and not to the cost of these programs in terms of their impact on national income accounts. When viewed in a budgetary context, these programs appear quite costly. However, when viewed in the context of their effect on national income, old-age programs appear relatively cost-free because, rather than depleting economic resources, they only transfer these resources from one sector of the economy to another. Consequently, by paying attention only to budgetary considerations, the current debate overestimates the economic costs of old-age policies.

13. Robert Binstock, "A Policy Agenda on Aging for the Eighties," in *Aging: Agenda for the Eighties—A National Journal Issues Book*, ed. J. P. Hubbard (Washington, D.C.: Government Research Corporation, 1979).

14. U. S., Congress, House, Select Committee on Aging, *Retirement: The Broken Promise* (Washington, D.C.: Government Printing Office, 1981).

15. P. L. Grimaldi, *Supplemental Security Income* (Washington, D.C.: American Enterprise Institute, 1980).

16. Robert B. Hudson, "Old Age Politics in a Time of Change," in *Aging and Society: Current Research and Policy Perspectives*, ed. E. F. Borgatta and M. G. McCluskey (Beverly Hills: Sage, 1980).

17. B. Neugarten, "Policy for the 1980s: Age or Need Entitlement," in Hubbard, *Aging*.

18. Estes, *Aging Enterprise*.

19. A shift to need entitlement, especially in retirement income programs, may have a negative effect on incentives to save for retirement. If an individual can count on receiving a generous public pension at age sixty-five, he or she may have no incentive to save for retirement during their working years. Accordingly, incentive effects may require low benefit levels in need-based programs. Hudson, "Graying of the Federal Budget"; Neugarten, "Policy for the 1980s."

20. J. H. Schulz, "Pension Policy at a Crossroads: What Should Be the Pension Mix?" *Gerontologist* 21 (February 1981): 46–53; J. H. Schulz, *The Economics of Aging*, 2nd ed. (Belmont, Cal.: Wadsworth, 1980).

21. U. S., Congressional Budget Office, *Paying for Social Security: Funding Options for the Near Term* (Washington, D.C.: Congressional Budget Office, 1981).

22. Munnell, *Future of Social Security*.

23. M. S. Feldstein, "Facing the Social Security Crisis," *Public Interest* 47 (1977): 88–100.

24. P. J. Ferrara, *Social Security* (San Francisco: Cato Institute, 1980).

25. Also see Milton Friedman, *Social Security: Universal or Selective?* (Washington,

25. Also see Milton Friedman, *Social Security: Universal or Selective?* (Washington, D.C.: American Enterprise Institute, 1972).

26. Derthick, *Policymaking for Social Security*.

27. Ibid.

28. U. S. Advisory Council on Social Security, *Report of the 1979 Advisory Council on Social Security* (Washington, D.C.: Government Printing Office, 1979).

29. Congressional action in 1977 to decouple benefit increases for active workers from those for retired workers and to shift the indexing of benefits for active workers from the movement of prices to changes in wages represented a benefit cut for those who retired after the new formula became effective.

30. R. M. Ball, *Social Security: Today and Tomorrow* (New York: Columbia University Press, 1978); and R. M. Ball, testimony before U. S. House Committee on Ways and Means, Subcommittee on Social Security, *Social Security Financing*, 97th Cong., 1st Sess. (Washington, D.C.: Government Printing Office, 1981).

31. Munnell, *Future of Social Security*.

32. The controversy over the minimum benefit is, in fact, a red herring. Existing law freezes the minimum benefit at $122 per month. Consequently, its significance will diminish with increases in the cost of living and the upward adjustment of normal Social Security benefits.

33. National Commission on Social Security, *Social Security in America's Future* (Washington, D.C.: Government Printing Office, 1981).

34. Consultant Panel on Social Security, *Report of the Consultant Panel on Social Security to the Congressional Research Service*, Prepared for the use of the Senate Committee on Finance and the House Committee on Ways and Means, 94th Cong., 2nd Sess. (Washington, D.C.: Goverment Printing Office, 1976). In most years, the growth of wages has exceeded the growth in prices. Thus, under wage indexing, replacement rates remain stable but Social Security as a percentage of GNP would rise. In contrast, under price indexing, replacement rates fall while Social Security taxes and expenditures as a percentage of GNP remain stable. Derthick, *Policymaking For Social Security*.

35. Under current law, beneficiaries age sixty-five to seventy-two (sixty-five to seventy in 1982) lose one dollar of their Social Security retirement benefit for every two dollars they earn in excess of an annual exempt amount—$5,500 in 1981 and $6,000 in 1982.

36. Among those advocating repeal are NRTA/AARP, whereas NCOA advocates liberalizing the earnings test for low-income workers. U.S., Congress, Select Committee on Aging, House Subcommittee on Retirement Income and Employment, Social Security Earnings Test, *Hearings*, 96th Cong., 2nd Sess. (Washington, D.C.: Government Printing Office, June 21, 1980).

37. Testimony of David Stockman, in U.S., Congress, House Committee on Ways and Means, Subcommittee on Social Security, *Social Security Financing*, 97th Cong. 1st Sess. (Washington, D.C.: Government Printing Office, 1981), p 711.

38. Derthick, *Policymaking for Social Security*.

39. For examples of proposals calling for a separation of individual equity and social adequacy functions, see Munnell, *Future of Social Security*; Michael J. Boskin, ed., *The Crisis in Social Security: Problems and Prospects* (San Francisco: Institute for Contemporary Studies, 1977); Grimaldi, *Supplemental Security Income*.

40. For examples of proposals recommending an expansion of private pensions see Feldstein, "Facing the Social Security Crisis"; Boskin, *The Crisis in Social Security*; Ferrara, *Social Security*; President's Commission on Pension Policy, *Coming of Age: Toward a National Retirement Income Policy* (Washington, D.C.: The Commission, 1981; and Friedman, *Social Security*.

41. Testimony of P. McColough, in U.S., Congress, House, Committee on Ways and Means, Subcommittee on Social Security, *Social Security Financing*.

42. President's Commission on Pension Policy, *Coming of Age*.

43. National Commission on Social Security, *Social Security in America's Future*.

44. The absence of private plan benefits can have a significant impact on the adequacy of postretirement income. In a projection of retirement income, Schulz, *Economics of Aging*, reports that 23 percent of retired couples and 77 percent of retired individuals with Social Security as their sole source of benefits will have retirement incomes below 125 percent of the official poverty line. In contrast, only 5 percent of the couples and 26 percent of the individuals receiving benefits from both private and public plans will have retirement incomes below or slightly above the poverty line. Dual recipients can also expect higher replacement rates. While 22 percent of the couples and 1 percent of the individuals receiving Social Security alone will replace at least 65 percent of their preretirement earnings, 56 percent of the couples and 36 percent of the individuals with more than one source of retirement benefits will have replacement rates at or above this level.

45. McColough, testimony, p. 409.

46. In 1967, Medicare expenditures approached $4 billion and had increased to $34 billion by 1980. Expenditures for Medicaid followed a similar pattern, increasing from approximately $3.5 billion in 1968 to $27 billion in 1980, with 40 percent of this amount paid on behalf of older persons.

47. K. Davis and C. Schoen, *Health and the War on Poverty: A Ten Year Appraisal* (Washington, D.C.: Brookings Institution, 1978).

48. National Commission on Social Security, *Social Security in America's Future*.

49. Binstock, "Policy Agenda on Aging"; Estes, *Aging Enterprise*.

Bibliography

SOCIAL POLICY ISSUES: INTERDISCIPLINARY COLLECTIONS AND OVERVIEWS

Achenbaum, Wilbert Andrew. "Old Age in the U.S., 1790 to the Present." Ph.D. diss., University of Michigan, 1976.

_____. *Old Age in the New Land*. Baltimore: Johns Hopkins University Press, 1978.

Barron, Milton. "Minority Group Characteristics of the Aged in American Society." *Journal of Gerontology* 8 (1953):477-81.

Binstock, Robert H. "Aging and the Future of American Politics," *Annals* 415 (1974):199-212.

Binstock, Robert H., and Shanas, Ethel, eds. *Handbook of Aging and the Social Sciences*. New York: Van Nostrand Reinhold, 1976.

Borgatta, E. F., and McCluskey, M. G., eds. *Aging and Society: Current Research and Policy Perspectives*. Beverly Hills: Sage, 1980.

Brotman, Herman A. "The Aging of America: A Demographic Profile," *National Journal* (October 1978):1622-27.

Brown, Leo E., ed. *Quality of Life*. Acton, Mass.: Publishers Science Group, 1975.

Brown, M. R., ed. *Readings in Gerontology*. 2d ed. St. Louis: C. V. Mosby, 1978.

Butler, Robert N. "Pacification and the Politics of Aging." *Aging and Human Development* 5 (1974).

_____. *Why Survive? Being Old in America*. New York: Harper & Row, 1975.

Califano, Joseph A., Jr. "Aging of America: Questions for the Four-Generation Society." *Annals* 438 (July 1978):96-97.

_____. "United States Policy for the Aging—A Commitment to Ourselves." *National Journal* 10 (September 1978):1575-87.

Cowgill, Donald, and Holmes, Lowell. *Aging and Modernization*. New York: Appleton-Century-Crofts, 1972.

Crandall, Richard C. *Gerontology: A Behavioral Science Approach*. Reading, Mass.: Addison-Wesley, 1980.

Dahlin, Michael. "Problems of Old Age in America, 1890-1929." Ph.D. diss., Stanford University, 1977.

Delgado, Maria, and Finley, Gordon E. "The Spanish-Speaking Elderly: A Bibliography." *Gerontologist* 18 (August 1978):387-94.

Donahue, Wilma, and Tibbetts, Clark, eds. *Politics of Age*. Ann Arbor: University of Michigan Press, 1962.

Drake, Joseph T. *The Aged in American Society*. New York: Ronald Press, 1958.

Eisele, Frederick R., ed. *Political Consequences of Aging*. American Academy of Political and Social Science Annals 415 (September 1974).

Epstein, Abraham. *Facing Old Age*. New York: Knopf, 1922.

Etzioni, A. "Old People and Public Policy," *Social Policy* 7 (1976):21–29.

Fischer, David Hackett. *Growing Old in America*. New York: Oxford University Press, 1977.

Fowles, Donald G. *Statistical Reports on Older Americans: Some Prospects for the Future Aging Population*. Washington, D.C.: Department of Health, Education, and Welfare, 1978.

Gelfand, Donald E., and Olsen, Jody K. *The Aging Network: Programs and Services*. New York: Springer, 1980.

Harris, Diana, and Cole, William E. *Sociology of Aging*. Boston: Houghton Mifflin, 1980.

Harris, Louis, and Associates, Inc. *The Myth and Reality of Aging in America*. Washington, D.C.: National Council on the Aging, July 1976.

Hendricks, Jon, and Hendricks, Davis C. *Aging in Mass Society: Myths and Realities*. Cambridge, Mass.: Winthrop, 1977.

_____, eds. *Dimensions of Aging: Readings*. Cambridge, Mass: Winthrop, 1979.

Hessel, Dieter, ed. *Maggie Kuhn on Aging*. Philadelphia: Westminster Press, 1977.

Hill, Robert, "A Demographic Profile of the Black Elderly." *Aging* nos. 287–288 (1978):2–9.

Hubbard, J. P., ed. *Aging: Agenda for the Eighties—A National Journal Issues Book*. Washington, D.C.: Government Research Corporation, 1979.

Hudson, Robert B. "Emerging Pressures on Public Policies for the Aging." *Society* (July–August 1978): 30–34.

_____. "The 'Graying' of the Federal Budget and Its Consequences for Old-Age Policy." *Gerontologist* 18, part 1 (October 1978): 428–40.

_____. "Political and Budgetary Consequences of an Aging Population." *National Journal* (October 1978): 1699–1705.

_____, ed. *The Aging in Politics: Process and Policy*. Springfield, Ill.: Charles C. Thomas, 1981.

Jackson, Jacquelyne Johnson. *Double Jeopardy: The Older Negro in America Today*. New York: National Urban League, 1964.

_____. *Minorities and Aging*. Belmont, Calif.: Wadsworth, 1980.

_____. "Morality Patterns for Aged Blacks and Whites, United States, 1964–1978." *Black Scholar* (Winter 1982).

Jones, Rochelle. *The Other Generation: The New Power of Older People*. Englewood Cliffs, N.J.: Prentice-Hall, 1977.

Kart, Cary S., and Manard, Barbara B., eds. *Aging in America: Readings in Social Gerontology*. New York: Knopf, 1975.

Kolko, Gabriel. *Main Currents in American History*. New York: Harper & Row, 1976.

Kuhn, Maggie. "Open Letter." *Gerontologist* 18 (October 1978): 422–24.

Kutza, Elizabeth Ann. *The Benefits of Old Age*. Chicago: University of Chicago Press, 1981.

Levin, Jack, and Levin, William C. *Ageism: Prejudice and Discrimination Against the Elderly*. Belmont, Calif: Wadsworth, 1980.

Lowy, Louis. *Social Policies and Programs on Aging*. Lexington, Mass.: Heath-Lexington Books, 1980.

Markson, Elizabeth, and Batra, Gretchen. *Public Policies for an Aging Population*. Lexington, Mass: Heath-Lexington Books, 1980.

McMillan, Alma W., and Bixby, Ann Kallman. "Social Welfare Expenditures, Fiscal Year 1978." *Social Security Bulletin* 43 (May 1980):3–17.

Morgan, John C. *Becoming Old: An Introduction to Social Gerontology*. New York: Springer, 1979.

National Council on Aging. *Fact Book on Aging: A Profile of America's Older Population*. Washington, D.C.: National Council on Aging, 1979.

Neugarten, Bernice. "Patterns of Aging: Past, Present and Future." *Social Service Review* (December 1973):571–80.

———. *Social Policy, Social Ethics and the Aging Society*. Chicago: University of Chicago Press, 1976.

O'Connor, James. *The Fiscal Crisis of the State*. New York: St. Martin's Press, 1973.

Olson, Laura Katz, *The Political Economy of Aging: The State, Private Power and Social Welfare*. New York: Columbia University Press, 1982.

Orbach, Harold L., and Tibbitts, Clark, eds. *Aging and the Economy*. Ann Arbor: University of Michigan Press, 1963.

Oriol, William E. "The Donald P. Kent Memorial Lecture: 'Modern' Age and Public Policy." *Gerontologist* 21 (February 1981): 35–45.

Osterbind, Carter C., ed. *Social Goals, Social Programs and the Aging*. Gainesville: University Presses of Florida, 1975.

Pampel, Fred C. *Social Change and the Aged: Recent Trends in the U.S.* Lexington, Mass: Heath-Lexington Books, 1980.

Pechman, Joseph A., ed. *The 1978 Budget: Setting National Priorities*. Washington, D.C.: Brookings Institution, 1977.

Quidagno, Jill S., ed. *Aging, the Individual and Society*. New York: St. Martin's Press, 1980.

Radosh, Ronald, and Rothbard, Murray N., eds. *New History of Leviathan*. New York: Dutton, 1972.

Riesman, Frank. *Older Persons: Unused Resources for Unmet Needs*. Los Angeles: Sage, 1977.

Riley, Matilda White, and Foner, Anne, eds. *Aging and Society: An Inventory of Research Findings*. Vol. 1. New York: Russell Sage, 1968.

Riley, Matilda White; Riley, John W., Jr.; and Johnson, Marilyn E. *Aging and Society: Aging and the Professions*. Vol. 2. New York: Russell Sage, 1969.

Riley, Matilda White; Johnson, Marilyn; and Foner, Anne, eds. *Aging and Society: A Sociology of Age Stratification*. Vol. 3. New York: Russell Sage, 1972.

Schwartz, Arthur N., and Peterson, James A. *Introduction to Gerontology*. New York: Holt, Rinehart and Winston, 1979.

Seltzer, Mildred M.; Corbett, Sherry L.; and Atchley, Robert C., eds. *Social Problems of the Aging: Readings*. Belmont, Cal: Wadsworth, 1978.

Spencer, Marian G., and Dorr, Caroline J., eds. *Understanding Aging: A Multi-disciplinary Approach*. New York: Appleton-Century-Crofts, 1975.

Stanford, Percil, ed. *Minority Aging and the Legislative Process*. San Diego, Cal.: Center on Aging, 1977.

Tenenbaum, Frances. *Over 55 Is Not Illegal*. Boston: Houghton Mifflin, 1979.

Tibbetts, Clark, ed. *Handbook of Social Gerontology*. Chicago: University of Chicago Press, 1960.

Townsend, C. *Old Age: The Last Segregation*. New York: Bantam Books, 1971.

Turner, Judith. "White House Report: Conference on Elderly Seeks Change in Attitude Toward Elderly." *National Journal* (September 15, 1971).

U.S. Congress. House. Select Committee on Aging. *Funding of Federal Programs for Older Americans*. 94th Cong., 2nd sess. Washington, D.C.: Government Printing Office, September 1976.

U.S. Congress. Senate. Special Committee on Aging. *Developments in Aging: 1977*, parts 1, 2. 95th Cong., 2nd sess. Washington, D.C.: Government Printing Office, April 27, 1978.

————. *Developments in Aging: 1978*, parts 1, 2. 96 Cong., 1st sess. Washington, D.C.: Government Printing Office, March 30, 1979.

————. *Developments in Aging: 1979*, parts 1, 2. 96th Cong., 2nd sess. Washington, D.C.: Government Printing Office, February 28, 1980.

————. *The Proposed Fiscal 1981 Budget: What It Means for Older Americans*. 96th Cong., 2nd sess. Information paper prepared by the staff. Washington, D.C.: Government Printing Office, February 1980.

U.S. Congress. Senate. Committee on Labor and Public Welfare. Subcommittee on Aging, and Special Committee on Aging. *Post-White House Conference on Aging Reports*. 93rd Cong., 1st sess., 1973. Washington, D.C.: Government Printing Office, April 1973.

U.S. Department of Health, Education, and Welfare. *The Nation and Its Older People: Report of the White House Conference on Aging, January 9–12, 1961*. Washington, D.C.: Government Printing Office, April 1961.

U.S. Federal Council on the Aging. *National Policy Concerns for Older Women*. Washington, D.C.: Government Printing Office, 1975.

————. *Annual Report to the President, 1976*. Washington, D.C.: Government Printing Office, January 14, 1977.

U.S. National Advisory Committee for the 1961 White House Conference on Aging. *Aging in the States*. Washington, D.C.: Government Printing Office, January 1961.

Vinyard, Dale. "The Senate Special Committee on the Aging. *Gerontologist* 12, part 1 (Autumn 1972):298–303.

————. "Senate Committee on the Aging and Development of a Policy System." *Michigan Academician* (Winter 1973).

————. *A Policy System for the Aged: Some Preliminary Observations*. Occasional Papers in Gerontology. Ann Arbor. Wayne State University-University of Michigan Institute of Gerontology, 1975.

————. "Rediscovery of the Aged: Senior Power and Public Policy." *Society* (July-August 1978): 24–27.

————. "White House Conferences and the Aged." *Social Service Review* (December 1979): 655–71.

————. "The House Select Committee on the Aging." *Long Term Care and Health Sevices Administration Quarterly* 3 (Winter 1979): 317–24.

————. "Public Policy and the Elderly: Some Additional Considerations." *Social Thought* (Spring 1980): 37–40.

Ward, Russell A. *The Aging Experience: An Introduction to Social Gerontology.* New York: Lippincott, 1979.

Wiles, Marilyn M. *Old Age and Ruralism: A Case of Double Jeopardy.* Albany: New York Senate Research Service, 1980.

Witmer, T. R. "The Aging of the House." *Political Science Quarterly* 79 (1964): 526–41.

Woodruff, Diana S., and Birren, James E., eds. *Aging: Scientific Perspectives and Social Issues.* New York: D. Van Nostrand, 1975.

POLITICAL PARTICIPATION AND POLITICAL BEHAVIOR OF OLDER PEOPLE

Abramson, Paul R. *Generational Change in American Politics.* Lexington, Mass.: Heath, 1975.

Agnello, Thomas J. "Aging and the Sense of Political Powerlessness." *Public Opinion Quarterly* 37 (1973): 251–59.

Alford, Robert R., and Friedland, R. "Political Participation and Public Policy." *Annual Review of Sociology* (1975): 429–79.

Atchley, Robert C. *The Social Forces in Later Life.* 2d ed. Belmont, Calif.: Wadsworth, 1977.

Binstock, Robert. "Interest-Group Liberalism and the Politics of Aging." *Gerontologist* 12 (Autumn 1972): 265–80.

Cain, Leonard, "The Young and the Old: Coalition or Conflict Ahead?" *American Behavioral Scientist* 19 (1975) 166–75.

Cameron, Sandra W. "The Politics of the Elderly." *Midwest Quarterly* (Winter 1974):141–53.

Campbell, Angus. "Politics Through the Life Cycle." *Gerontologist* 11 (Summer 1971):112–117.

Carlie, Michael K. "The Politics of Age: Interest Group or Social Movement." *Gerontologist* 9 (Winter 1969):259–63.

Clemente, F. "Age and the Perception of National Priorities." *Gerontologist* 15 (1975):61–63.

Critenden, John. "Aging and Party Affiliation." *Public Opinion Quarterly* 26 (1962):648–57.

Cumming, Elaine, and Henry, William E. *Growing Old: The Process of Disengagement.* New York: Basic Books, 1961.

Cutler, Neal E. "Generation, Maturation and Party Affiliation." *Public Opinion Quarterly* 33 (1969–70):513–88.

———. "Demographic, Social-Psychological, and Political Factors in the Politics of Aging: A Foundation for Research in 'Political Gerontology.'" *American Political Science Review* 71 (September 1977):1011–25.

———. "The Impact of Population Dynamics on Public Policy: The Perspective of Political Gerontology." *Policy Studies Journal* 6 (Winter 1977):167–74.

———, and Bingston, Vern L. "Age and Political Alienation: Maturation, Generation, and Period Effects." *Annals* 415 (September 1974):160–75.

Cutler, Stephen J., and Kaufman, Robert L. "Change in Political Attitudes: Tolerance of Ideological Nonconformity," *Public Opinion Quarterly* (September 1975):69–81.

Dawson, Richard. *Public Opinion and Political Disarray*. New York: Harper & Row, 1973.

Dobson, Douglas, and Karns, David A. *Public Policy and Senior Citizens: Policy Formulation in the American States*. Washington, D.C., Administration on Aging, 1979.

Dobson, Douglas, and St. Angelo, Douglas. *Politics and Senior Citizens: Advocacy and Policy Formation in a Local Context*. Washington, D.C.: Administration on Aging, 1980.

Dodge, Richard W., and Uyeki, Eugene S. "Political Affiliation and Imagery Across Two Related Generations." *Midwest Journal of Political Science* (1963): 266–76.

Douglass, Elizabeth; Cleveland William; and Maddox, George. "Political Attitudes, Age and Aging." *Journal of Gerontology* (1974):666–75.

Dreyer, Edward, and Rosenbaum, Walter, eds. *Political Opinion and Behavior*. 3rd ed. Belmont, Calif.: Duxbury Press, 1976

Eisele, Frederick R., ed. "Political Consequences of Aging," *Annals* 415 (September 1974).

Estes, Carroll L. "Political Gerontology." *Society* (July–August 1978):43–49.

Flanigan, William, and Zingale, Nancy. *Political Behavior of the American Electorate*. Boston, Mass.: Allyn and Bacon, 1978.

Foner, Ann. "Age Stratification and Age Conflict in Political Life." *American Sociological Review* 39 (April 1974):187–96.

———. "Age and Society: Structure and Change." *American Behavioral Scientist* 19 (1975): 144–65.

Free, Lloyd, and Cantril, Hadley. *The Political Beliefs of Americans: A Study of Public Opinion*. New York: Simon & Schuster, 1968.

Gelb, Betsy D. "Gray Power: Next Challenge to Business?" *Business Horizons* 20 (April 1977):38–45.

Gergen, Kenneth, and Bach, Kurt. "Aging, Time Perspective and Preferred Solution to International Conflict." *Journal of Conflict Resolution* (June 1965): 176–86.

———. "Communication in the Interview and the Disengaged Respondent." *Public Opinion Quarterly* 30 (1966):385–98.

Glamser, F. "The Importance of Age to Conservative Opinions: A Multivariate Analysis." *Journal of Gerontology* 29 (1974):549–54.

Glenn, Norval D. "Aging, Disengagement and Opinionation." *Public Opinion Quarterly* 33 (1969):17–33.

———. "Aging and Conservatism." *Annals* 415 (1974): 176–86.

Glenn, Norval, and Grimes, Michael. "Aging, Voting and Political Interest." *American Sociological Review* 33 (August 1968):563–75.

Glenn, Norval D., and Hefner, Ted. "Further Evidence on Aging and Party Identification." *Public Opinion Quarterly* 36 (1972): 31–47.

Gubrium, Jaber. "Continuity in Social Support, Political Interest and Voting in Old Age." *Gerontologist* 12 (Winter 1972):418–22.

Henretta, J. C. "Political Protest by the Elderly: An Organizational Study." Ph.D. diss., Harvard University, 1973.

Hess, Clinton, and Kerschner, Paul. *Silver Lobby*. Los Angeles: University of Southern California Press, 1978.

Holtzman, Abraham. "Analysis of Old Age Political Behavior in the United States." *Journal of Gerontology* 9 (1954):56–66.

———— . *The Townsend Movement*. New York: Bookman Association, 1963.

House J. S., and Mason, W. M. "Political Alienation in America, 1952–1968." *American Sociological Review* 40 (1975): 123–47.

Jacobs, Ruth, and Hess, Beth. "Panther Power: Symbol and Substance."*Long-Term Care and Health Services Administration Quarterly* (Fall 1979):238–44.

Kerschner, Paul. *Advocacy and Age*. Los Angeles: Andrus Gerontology Center, 1976.

Kirkpatrick, Samuel. "Aging Effects and Generational Differences in Social Welfare Attitude Constraint in Mass Public, 1952–1972." *Western Political Quarterly* (March 1976):45–58.

Kleyman, P. *Senior Power*. San Francisco: Glide Press, 1974.

Knoke, David. "Social and Demographic Factions in Party Affiliation." *American Sociological Review* (1974):700–713.

Leotta, Louis. "Abraham Epstein and Movement for Old Age Security." *Labor History* (Summer 1975):359–77.

Martin, William; Bengtson, Vern; and Acock, Al. "Alienation and Age: A Context Specific Approach." *Social Forces* 53 (November 1974): 267–84.

Milbrath, Lester W., and Goel, M. L. *Political Participation*. Chicago: Rand McNally, 1977.

Miller, Arthur H.; Gurin, Patricia; and Gurin, Gerald. "Age Consciousness and Political Mobilization of Older Americans," *Gerontologist* 20 (December 1980):691–700.

Nie, Norman, and Verba, S. "Political Participation and the Life Cycle." *Comparative Politics* (April 1974):319–40.

Nie, Norman; Verba, S.; and Petrocik, J.R. *The Changing American Voter*. Cambridge: Harvard University Press, 1976.

Pederson, Johannes. "Age and Change in Public Opinion." *Public Opinion Quarterly* (Summer 1976):143–53.

Pinner, Frank; Jacobs, Paul; and Selznick, Philip. *Old Age and Political Behavior: Case Study*. Berkeley: University of California Press, 1959.

Polner, Walter. "The Aged in Politics: Passage of the Railroad Retirement Act of 1934." *Gerontologist* (1962):207–15.

Pomper, Gerald. *Voter's Choice*. New York: Harper & Row, 1975.

Pratt, Henry J. "Old Age Associations in National Politics. *Annals* 415 (1974):106–19.

———— . *The Gray Lobby: Politics of Old Age*. Chicago: University of Chicago Press, 1976.

———— . "Symbolic Politics and the Aged." *Society* (July–August 1978):67–72.

———— . "Political Science and the Politics of Aging as a Field of Study." *Research in Aging* 1 (June 1979):155–86.

———— . "The Aged Agitation and Advocacy." *Generations* (May 1980):33–34.

Prothro, James, and Grigg, Charles. "Fundamental Principles of Democracy: Bases of Agreement and Disagreement." *Journal of Politics* 22 (1960): 276–94.

Putnam, Jackson. *Old Age Politics in California: From Richardson to Reagan*. Stanford, Cal.: Stanford University Press, 1970.

Ragan, Pauline. "Another Look at the Politicizing of Old Age." *Urban and Social Change Review* 10 (1977):6–13.

Ragan, Pauline, and Davis, William J. "Diversity of Older Voters." *Society* (July–August 1978):50–53.

Ragan, Pauline, and Dowd, James J. "The Emerging Political Consciousness of the Aged: A Generational Interpretation." *Journal of Social Issues* 39 (1974):137–58.

Riemer, Yosef, and Binstock, Robert M. "Campaigning for the Senior Vote: A Case Study of Carter's 1976 Campaign." *Gerontologist* 18 (December 1978): 517–24.

Riley, Matilda. "Aging and Cohort Succession: Interpretations and Misinterpretations." *Public Opinion Quarterly* 37 (1973):35–49.

Rose, Arnold, and Peterson, Warren, eds. *Older People and Their Social World.* Philadelphia: F. A. Davis, 1965.

Sanders, Daniel S. *Impact of Reform Movements on Social Policy Change: Case Study of Social Insurance.* Fair Lawn, N.J.: R. E. Burdick, 1973.

Schmidhauser, John. "The Political Behavior of Older Persons." *Western Political Quarterly* 2 (1958):113–24.

———. "The Political Influence of the Aged." *Gerontologist* (Spring 1968): 44–49.

Torres-Gil, Fernando, and Becerra, Rosina M. "The Political Behavior of the Mexican-American Elderly." *Gerontologist* 17 (October 1977):392–99.

Trela, James. "Some Political Consequences of Senior Centers and Other Old Age Group Memberships." *Gerontologist* (Summer 1971): 118–23.

———. "Age Structure of Voluntary Associations and Political Self-Interest Among the Aged." *Sociological Quarterly* (Spring 1972): 244–52.

———. "Social Class and Association Membership." *Journal of Gerontology* (March 1976): 198–203.

Walker, David B. "The Age Factor in the 1958 Congressional Elections." *Midwest Journal of Political Science* 4 (1960):1–25.

Zody, Richard. "Age and Political Behavior: Search for an Operational Methodology." Ph.D. diss., Southern Illinois University, 1968.

INCOME SUPPORT PROGRAMS AND ECONOMIC RESOURCES OF OLDER PEOPLE

INCOME AND POVERTY

Borziller, Thomas C. "In-kind Benefit Programs and Retirement Income Adequacy." *National Journal* 12 (1980):1821–25.

Brotman, Herman B. "Income and Poverty in the Older Population in 1975." *Gerontologist* 17 (February 1977):23–26.

Cook, Fay Lomax. "The Disabled and the Poor Elderly: Preferred Groups for Public Support?" *Gerontologist* 19 (August 1979):344–53.

Grad, Susan, and Foster, Karen. "Income of the Population 55 and Older, 1976." *Social Security Bulletin* 42 (July 1979):16–32.

Grimaldi, P. L. *Supplemental Security Income.* Washington, D.C.: American Enterprise Institute, 1980.

Harrington, Michael. *The Other America: Poverty in the United States*. Baltimore, Penguin Books, 1971.

──── . "Hiding the Other America." *New Republic* (February 1977):15–17.

Hawkins, Sue C. "SSI: Trends in State Supplementation, 1974–1978." *Social Security Bulletin* 43 (July 1980):19–27.

Moon, Marilyn. *The Management of Economic Welfare: Its Application to the Aged Poor*. New York: Academic Press, 1977.

Orshansky, Mollie, "Counting the Poor: Another Look at the Poverty Profile." *Social Security Bulletin* 28 (1965):3–29.

Pension Rights Center. *Retirement Income—A Report*. Washington, D.C.: Pension Rights Center, Fall 1979.

Piven, Francis Fox, and Cloward, Richard. *Regulating the Poor: The Functions of Public Welfare*. New York: Vintage Books, 1971.

Rigby, Donald E., and Ponce, Elsa Orley. "Supplemental Security Income: Optional State Supplementation, October 1977." *Social Security Bulletin* 42 (October 1979):11–17.

Rodgers, Harrell R., Jr. *Poverty amid Plenty: A Political and Economic Analysis*. Reading, Mass.: Addison-Wesley, 1979.

Rose, Stephen J. *Social Stratification in the U.S.: An Analytic Guidebook*. Baltimore: Social Graphics, 1979.

Tissue, Thomas. "The Survey of the Low-Income Aged and Disabled: An Introduction." *Social Security Bulletin* 40 (February 1977):3–11.

──── . "Low-Income Widows and Other Aged Singles." *Social Security Bulletin* 42 (December 1979):3–10.

U.S. Bureau of the Census. "Characteristics of the Population Below the Poverty Level, 1978." *Current Population Reports*, Series P-60, No. 124. Washington, D.C., Government Printing Office, 1980.

U.S. Congress, House, Select Committee on Aging. *Poverty Among America's Aged*. Hearing, 95th Cong., 2nd sess. Washington, D.C.: Government Printing Office, August 9, 1978.

U.S. Congressional Budget Office. "Poverty Status of Families Under Alternative Definitions of Income." Background Paper no. 17, rev. Washington, D.C., June 1977.

U.S. Department of Health, Education, and Welfare. "The Measure of Poverty, Administrative and Legislative Uses of the Terms 'Poverty,' 'Low-Income,' and Other Related Terms." Technical Paper no. 2. Washington, D.C., 1976.

U.S. Federal Council on the Aging. *The Impact of the Tax Structure on the Elderly*. Washington, D.C.: Government Printing Office, December 29, 1975.

WORK, UNEMPLOYMENT, AND RETIREMENT

Barker, David T., and Clark, Robert L. "Mandatory Retirement and Labor-Force Participation of Respondents in the Retirement History Study." *Social Security Bulletin* 43 (November 1980):20–29.

Batten, M. D., and Kastenbaum, S. "Older People, Work, and Full Employment." *Social Policy* 7 (1976):30–33.

Braverman, Harry. *Labor and Monopoly Capital: The Degradation of Work in the Twentieth Century*. New York: Monthly Review Press, 1976.

Campbell, Shirley. "Delayed Mandatory Retirement and the Working Women." *Gerontologist* 19 (June 1979):257–63.

Cantrell, Stephen R., and Clark, Robert L. "Retirement Policy and Promotional Prospects." *Gerontologist* 20 (October 1980):575–80.

Clark, Robert L., ed. *Retirement Policy in an Aging Society*. Durham, N.C.: Duke University Press, 1980.

Ford, Laura C. "The Implications of the Age Discrimination in Employment Act Amendments of 1978 for Colleges and Universities." *Journal of College and University Law* 5 (1978–1979).

Garraty, John A. *Unemployment in History: Economic Thought and Public Policy*. New York: Harper & Row, 1978.

Henretta, John C., and O'Rand, Angela M. "Labor-Force Participation of Older Married Women." *Social Security Bulletin* 43 (August 1980):10–16.

Ireland, L. M. "Retirement History Study: An Introduction." *Social Security Bulletin* 35 (November 1972):3–8.

Kreps, Juanita M., ed. *Employment, Income, and Retirement Problems of the Aged*. Durham, N.C.: Duke University Press, 1963.

Morgan, Leslie A. "Work in Widowhood: A Viable Option?" *Gerontologist* 20 (October 1980):581–87.

Timmerman, Sandra. "Inequities of Mandatory Retirement: An Overview." *Journal of the Institute for Socioeconomic Studies* (Winter 1977):30–43.

U.S. Congress, Senate, Special Committee on Aging. *Emerging Options for Work and Retirement Policy*. Washington, D.C.: Government Printing Office, 1980.

THE ECONOMICS OF AGING: OVERVIEWS

Clark, Robert L., and Menefee, John. "Federal Expenditures for the Elderly: Past and Future." *Gerontologist* 21 (1981):132–37.

Greenough, W. C., and King, F. P. *Pension Plans and Public Policy*. New York: Columbia University Press, 1976.

Harris, Louis, and Associates, Inc. *Study of American Attitudes Toward Retirement*. Commissioned by Johnson and Higgins. New York. February 1979.

McGill, Dan M. *Social Security and Private Pension Plans: Competitive or Complementary?* Homewood, Ill.: Irwin-Dorsey, 1976.

Samuelson, Robert. "Busting the U.S. Budget: The Costs of an Aging America." *National Journal* (February 18, 1978):256–60.

──── . "Aging America—Who will Shoulder the Growing Burden?" *National Journal* 10 (1978):1712–17.

Schulz, James H. *The Economics of Aging*. 2nd ed. Belmont, Cal.: Wadsworth, 1980.

──── . "Pension Policy at a Crossroads: What Should Be the Pension Mix?" *Gerontologist* 21 (February 1981):46–53.

Thompson, Gayle B. "Pension Coverage and Benefits, 1972: Findings from the Retirement History Study." *Social Security Bulletin* 41 (February 1978):3–17.

U.S. Congress. House. Select Committee on Aging. *Pension Problems of Older Women*. 94th Cong., 1st sess. Washington, D.C.: Government Printing Office, October 21, 1975.

──── . *Retirement: The Broken Promise*. Washington, D.C.: Government Printing Office, 1981.

U.S. President's Commission on Pension Policy. *Coming of Age: Toward a National Retirement Income Policy*. Washington, D.C.: President's Commission on Pension Policy, February 26, 1981.

THE SOCIAL SECURITY SYSTEM

Abbott, Grace. *From Relief to Social Security*. New York: Russell and Russell, 1966.

Ball, Robert M. *Social Security: Today and Tomorrow*. New York, Columbia University Press, 1978.

Bartlett, Dwight K. "Current Developments in Social Security Financing." *Social Security Bulletin* 43 (September 1980): 10–20.

Boskin, Michael J., ed. *The Crisis in Social Security: Problems and Prospects*. San Francisco: Institute for Contemporary Studies, 1977.

Brown, J. D. *Essays on Social Security*. Princeton: Princeton University Press, 1977.

Burkhauser, Richard V. "Are Women Treated Fairly in Today's Social Security System?" *Gerontologist* 19 (June 1979): 242–49.

Burkhauser, Richard, and Holden, Karen, eds. *A Challenge to Social Security: The Changing Roles of Men and Women in American Society*. New York: Academic Press, 1982.

Campbell, R. R. *Social Security: Promise and Reality*. Stanford: Hoover Institute Press, 1977.

Derthick, Martha. *Policymaking for Social Security*. Washington, D.C.: Brookings Institution, 1979.

Douglas, Paul H. *Social Security in the United States: An Analysis and Appraisal of the Federal Social Security Act*. New York: McGraw-Hill, 1936.

Esposito, Louis; Podoff, David; and Prero, Aaron J. "Changing the Taxable Maximum: Effect on Social Security Taxes by Industry and Firm Size." *Social Security Bulletin* 43 (July 1980):3–18.

Esposito, Louis; Mallan, Lucy B.; and Podoff, David. "Distribution of Increased Benefits Under Alternative Earnings Tests." *Social Security Bulletin* 43 (September 1980):3–9.

Feldstein, Martin S. "Social Security, Induced Retirement, and Aggregate Capital Accumulation." *Journal of Political Economy* 82 (September–October 1974): 905–26.

――――. "Facing the Social Security Crisis." *Public Interest* 47 (1977): 88–100.

Ferrara, P. J. *Social Security*. San Francisco, Cato Institute, 1980.

Flowers, R. M. *Women and Social Security: An Institutional Dilemma*. Washington, D.C.: American Enterprise Institute for Public Policy Research, 1977.

Friedman, Milton. *Social Security: Universal or Selective?* Washington, D.C.: American Enterprise Institute 1972.

Gordon, Josephine G., and Schoeplein, Robert N. "Tax Impact from Elimination of the Retirement Test." *Social Security Bulletin* 42 (September 1979):22–32.

Henle, Peter. "Social Security Reform: A Look at the Problems." *Monthly Labor Review* 100 (February 1977):55–58.

Hogan, Timothy. "The Implications of Population Stationarity for the Social Security System." *Social Science Quarterly* (June 1974):151–58.

Holden, Karen C. "The Inequitable Distribution of OASI Benefits Among Homemakers." *Gerontologist* 19 (1979):250–56.

Lingg, Barbara A. "Beneficiaries Affected by the Annual Earnings Test in 1977." *Social Security Bulletin* 43 (December 1980):3–15.

Lubove, Roy. *The Struggle for Social Security*. Cambridge: Harvard University Press, 1968.

Munnell, Alicia H. *The Future of Social Security*. Washington, D.C.: Brookings Institution, 1977.

Sanders, Daniel. *The Impact of Reform Movements on Social Policy Change: The Case of Social Insurance*. Fair Lawn, N.J.: R. E. Burdick, 1973.

Sass, Tim. "Demographic and Economic Characteristics of Nonbeneficiary Widows: An Overview." *Social Security Bulletin* 42 (November 1979): 3–14.

Somers, Tish. "Commentary on Report of the Health, Education, and Welfare Task Force on the Treatment of Women Under Social Security." Washington, D.C.: National Organization of Women, Older Women's Rights Committee, February 1978.

U.S. Advisory Council on Social Security. *Report of the 1979 Advisory Council on Social Security*. Washington, D.C.: Government Printing Office, 1979.

U.S. Department of Health, Education, and Welfare. *Report of the Task Force on the Treatment of Women Under Social Security*. Washington, D.C.: Government Printing Office, February 1978.

———. *Social Security and the Changing Roles of Men and Women*. Washington, D.C.: Government Printing Office, February 1979.

Witte, Edwin, E. *Social Security Perspectives*. Madison: University of Wisconsin Press, 1962.

PRIVATE- AND PUBLIC-SECTOR RETIREMENT SYSTEMS

Barfield, Richard E. *The Automobile Worker and Retirement: A Second Look*. Ann Arbor: University of Michigan, Institute for Social Research, 1970.

Bartell, Robert H., and Simpson, Elizabeth T. *Pension Funds of Multiemployer Industrial Groups, Unions and Nonprofit Organizations*. National Bureau of Economic Research. Occasional Paper 105. New York: Columbia University Press, 1968.

Beier, Emerson. "Incidence of Private Retirement Plans." *Monthly Review Press* 74 (July 1971).

Bell, D. R. "Prevalence of Private Retirement Plans." *Monthly Labor Review* 98 (1975):17–20.

Bernstein, Merton C. *The Future of Private Pensions*. New York: Free Press of Glencoe, 1964.

Bureau of National Affairs. *Highlights of the New Pension Reform Law*. Washington, D.C.: Bureau of National Affairs, 1974.

Chadwick, William J. "The Implementation of ERISA: Progress Made by the Department of Labor." *Labor Law Journal* 28 (February 1977):67–76.

Clark, Robert. *The Role of Private Pensions in Maintaining Living Standards in Retirement*. Washington, D.C.: National Planning Association, October 1977.

Conference Board, Inc. *Financial Management of Company Pension Plans*. Report no. 611. New York: Conference Board, 1973.

Dearing, Charles. *Industrial Pensions*. Washington, D.C.: Brookings Institution, 1954.

Drucker, Peter F. *The Unseen Revolution: How Pension Fund Socialism Came to America*. New York: Harper & Row, 1976.

Glasson, William H. *Federal Military Pensions in the United States*. New York: Oxford University Press, 1918.

Meir, Elizabeth L., and Bremberg, Helen K. *ERISA: Progress and Problems*. Washington, D.C.: National Institute of Industrial Gerontology, National Council on the Aging, 1977.

Melone, Joseph J. *Collectively Bargained Multi-Employer Pension Plans*. Homewood, Ill.: Irwin, 1963.

Olson, Laura Katz "The Political Economy of Worker Pension Funds." In *Employment and Labor-Relations Policy*. Edited by Charles Bulmer and John L. Carmichael, Jr. Lexington, Mass.: Heath, Lexington Books, 1980.

_____ . "Pension Power in the Public Sector." In *The Public Sector Crisis Reader*. Edited by the Union of Radical Political Economists. New York: Monthly Review Press, 1982.

Rifkin, Jeremy, and Barber, Randy. *The North Will Rise Again: Pensions, Politics and Power in the 1980s*. Boston: Beacon Press, 1978.

Rosen, Kenneth T. *The Role of Pension Funds in Housing Finance*. Working Paper no. 35. Boston: Joint Center for Urban Studies of the Massachusetts Institute of Technology and Harvard University, June 1975.

Skolnik, Alfred M. "Private Pension Plans, 1950–1974." *Social Security Bulletin* 39 (June 1976):3–17.

Soldofsky, Robert M. *Institutional Holdings of Common Stock, 1900–2000: History, Projection, and Interpretation*. Ann Arbor: University of Michigan Press, 1971.

Somers, Gerald G., ed. *Proceedings of the Eighteenth Annual Winter Meeting, Industrial Relations Research Association*. Madison, Wisc.: Industrial Relations Research Association, 1965.

Tilove, Robert. *Public Employee Pension Funds*. New York: Columbia University Press, 1976.

Treynor, Jack L.; Regan, Patrick J.; and Priest, William W., Jr. *The Financial Reality of Pension Funding Under ERISA*. Homewood, Ill.: DOW Jones–Irwin, 1976.

U.S. House. Committee on Education and Labor. *Pension Task Force Report on Public Employee Retirement Systems*. 59th Cong., 2nd sess. Washington, D.C.: Government Printing Office, March 15, 1978.

U.S. Senate. Committee on Governmental Affairs. Subcommittee on Reports, Accounting, and Management. *Voting Rights in Major Corporations*. 95th Cong., 1st sess. Washington, D.C.: Government Printing Office, January 1978.

Webb, Lee, and Schweke, William, eds. *Public Employee Pension Funds: New Strategies for Investment*. Washington, D.C.: Conference on Alternative State and Local Policies, July 1979.

HEALTH CARE AND THE ELDERLY

Alford, Robert R. *Health Care Politics*. Chicago: University of Chicago Press, 1975.

Berliner, Howard. "Origins of Health Insurance for the Aged." *International Journal of Health Services* (1973):465–73.

Brown, E. Richard. *Rockefeller Medicine Men: Medicine and Capitalism in America.* Berkeley: University of California Press, 1979.

Carlson, Rick J. *The End of Medicine.* New York: Wiley, 1975.

Clark, Robert Charles. "Does the Nonprofit Form Fit the Hospital Industry." *Harvard Law Review* 93 (May 1980):1407–90.

Cohen, Harris. "Regulating Politics and American Medicine." *American Behavioral Scientist* 19 (September–October 1975):122–36.

Conrad, Fran. "Society May Be Dangerous to Your Health." *Science for the People* 11 (March–April 1979):14–20, 32–34.

Davis, Karen. "Hospital Costs and the Medicare Program." *Social Security Bulletin* 36 (August 1973):18–36.

————. *National Health Insurance.* Washington, D.C.: Brookings Institution, 1975.

————, and Schoen, Cathy. *Health and the War on Poverty.* Washington, D.C.: Brookings Institution, 1978.

Donabedian, Avedis. "Effects of Medicare and Medicaid on Access to and Quality of Health Care." *Public Health Reports* 91 (July–August 1976):322–31.

Ehrenreich, John, ed. *The Cultural Crisis of Modern Medicine.* New York: Monthly Review Press, 1978.

————, and Ehrenreich, Barbara. *The American Health Empire: Power, Profits and Politics.* New York: Vintage Press, 1971.

Epstein, Samuel S. *The Politics of Cancer.* San Francisco: Sierra Club Books, 1978.

Feder, Judith M. *Medicare: The Politics of Federal Hospital Insurance.* Lexington, Mass.: Heath, Lexington Books, 1977.

————; Holahan, John; and Marmor, Theodore, eds. *National Health Insurance.* Washington, D.C.: Urban Institute, 1980.

Feingold, Eugene. *Medicare: Policy and Politics.* San Francisco: Chandler, 1966.

Friedman, Kenneth M., and Rakoff, Stuart H., eds. *Toward a National Health Policy: Public Policy and the Control of Health-Care Costs.* Lexington, Mass.: Heath, Lexington Books, 1977.

Ginsburg, Paul P. "Resource Allocation in the Hospital Industry: The Role of Capital Financing." *Social Security Bulletin* 35 (October 1972):20–30.

Glaser, William A. *Paying the Doctor: Systems of Remuneration and Their Effects.* Baltimore: John Hopkins University Press, 1970.

Gornick, Marian. "Ten Years of Medicare: Impact on the Covered Population." *Social Security Bulletin* 39 (July 1976):3–17.

Harris, Richard. *A Sacred Trust.* New York: New American Library, 1966.

Hirshfield, Daniel S. *The Lost Reform: The Campaign for Compulsory Health Insurance in the U.S. from 1932 to 1943.* Cambridge: Harvard University Press, 1970.

Hoyt, Edwin P. *Condition Critical: Our Hospital Crisis.* New York: Holt, Rinehart and Winston, 1966.

Inglehart, John K. "Health Report: Explosive Rise in Medical Costs Puts Government in Quandary." *National Journal* (September 1975):1319–28.

Jackson, Jacquelyn J. "Special Health Problems of Aged Blacks." *Aging* Nos. 287–88 (1978):15–20.

Kane, Robert L.; Kasteler, Josephine M.; and Gray, Robert M., eds. *The Health Gap: Medical Services and the Poor.* New York: Springer, 1976.

Kass, Leon R. "Regarding the End of Medicine and the Pursuit of Health." *Public Interest* 40 (Summer 1975):11–42.

Kolodrubetz, Walter W. "Group Health Insurance Coverage of Full-Time Employees, 1972." *Social Security Bulletin* 37 (April 1974):17–35.

Loewenstein, Regina. "Early Effects of Medicare on the Health Care of the Aged." *Social Security Bulletin* 34 (April 1971):3–20.

Marmor, Theodore R. *The Politics of Medicare.* Chicago: Aldine, 1973.

Mueller, Marjorie Smith, Gibson, Robert M.; and Fisher, Charles R. "Age Differences in Health Care Spending, Fiscal Year 1976." *Social Security Bulletin* 40 (August 1977):3–14.

Munts, Ray. *Bargaining for Health: Labor Unions, Health Insurance and Medical Care.* Madison: University of Wisconsin Press, 1967.

Myers, Robert J. *Medicare.* Homewood, Ill.: Irwin, 1970.

Pegels, Carl C. *Health Care and the Elderly.* Gaithersburg, Md.: Aspen Systems, 1980.

Ribicoff, Abraham. *The American Medical Machine.* New York: Saturday Review Press, 1972.

Somers, Herman M., and Somers, Anne R. *Medicare and the Hospitals: Issues and Prospects.* Washington, D.C.: Brookings Institution, 1967.

Spiegelman, Mortimer. *Ensuring Medical Care for the Aged.* Homewood, Ill.: Irwin, 1960.

Stevens, Robert, and Stevens, Rosemary. *Welfare Medicine in America: A Case Study of Medicaid.* New York: Free Press, 1974.

U.S. Congress. House. Committee on the Judiciary. Subcommittee on Civil Rights and Constitutional Rights. *Title VI Enforcement in Medicare and Medicaid Programs, Hearings before the Subcommittee.* 93rd Cong., 1st sess. Washington, D.C.: Government Printing Office, 1974.

U.S. Congress. House. Committee on Ways and Means. *Medical Care for the Aged: Executive Hearings Before the Comittee on H.R. 1 and Other Proposals for Medical Care for the Aged.* 89th Cong., 1st sess. Washington, D.C.: Government Printing Office, 1965.

U.S. Congress. Senate. Committee on Aging. *Costs and Delivery of Health Services to Older Americans: Hearings.* 90th Cong., 1st and 2nd sess. Washington, D.C.: Government Printing Office, 1968 and 1969.

U.S. Congress. Senate. Committee on Finance. Subcommittee on Health. *Medicare–Medicaid Administrative and Reimbursement Reform: Hearings Before the Subcommittee.* 94th Cong., 2nd sess. Washington, D.C.: Government Printing Office, July 1976.

U.S. Department of Health, Education, and Welfare. *Health United States, 1976–77.* Washington, D.C.: Government Printing Office, 1977.

———. Social Security Administration. *Background on Medicare 1957–1962: Reports, Studies and Congressional Considerations on Health Legislation.* 85th to 87th Congs., 2 vols. Washington, D.C.: Government Printing Office, 1963.

Waitzkin, Howard B., and Waterman, Barbara. *The Exploitation of Illness in Capitalist Society.* Indianapolis: Bobbs-Merrill, 1974.

Weaver, Jerry. "Elderly as a Political Community: Case of National Health Policy." *Western Political Quarterly* (1976):61–69.

———. *National Health Policy and the Underserved.* St. Louis: Mosby, 1976.

SOCIAL SERVICES AND OTHER PUBLIC PROGRAMS

Avant, W. Ray, and Dressel, Paula L. "Perceiving Needs by Staff and Elderly Clients: The Impact of Training and Client Contact." *Gerontologist* 20 (1980):71–77.

Bailey, J. *Social Theory for Social Planning*. London: Routledge and Kegan Paul, 1975.

Benton, B.; Feild T.; and Millar, R. *State and Area Agency on Aging Intervention in Title XX*. Washington, D.C.: Urban Institute, 1977.

Coberly, Sally; Fleisher, Dorothy; and Fritz, Dan. "A Policy Note on the 1978 Amendments to the Older Americans Act." *Gerontologist* 20 (April 1980): 140–47.

Coward, Raymond T. "Planning Community Services for the Rural Elderly: Implications from Research." *Gerontologist* 19 (June 1979):275–82.

Cutler, Neil E., and Steinburg, Raymond M. *A Longitudinal Analysis of 97 Area Agencies on Aging*. Los Angeles: University of Southern California, Andrus Gerontology Center, May 1976.

Estes, Carroll L. "Barriers to Effective Community Planning for the Elderly," *Gerontologist* 13 (1973):178–83.

————— . "Community Planning for the Elderly: A Study of Goal Displacement." *Gerontologist* 29 (1974):684–91.

————— . *The Aging Enterprise*. San Francisco: Jossey-Bass, 1979.

Fritz, Dan. "The Administration on Aging as an Advocate: Progress, Problems, and Prospects." *Gerontologist* 19 (April 1979):141–57.

Galper, Jeffrey H. *The Politics of Social Services*. Englewood Cliffs, N.J.: Prentice-Hall, 1975.

Gilbert, Neil. "The Transformation of Social Services." *Social Service Review* 51 (1977):624–41.

————— , and Specht, Harry. "Title XX Planning by Area Agencies on Aging: Efforts, Outcomes and Policy Implications." *Gerontologist* 19 (June 1979): 264–74.

Golant, Stephen M., and McCaslin, Rosemary. "A Functional Classification of Services for Older People." *Journal of Gerontological Social Work* 1 (1979):187–209.

Gottesman, Leonard E.; Ishizaki, Barbara; and MacBride, Stacey. "Service Management–Plan and Concept in Pennsylvania." *Gerontologist* 19 (August 1979):379–85.

Hardy, Richard E., and Cull, John G. *Organization and Administration of Service Programs for the Older American*. Springfield, Ill.: Charles C. Thomas, 1975.

Havens, Betty. "The Potential for Determining the Predictive Validity of Assessed Needs." *Aging and Leisure Living* 3 (1980):5–8.

Hayslip, Bert; Ritter, Mary Lou; Oltman, Ruth M.; and McDonnell, Connie. 'Home Care Services and the Rural Elderly," *Gerontologist* 20 (April 1980):192-99.

Health Facilities Services, Inc. *A Technical Assistance Guide for Directors and Personnel of Regional, State, and Area Agencies on Aging in the Supplementation of Title III and Title VII Programs*. Washington, D.C.: Health Facilities Resources, May 1976.

Howenstine, R. A.; Miller, J.; and Tucker, R.C. *Research on Social Systems and Inter-Agency Relations: A Study of the Area Agencies on Aging*. New Haven: Yale University Press, 1975.

Hudson, Robert, "Rational Planning and Organizational Imperatives: Prospects for Area Agencies on Aging," *Annals* 415 (September 1974):41–54.

———— , and Veley, M. B. "Federal Funding and State Planning: Case of State Units on Aging." *Gerontologist* 14 (1978):122–28.

Ishizaki, Barbara; Gottesman, Leonard E.; and MacBride, Stacey Mong. "Determinants of Model Choice for Service Management Systems." *Gerontologist* 19 (August 1979):385–88.

Kane, R. L., and Kane, R. A. "Care of the Aged: Old Problems in Need of New Solutions." *Science* 200 (1978):913–19.

Kasschau, P. L. "The Elderly as Their Planners See Them." *Social Policy* (1976):13–20.

Lawton, M. Powell; Newcomer, J.; and Byerts, Thomas O., eds. *Community Planning for an Aging Society.* Stroudsburg, Penn.: Dowden, Hutchinson, and Ross, 1976.

Little, Virginia C. "Assessing the Needs of the Elderly: State of the Art." *International Journal of Aging and Human Development* 11(1980):65–76.

Marmor, Theodore R., and Kutza, Elizabeth Ann. *Analysis of Federal Regulations Related to Aging: Legislative Barriers to Coordination Under Title III.* Washington, D.C.: Department of Health, Education and Welfare, Administration on Aging, October 1975.

McConnell, Stephen. "Income vs. In-kind Services for Elderly." *Social Service Review* 51 (June 1977):337–56.

McKnight, J. "Professional Service Business." *Social Policy* 8 (1977):110–16.

Murdock, Steve H.; Schwartz, Donald F.; Hwang, Sean. "The Effects of Socioeconomic Characteristics and Off-Reservation Contacts on the Service Awareness and Usage Patterns of Elderly Native Americans." *Long Term Care and Health Services Administration Quarterly* 4 (1980):64–76.

Nelson, Gay. "Social Services to the Urban and Rural Aged: The Experience of Area Agencies on Aging." *Gerontologist* 20 (April 1980):200–207.

Ochs, Sytske, and Moorhus, Donita. "Serving the Frail Elderly in the Community." *Aging* 293–94 (March–April, 1979):10–11, 21–23.

Pippin, Roland N. "Assessing the Needs of the Elderly with Existing Data." *Gerontologist* 20 (1980):65–70.

Posner, Barbara Miller. *Nutrition and the Elderly: Policy Development, Program Planning and Evaluation.* Lexington, Mass.: Heath, Lexington Books, 1979.

Ramerman, Sheila B., and Kohn, Alfred J. *Social Services in the United States: Policies and Programs.* Philadelphia: Temple University Press, 1976.

Riesenfeld, Mark J.; Newcomer, Robert; Berlant, Paul; and Dempsey, William. "Perception of Public Service Needs: The Urban Elderly and the Public Agency." *Gerontologist* 12 (Summer 1972):185–90.

Sanier, Janet S.; Ochs, Sytske; and McGloin, Joanne M. "Reaching and Serving the Mentally Frail Elderly." *Aging* 293–94. (March–April, 1979):10–17.

Schmandt, Jurgen; Bach, Victor; and Radin, Beryl A. "Information and Referral Services for Elderly Welfare Recipients." *Gerontologist* 19 (February 1979): 21–27.

Schneider, Robert L. "Barriers to Effective Outreach in Title VII Nutrition Programs." *Gerontologist* 19 (April 1979):163–69.

Sicker, Martin. "On Austerity and Accountability: The Double Bind." *Journal of Gerontological Social Work* 1 (1979):259–63.

Stanfield, R. L. "Services for the Elderly: A Catch-22." *National Journal* 10 (1978):1718–21.

Thurz, Daniel. *Social Service Delivery Systems: Meeting Human Needs*. Beverly Hills: Sage, 1975.

Tobin, Sheldon S.; Davidson, Steven M.; and Sack, Ann. *Effective Social Services for Older Americans*. Ann Arbor: Institute of Gerontology, University of Michigan–Wayne State University, 1976.

――――― . "The Future Elderly: Needs and Services." *Aging* 279–280 (January–February, 1978):22–26.

U.S. Comptroller General. *Local Area Agencies Help the Aging but Problems Need Correcting*. Washington, D.C.: Government Printing Office, August 2, 1977.

U.S. Department of Health, Education, and Welfare. Office of Human Development. Administration on Aging. *Programs for Older Americans: Objective Setting and Monitoring: A Reference Manual*. Washington, D.C., December 1975.

HOUSING

Aaron, Henry J. *Shelter and Subsidies: Who Benefits from Federal Housing Policies?* Washington, D.C.: Brookings Institution, 1972.

Barton, Stephen E. "The Urban Housing Problem: Marxist Theory and Community Organizing." *Review of Radical Political Economists* 9 (Winter 1977):16–30.

Buland, Robert A.; LeRay, N. L.; and Crawford, C. O. *Older American Households and Their Housing, 1975: A Metro-Nonmetro Comparison*. University Park: Pennsylvania State University Press, 1980.

Eckert, J. Kevin. "Urban Renewal and Redevelopment: High Risk for the Marginally Subsistent Elderly." *Gerontologist* 19 (October 1979):496–502.

Edel, Matthew. "Rent Theory and Working Class Strategy: Marx, George and the Urban Crisis." *Review of Radical Political Economists* 9 (Winter 1977):1–15.

Fairholm, Gilbert W., and Fairholm, Barbara. "Policy Implications of Property Tax Relief for the Elderly." *Gerontologist* 19 (October 1979):432–37.

Freedman, Leonard. *Public Housing: The Politics of Poverty*. New York: Holt, Rinehart and Winston, 1969.

Henig, Jeffrey R. "Gentrification and Displacement of the Elderly: An Empirical Analysis." *Gerontologist* 21 (February 1981):67–75.

Lawton, M. Powell. *Planning and Managing Housing for the Elderly*. New York: Wiley, 1975.

Meehan, Eugene J. *The Quality of Federal Policymaking: Programmed Failure in Public Housing*. Columbia: University of Missouri Press, 1979.

Montgomery, James E.; Stubbs, Alice C.; and Day, Savannah S. "The Housing Environment of the Rural Elderly." *Gerontologist* 20 (August 1980):444–51.

Montgomery, Roger, and Marshall, Dale R. "Symposium on Housing Policy." *Policy Studies Journal* 8 (1979):1–336.

Pynoos, John; Schafer, Robert; and Hartman, Chester W., eds. *Housing Urban America*. Chicago: Aldine, 1973.

Struyk, Raymond J., and Soldo, Beth J. *Improving the Elderly's Housing*. Cambridge, Mass.: Ballinger, 1980.

U.S. Advisory Commission on Intergovernmental Relations. *Property Tax Circuit Breakers: Current Status and Policy Issues.* Washington, D.C.: Government Printing Office, 1975.

U.S. Department of Commerce. Bureau of the Census. *General Housing Characteristics for the U.S. and Regions: 1976, Current Housing Reports.* Series H-150-76, Annual Housing Survey, part A. Washington, D.C.: Government Printing Office, 1978.

U.S. Department of Housing and Urban Development. National Housing Policy Review. *Housing in the Seventies.* Washington, D.C.: Government Printing Office, 1974.

Weiss, J. D. *Better Buildings for the Aged.* New York: McGraw-Hill, 1971.

Wolman, Harold. *Politics of Federal Housing.* New York: Dodd, Mead, 1974.

Yezer, Anthony. *How Well Are We Housed? The Elderly.* Washington, D.C., Department of Housing and Urban Development, Office of Policy Development and Research, May 1979.

Zimmer, Jonathan E. *From Rental to Cooperative: Improving Low and Moderate Income Housing.* Beverly Hills: Sage, 1977.

NURSING HOMES

Dunlop, Burton David. *The Growth of Nursing Home Care.* Lexington, Mass.: Heath, Lexington Books, 1979.

Gottesman, L., and Bourestrom, N. "Why Nursing Homes Do What They Do." *Gerontologist* 14 (1974):501–6.

Gubrium, Jabor. *Living and Dying at Murray Manor.* Springfield, Ill.: Charles C. Thomas, 1973.

Kane, Robert L., and Kane, Rosalie A. "Alternatives to Institutional Care of the Elderly: Beyond the Dichotomy." *Gerontologist* 20, part 1 (June 1980):249–59.

Koetting, Michael. *Nursing-Home Organization and Efficiency: Profit Versus Nonprofit.* Lexington, Mass.: Heath, Lexington Books, 1980.

Laird, Carobeth. *Limbo: A Memoir about Life in a Nursing Home.* Novato, Cal.: Chandler and Sharp, 1979.

Manard, Barbara Bolling; Woehle, Ralph E.; and Heilman, James M. *Better Homes for the Old.* Lexington, Mass.: Heath, Lexington Books, 1977.

Mendelson, Mary A. *Tender Loving Greed.* New York: Random House, 1975.

Thomas, William C. *Nursing Homes and Public Policy.* Ithaca, N.Y.: Cornell University Press, 1969.

U.S. Congress. Senate. Special Committee on Aging. *Hearings on the Federal-State Effort in Long-Term Care for Older Americans: Nursing Homes and "Alternatives."* 95th Cong., 2nd sess. Washington, D.C.: Government Printing Office, 1979.

———. Subcommittee on Long-Term Care. *Nursing Home Care in the United States: Failure in Public Policy.* Introductory Report. 94th Cong., 1st sess. Washington, D.C.: Government Printing Office, November 19, 1974.

———. *Nursing Home Care in the United States; Failure in Public Policy, the Litany of Nursing Home Abuses and an Examination of the Roots of Controversy.* 94th Cong., 1st sess. Washington, D.C.: Government Printing Office, December 17, 1974.

————— . *Nursing Home Care in the United States: Failure in Public Policy, Drugs in Nursing Homes: Misuse, High Costs, and Kickbacks*. 94th Cong., 1st sess. Washington, D.C.: Government Printing Office, January 1975.

————— . *Nursing Homes in the United States: Failure in Public Policy, Doctors in Nursing Homes: The Shunned Responsibility*. Supporting Paper no. 3. 94th Cong., 1st sess. Washington, D.C.: Government Printing Office, March 1975.

————— . *Nursing Home Care in the United States: Failure in Public Policy, Nurses in Nursing Homes: The Heavy Burden*. Supporting Paper no. 4. 94th Cong., 1st sess. Washington, D.C.: Government Printing Office, April 1975.

————— . *Nursing Home Care in the United States: Failure in Public Policy, the Continuing Chronicle of Nursing Home Fires*. Supporting Paper no. 5. 94th Cong., 1st sess. Washington, D.C.: Government Printing Office, August 1975.

————— . *Nursing Home Care in the United States: Failure in Public Policy, What Can Be Done in Nursing Homes: Positive Aspects in Long-Term Care*. Supporting Paper no. 6. 94th Cong., 1st sess. Washington, D.C.: Government Printing Office, September 1975.

————— . *Nursing Home Care in the United States: Failure in Public Policy, the Role of Nursing Homes in Caring for Discharged Mental Patents (and the Birth of a For-Profit Boarding Home Industry)*. Supporting Paper no. 7. 94th Cong., 2nd sess. Washington, D.C.: Government Printing Office, March 1976.

————— . *Nursing Home Care in the United States: Failure in Public Policy, Access to Nursing Homes by U.S. Minorities*. Supporting Paper no. 8. 94th Cong., 2nd sess. Washington, D.C.: Government Printing Office, 1976.

————— . *Nursing Home Care in the United States: Failure in Public Policy, Profits and the Nursing Homes: Incentives in Favor of Poor Care*. Supporting Paper no. 9. 94th Cong., 2nd sess. Washington, D.C.: Government Printing Office, 1976.

U.S. Congressional Budget Office. *Long-Term Care for the Elderly and Disabled*. Washington, D.C.: Government Printing Office, 1977.

U.S. General Accounting Office. *State Audits to Identify Medicaid Overpayment to Nursing Homes*. Washington, D.C.: Government Printing Office, January 24, 1977.

Vladick, Bruce. *Unloving Care: The Nursing Home Tragedy*. New York: Basic Books, 1980.

Wilson, Sally Hart. "Nursing Home Patient's Rights: Are They Enforceable?" *Gerontologist* 18 (June 1978):255–61.

OLDER PEOPLE IN OTHER NATIONS: COMPARATIVE APPROACHES

Bratthall, Kenneth. "Flexible Retirement and the New Swedish Partial-Pension Scheme." *Industrial Gerontology* 3 (1976):157–65.

Bryden, Kenneth. *Old Age Pensions and Policy-Making in Canada*. Montreal: McGill University Press, 1974.

Dieck, Margret. "Residential and Community Provisions for the Frail Elderly in Germany—Current Issues and Their History." *Gerontologist* 20, part 1, (June 1980):260–72.

Foolgraff, Barbara. "Social Gerontology in West Germany: A Review of Recent and Curent Research." *Gerontologist* 18 (February 1978):42–58.

Flynn, Marilyn L. "Coordination of Social and Health Care for the Elderly: The British and Irish Examples." *Gerontologist* 20, part 1 (June 1980):300-307.

Grunow, Dieter. "Sozialstationen: A New Model for Home Delivery of Care and Service (West Germany)." *Gerontologist* 20, part 1 (June 1980):308-17.

Heclo, Hugh. *Modern Social Policies in Britain and Sweden*. New Haven: Yale University Press, 1974.

Horlick, Max, and Skolnik, Alfred M. *Mandating Private Pensions: A Study of European Experience*. Research Report no. 1. Washington, D.C.: Department of Health, Education, and Welfare, Social Security Administration, Office of Policy, 1979.

Kassalow, Everett M., ed. *The Role of Social Security in Economic Development*. Research Report no. 27 Washington, D.C.: Department of Health, Education, and Welfare, Social Security Administration, 1968.

Noam, Ernst. *Homes for the Aged: Supervision and Standards*. Washington, D.C.: Department of Health, Education, and Welfare, Office of Human Development, 1975.

Pinker, Robert A. "Facing up to the Eighties: Health and Welfare Needs of British Elderly." *Gerontologist* 20, part 1 (June 1980):273-82.

Ross, Stanford G. "Social Security: A Worldwide Issue." *Social Security Bulletin* 42 (August 1979):3-10.

Schulz, James; Carrin, Guy; Krupp, Hans; Peschke, Manfred; Sclar, Elliott; and Steenberge, J. van, eds. *Providing Adequate Income: Pension Reform in the U.S. and Abroad*. Waltham, Mass.: Brandeis University Press, 1974.

Simanis, Joseph G. "Worldwide Trends in Social Security, 1979." *Social Security Bulletin* 43 (August 1980):6-9.

Treas, Judith. "Socialist Organization and Economic Development in China: Latent Consequences for the Aged." *Gerontologist* 19 (February 1979):34-43.

U.S. Department of Health, Education, and Welfare. Social Security Administration. *Social Security in a Changing World*. Washington, D.C., September 1979.

———. Office of Policy. *Social Security Programs Throughout the World, 1979*. Research Report no. 54. Washington, D.C., 1979.

Wilson, Thomas, ed. *Pensions, Inflation and Growth: A Comparative Study of the Elderly in the Welfare State*. London: Heinemann Educational Books, 1974.

Index

About the Contributors

DAVID K. BROWN is Associate Professor of Gerontology and Coordinator of Academic Programs with the Center for the Study of Aging at the University of Alabama, Tuscaloosa. He also serves as a faculty member to the University of Alabama Management Institute. He has conducted and directed numerous management training conferences and workshops to human services executives nationwide. He has served as Project Director and Coordinator to a number of projects involving elderly issues throughout Alabama and the Southeast. He has published both nationally and internationally in the field of development planning and program management.

WILLIAM P. BROWNE is Professor of Political Science and Coordinator of Public Administration Programs, Central Michigan University, where he has taught, has served in various administrative capacities, organized several conferences, and done consulting work for governmental institutions and universities. His publications have appeared in several journals, including the *Public Administration Review; Policy Studies Journal; Western Political Quarterly; Ethnicity; Education; Midwest Public Administration Review; Polity; and Policy Studies Review and Urban Affairs Annual.* He also authored two monographs on local government, several book chapters, *Politics, Programs and Bureaucrats,* and three other books on policy and politics. His research and personal interests are mostly concerned with the impact of bureaucracies and interest groups on governmental policymaking.

ROBERT H. BINSTOCK is Louis Stuberg Professor of Law and Politics and Director of the Program in the Economics and Politics of Aging at Brandeis University. A former President of the American Gerontological Society (1975-1976), he served as Director of the White House Task Force on Older Americans in 1967-1968 and as Chairman of the Adult Development and Aging Research and Training Committee, National Institutes of Health, 1971-1972. He is the author of numerous articles on the politics and policies affecting aging. His books include *Feasible Planning for Social Change, The Politics of the Powerless, America's Political System,* and

Handbook of Aging and the Social Sciences. Among the honors he has received is the Donald P. Kent Award from the Gerontological Society of America for "exemplifying the highest standards of professional leadership in gerontology through teaching, service, and interpretation of gerontology to the larger society."

DAVID M. BRODSKY is Associate Professor and former Department Head of Political Science at the University of Tennessee at Chattanooga. He has broad experience in gerontology, including the 1981 White House Conference, consultant to both the Congress and the Tennessee Commission on Aging, as well as research and publications in the field.

DOUGLAS DOBSON is Associate Professor of Political Science and Director of the Center of Governmental Studies, Northern Illinois University. His research for the U.S. Administration on Aging has provided much of the basic data for understanding the political behavior of the elderly. He has extensive research experience and several publications in the field of political science.

JACQUELYNE JOHNSON JACKSON is Professor of Human Development at Howard University and Associate Professor of Medical Sociology at Duke University. Author of a number of works on aged blacks, her *Minorities and Aging* (Wadsworth, 1980) represents an important work in ethnogerontology. A founder of the *National Caucus on the Black Aged*, Dr. Jackson was a delegate to the 1971 White House Conference on Aging and the principal author of the report on aging and aged blacks which emerged from that conference. Among her awards are those from the American Association of Homes for the Aging (1972), the American Psychiatric Association (1978), and Prairie View A&M University (1981).

PAUL K. H. KIM is Professor and Acting Director of the Florida International University Social Work Department and Coordinator of the MSW/Gerontology Specialization Program. He is the author of numerous articles on social work and aging. Recently he published a coedited book on the rural elderly.

LAURA KATZ OLSON is Associate Professor of Government at Lehigh University. She has been awarded a Fulbright-Hays Fellow, Gerontological Fellow, and a NASPAA Fellow and has served for a year at the Social Security Administration as a policy analyst. In addition to articles and research grants in the field of aging policy, she is the author of *The Political Economy of Aging: Private Power, the State and Social Welfare.*

HENRY J. PRATT is Professor of Political Science at Wayne State University and holds Fellowship status in the Gerontological Society of

America. He has published extensively in the field of politics and aging, including a book, *The Gray Lobby* (1976), and articles in such journals as *The Annals of the American Academy of Political and Social Science; Transaction/Society;* and *Research on Aging: A Quarterly in Social Gerontology.* He has recently collaborated on a study of the impact of the 1978 Amendments to the Age Discrimination in Employment Act on American colleges and universities, which is tentatively titled *Mandatory Retirement and Federal Regulation* and is forthcoming from the University of Wisconsin Press.

DALE VINYARD is Professor of Political Science at Wayne State University. He has written books on Congress and the presidency and journal articles on the legislative process and the politics of the elderly.

JENNIFER L. WARLICK is Assistant Professor of Economics at the University of Notre Dame. From 1976 to 1979 she served as an economist in the Office of Income Security Policy, U.S. Department of Health, Education, and Welfare, where she was responsible for the formulation and evaluation of policy regarding social insurance and income maintenance for the aged and disabled. From 1979 to 1982 she was an Assistant Professor of Economics and Research Associate in the Institute for Research on Poverty, University of Wisconsin. She has published in both national (*Journal of Human Resources, Review of Income and Wealth*) and foreign journals and in numerous books regarding income maintenance policy and aging.